Economic Progress and Policy in Developing Countries

By The Same Author

ECONOMIC GROWTH IN THE WEST
(Norton Library Paperback, N423)

ECONOMIC GROWTH IN JAPAN AND THE USSR
(Norton Paperback)

Angus Maddison

Economic Progress and Policy in Developing Countries

W·W·Norton & Company·Inc·
NEW YORK

SBN 393 09961 X (Cloth Edition)
SBN 393 09976 8 (Paper Edition)

Library of Congress Catalog Card No. 73–131994

PRINTED IN THE UNITED STATES OF AMERICA

1 2 3 4 5 6 7 8 9 0

Acknowledgments

In writing this book, I received helpful advice from a large number of people. Those who were kind enough to criticize earlier drafts were Christopher Beringer, Helmuth Führer, Benjamin Higgins, Sir Arthur Lewis, Harold Pilvin, Murray Rossant, George Simantov, Victor Urquidi, Barend de Vries, and Montagu Yudelman. I gained a great deal from discussions with Tibor Scitovsky. I was also able, as a visiting Professor, to try out my ideas on my students in the University of California at Berkeley, and Sir George Williams University in Montreal. David Horowitz, Witold Marczewski, Jan Tumlir, the staff of the di Tella Institute, and the Vargas Institute provided help on several statistical questions. The Twentieth Century Fund provided generous financial support for my research. The book was completed before I joined the Development Advisory Service of Harvard University and in no way commits them.

Contents

List of Tables

TEXT TABLES

APPENDIX TABLES

Chapter I

Post-war Growth in Historical Perspective

The central issue of our times is the unequal income of nations. Its importance outweighs most of the domestic problems in rich countries, and the division of the world into rich and poor has become more significant than the ideological cleavage between communism and capitalism. There are twenty-five rich countries where real income is between $1,300 and $3,200 a year, but more than 100 countries where income ranges from $150 to $1,300 a year. Two-thirds of the world's population live in the latter group. Their poverty cannot be cured simply by transfers of income. The rich would have to give away more than half their income to achieve a levelling in consumption standards. Poverty can be abolished only by increasing output in the poor countries, and the limited aid which they receive must be used for this purpose.

The raising of income levels is generally called economic growth in rich countries, and in poor ones it is called economic 'development'. There are good reasons for differentiating the two processes. Economic 'growth' is less urgent. In rich countries, most people can now expect to live out their natural life-span medicated against preventable disease, with more than enough to eat, fairly adequate housing, reasonable working conditions, access to leisure, education and entertainment. In the post-war period they have been reasonably free of unemployment and major economic insecurity. There are still squalid cities and ugly pockets of poverty, and the desire for increased material comfort is far from satiated. But further progress is largely a matter of providing new frills. Improvement in the quality of life is a more pressing concern than the growth of output. In the rest of the world, problems are different. In Asia the average person dies fifteen years earlier than in Europe. Debilitating disease is still widespread. Famines have disappeared, but diets are inadequate.

Housing standards are miserable. Under-employment and unemployment are widely prevalent. Education is poor in quality and not available to many who could benefit from it. Disparities between the income of different groups and regions are much greater than in the developed world. In these countries, a 3 per cent increase in income means only $10 a year, in the rich countries an extra $60, but the $10 is more important than the $60 because the needs are greater.

The distinction between growth and development is also important because the problem of increasing incomes is more complicated in poor countries. In rich countries, resources are mobile, technical and managerial skills abound, organized scientific research has institutionalized technical progress, knowledge is easily diffused, there is a well articulated institutional and financial structure, and the fortune of the economy is not tied to a few commodities. In poor countries, problems of structural adjustment are much greater, skills are poor, resources are not so flexible, and the economies are more unstable. The modern sector is often a highly specialized enclave. They have a much more rapid population growth than most rich countries have ever experienced. Economic policy must not merely manage and modify growth forces which are already present. It must break the obstacles to growth and create the dynamism itself.

On the other hand, the very backwardness of poor countries presents opportunities which the developed world did not have when it operated at similar income levels. There is a much wider range of technological choice. Foreign aid can add substantially to growth potential. Government policy can play a bigger and more active role. The sequence of development will be different from that of the rich countries, and the post-war experience of several countries—Greece, Israel, Spain, Taiwan and Yugoslavia—has shown that the income gap between rich and poor can be reduced.

The treatment of 'developing' countries as a distinctive group occurred first in studies by international organizations which are the main providers of standardized economic statistics. The grouping was consolidated politically by the creation of the United Nations Conference on Trade and Development (UNCTAD), in which eighty-six politically independent countries constituted themselves as a pressure group, claiming special privileges in trade and aid on the grounds that they are underdeveloped.

But the group is very heterogeneous. Some countries which claim membership, such as Argentina, Chile, Israel, Spain and Venezuela, are closer to the rich than to most of the poor, and it is questionable whether current definitions of the 'developing world' are rational.

The distinction between rich and poor countries can only be made by reference to output or income per head. But the figures of national accounts statisticians are misleading when converted at official rates. Exchange rates reflect the purchasing power of currencies in terms of items entering international trade, whereas we need to measure differences in the price level for all goods and services. We have attempted to provide estimates of the type required for valid international comparisons in Appendix A, and the results are summarized in Table I–1. Real product per head in 1965 varied from about 5 per cent of the US level in Pakistan to over 40 per cent in Israel, i.e. the dispersion *within* the developing world is almost 1 to 9.[1] This is much wider than in the developed countries, where the income spread is less than 1 to 3.

It is interesting to see how the income gap between countries has changed over time. In 1870 Indian income was about a fifth of that in the USA and about half of that in Japan. In 1965 it was a seventeenth of the US level and an eighth of the Japanese level. India and Pakistan have always been very poor and their income level has less than doubled in the past century whereas in Japan income per head increased more than sevenfold.

Near the top end of the scale, Argentina has also had very slow growth. In 1870 Argentina was more prosperous than some European countries, and not far behind the United States. Its natural resources were so big in relation to population that it could pay wages high enough to attract seasonal immigrants from as far away as Italy. It is now relatively poor because of its retarded growth. It is a dropout from the developed world.

Most of the other countries have experienced fairly substantial

[1] The table shows levels of *domestic* product (GDP). The domestic product is usually produced with the help of foreign capital and the owners of this capital receive payments of interest and dividends. The amount remaining when foreigners have received interest and dividends is the *national* product (GNP). In developing countries this is usually smaller than GDP. However, developing countries normally use more resources than their GNP because they are net recipients of foreign capital and aid. Israel is a case where external resources are very large, so that real resources available per head were $1,538 in 1965 as compared with GDP per head of $1,340. Venezuela is another extreme case, where payments of profits to foreign investors were much larger than capital receipts, so that resources available per head were only $1,143 as compared with GDP per head of $1,264. All of these figures are at factor cost, i.e. they exclude indirect taxes and subsidies. They would all be higher at market prices.

long-run gains in income. In all cases, growth has been slower than in Japan or the United States, but they have not been stagnant economies, and some of them, such as Brazil, Colombia, Ghana, Malaya, Mexico, Taiwan and Yugoslavia have been fairly dynamic.

Table I–1

Level of Real Gross Domestic Product at Factor Cost Per Head of Population

Dollars at 1965 US relative prices

	1965	1950	1938	1913	1870
Argentina	1,272	1,036	865	788	412
Brazil	482	351	231	—	—
Ceylon	271	241	208	—	—
Chile	863	678	595	545	—
Colombia	375	305	263	182	—
Egypt	295	191	178	176	—
Ghana	230	184	—	117	—
Greece	676	301	432	315	—
India	182	149	156	138	103
Israel	1,340	572	—	—	—
Malaya	528	490	—	221	—
Mexico	423	283	205	178*	120†
Pakistan	152	126	133	117	88
Peru	397	255	—	147	—
Philippines	269	207	218‡	201	—
South Korea	255	158	—	—	—
Spain	975	374	520‡	419	—
Taiwan	573	267	348	206	—
Thailand	254	159	—	—	—
Turkey	289	203	201	—	—
Venezuela	1,264	828	493	—	—
Yugoslavia	736	312	279	217§	—
France	1,990	1,159	954	774	426
Germany	2,109	934	1,072	811	404
Italy	1,345	663	676	521	379
Japan	1,466	438	703	366	209‖
UK	1,985	1,394	1,236	1,037	658
USA	3,179	2,356	1,513	1,239	503
USSR	1,495	734	548	339	226

* 1910; † 1877; ‡ 1929; § 1909–12; ‖ 1879.

Source: Appendix A for 1965 levels, Appendix B figures for growth were used to estimate the levels for earlier years. Growth rates for developed countries derived from A. Maddison, *Economic Growth in Japan and the USSR*, Allen & Unwin, London, 1969.

The countries we are dealing with are therefore very different, both in their present level of development and in their economic history.

The main concern of this study is with the period since 1950. Our object is to analyse the reasons for the post-war acceleration in growth and for the variation in performance between countries. In this way we hope to demonstrate the role of economic policy in promoting development and to distil the essence of a practical strategy for future growth. In most respects, the circumstances in which these economies have operated in the post-war period are very different from those in the past. The leverage of their own policies is much greater and foreign aid has played a significant new role. They are not repeating 'stages' of growth already experienced by the developed world. It is not therefore necessary to analyse their economic history in any detail. However, it is useful to survey briefly the major historical reasons for their backwardness.

Most of them were late starters. When their modern growth started in the 1870s, the UK, USA and France had already had a century of rising per capita income. Their development was not due to spontaneous internal forces but was induced by the rapid development of cheap transport facilities for bulky cargoes. Steam shipping, refrigeration, the opening of the Suez Canal, the introduction of cable communications were a necessary complement to railways before they could fully exploit the benefits of international trade Once they entered the world market, their trade expanded rapidly. There were few tariff and no quantitative restrictions on trade. Foreign demand for primary products like cotton, coffee, rubber and cocoa expanded rapidly. Trade raised productivity by enabling them to specialize. In important cases it provided a profitable use for land and labour which had been idle before the transport revolution. The forces of expansion continued until 1929, and were not very seriously interrupted by the 1914–18 war.

The fortunes of different countries depended a good deal on the size of trade in relation to income, the natural resource endowment and the amount of foreign capital they received. In Ghana, a highly specialized cocoa industry was built up by peasant farmers, who were able to raise their income substantially without a great deal of investment. Malaya, specializing in rubber and tin, enjoyed rapid growth from the 1880s onwards, attracted nearly six million Chinese immigrants, and a limited amount of foreign capital. Ceylon was a similar type of economy, attracting Indian immigrants to rubber and tea plantations. The highly commercial export economies of Malaya and Ceylon needed to import food and this provided an opportunity for Thailand and Burma to use previously idle resources of land and labour to expand rice production and exports. Taiwan experienced rapid growth as a Japanese colony, with major increases in productivity of rice and sugar for export. In India, by contrast, there were no significant natural resources to exploit, and the expansion of trade had only a very marginal influence in raising income levels.

In most of the developing countries, the rate of investment generally remained low, and modern techniques of production did not spread throughout the economy. In no case were there deliberate policies of industrialization until the 1930s. They remained heavily dependent on imports for industrial goods, although in some cases they did develop a textile industry. Growth was therefore different in character from that in the developed world. It was diffused from outside rather than being autonomous. And it was generally slower. Trade rather than investment was the engine of growth.

The only late starter which made enough progress to become a 'developed' country was Japan. Initially, Japan was subject to the same colonial-type commercial treaty as the rest of Asia, so that the government could not impose protective tariffs. But the Japanese carried out a major institutional revolution in 1867 and created a tax structure, banking system, and legal framework that were highly conducive to growth. They introduced a modern system of compulsory education, a heavy armaments and shipping industry, carried out land reform, promoted agricultural research, started government enterprises and subsidized private industry. In the late nineteenth century the government carried out half the investment in the economy and by the 1920s Japan was investing 20 per cent of its GNP. Japan had certain peculiar features which helped such a development to take place. It had had a very large economic surplus in its old system of feudal rice levies, which was converted into government revenue by the Meiji reforms. Its lack of natural resources left it no alternative to industrial development. Finally it had a very large, well-educated class of *samurai*, who were politically willing to make basic institutional changes and to provide the bureaucratic expertise, technical capacity and business leadership required.

The Japanese model had no counterpart elsewhere until the 1930s, when the world crisis forced some of the countries into more vigorous development policies.

Until the 1930s, none of these countries made a positive attempt to stimulate local banking, shipping, insurance, export credit, technical education, or create government enterprise in fields where the initial risks were large. Agricultural research, where it took place, was confined to export crops and not extended to the subsistence sector.

The failure to follow the Japanese model was true of both independent countries and colonies. In Latin America, the institutional structure created by the Spanish and Portuguese was much less favourable to growth than that implanted in North America, and was not changed by political independence. Most of the Spanish speaking countries retained a system of serf labour. Nearly all land was divided into large scale properties (*latifundia*), and the masses had no access to land ownership. This system was eliminated in Western Europe between 1780 and 1810, and in Russia in 1860, but did not begin to change in Latin America until the Mexican revolution of 1910. The Brazilian economy was based on negro slavery until 1888. These societies benefited from international trade, but were slow to modernize their institutional structure and promote industrialization. Latin America was dominated by semi-feudal oligarchies and foreign commercial interests until the 1930s, when the world crisis brought about a collapse of the old regimes in Argentina and Brazil, and Cardenas consolidated the Mexican revolution.

In Asia and Africa, colonial regimes broke open traditional societies to international trade. By introducing law and order to countries which would otherwise have been in violent civil commotion (as in a good deal of Latin America), and by building railways, they opened up local markets. In places where there was surplus labour or land, *laissez-faire* and railways were enough to secure substantial growth. It is interesting to note that Marx, writing in the *New York Daily Tribune* in the middle of the nineteenth century, saw colonization in a dual role 'at once destructive and regenerative'.[1] In particular he expected it to spark off the development of a modern capitalist economy in India. It is not by any means clear that local nationalist regimes would have followed a much more energetic development policy than that of colonial regimes. Indian nationalist economists like Romesh Dutt and Dadhabhai Naraoji were liberals who would probably have raised tariffs but otherwise followed a largely *laissez-faire* policy. Mahatma

[1] See the discussion of Marx's views on India in J. Strachey, *The End of Empire*, London, 1959.

Gandhi had no great liking for modern economic development.

A good deal of the backwardness of poor countries is therefore due (*a*) to the fact that their development started when several of the developed countries had already a century of economic growth; (*b*) the fact that growth, once started, was due mainly to the productivity gains of international specialization—and not to high investment, industrialization and technical change, as in the developed world. However, there is a third reason for their backwardness. Many of these economies were dominated politically by the developed countries. Effectively, most of them were colonies until the 1930s, and for this reason they suffered from various forms of foreign exploitation. Some kinds of exploitation did not necessarily hinder their growth. The control of the economy by a colonial bureaucratic elite was not necessarily worse for development than control by a local semi-feudal oligarchy. The displaced local elite in colonies naturally had strong grievances at their loss of power and income, and the presence of a foreign ruling class may have helped destroy a few native industries producing luxury goods, such as the textile industry of Dacca. But the growth-impeding impact of foreign economic dominance was mainly due to certain characteristics which allowed the developed world to draw resources away from these economies.

In the first place, the nationals of developed countries who were engaged in commerce and investment, usually enjoyed special privileges. They often had extraterritorial legal status and tax privileges, and could nearly always count on the metropolitan country to use military pressure or gunboat diplomacy to enforce their claims. They usually had access to land and mineral rights on extremely favourable terms, and enjoyed a monopoly position in banking and shipping. In India, the managing agency system perpetuated the foreign commercial dominance originally introduced by the East India Company. The capital and enterprise of the developed world therefore creamed off a monopolistic surplus. This was a serious loss to countries in the first stage of capitalist development when the savings rate was still very low. These characteristics of foreign enterprise applied in Latin America as well as in the colonial economies. Under Porfirio Diaz, the privileges of foreign investors in Mexico were at least as great as in British India. However, the massive Latin American defaults on foreign debt in the 1930s did something to offset the earlier element of monopoly profit.

At various times in the past, colonial powers have levied direct tribute on subject nations, i.e. they remitted part of the local tax revenues to the metropolitan country. Thus when Mexico was a Spanish colony, half the public revenue was remitted to Madrid. This practice on the part of colonial governments had generally disappeared by the second half of the nineteenth century, though the UK did accept 'gifts' from India of $750 million during the first world war. Nevertheless, there was a steady outflow of funds from India because of the presence of a foreign government. This went to pay Indian army and civil service pensions and to finance home education for children of British parents in India. It included remittances of savings by British servants in India. We must include interest on non-railway public debt, in view of the fact that the debt was incurred to finance colonial wars. We must also add a rough estimate of the element of monopoly profit in private dividend remittances. There has been a good deal of argument about the size of this burden on the Indian economy, but the latest evidence suggests that it amounted to about 1.7 per cent of GNP a year from 1921 to 1938.[1]

We know that colonial regimes inhibited the development of human resources. In 1911, there were 66,000 British in the Indian army and police and 4,000 in the civil government. At that time, there were only sixty Indians in the top rank of the civil service and even fewer Indian officers in the army. Foreign investors were also reluctant to develop local technical and managerial competence. Privileged employment opportunities were reserved for nationals of the metropolitan country. Thus they blocked Indian access to managerial skills in large-scale commerce, shipping, railways, banking and jute. A quarter of the managerial personnel in the Indian textile industry in the 1920s were foreigners supplied by the managing agencies.[2] In Egypt, the Suez Canal Company did not use Egyptian pilots; in Ceylon and Malaya, most of the supervisory personnel in

[1] See A. K. Banerji, *India's Balance of Payments*, Asia Publishing House, London, 1963, pp. 80, 115, and 137. We have included private remittances for education, savings remitted by public servants, government pension payments, interest on non-railway public debt, and a third of private dividend remittances. National income figures were taken from S. Sivasubramonian, *National Income of India*, Delhi School of Economics, Delhi, 1965. They were adjusted upwards by 12·5 per cent to approximate to GNP.

[2] Details on India in this paragraph are from *Census of India 1911*, Vol. I, Pt. II, pp. 374–6, Calcutta, 1913; P. Woodruff, *The Men Who Ruled India, The Guardians*, Cape, London, 1963, p. 363; D. H. Buchanan, *The Development of Capitalistic Enterprise in India*, Cass, London, 1966.

plantation agriculture were expatriates until relatively recently. The opportunities for local people were even worse in Belgian, Dutch and French colonies than they were in these British controlled countries. All of this is in striking contrast with the intensive Japanese pursuit of Western skills, knowledge and education.

In general, colonial governments followed conservative fiscal, monetary and exchange rate policies. They tended to have balanced budgets, to maintain excessive foreign exchange reserves, and did not set up national monetary authorities until a very late stage. They did not impose exchange controls, allow debt moratoria or devaluation, unless it suited their own interest. In this respect India suffered by comparison with Latin American countries which followed much more expansionist policies in the 1920s and 1930s when India was trying to adjust to an over-valued currency by deflationary methods.

Finally the commercial policy of colonialism allowed no scope for tariff protection as a way of building up domestic industry. This was a weapon which had been used by all of the industrial powers at some stage in their own development, particularly by the USA and Russia, but it was not permitted in British colonies until the 1920s, and low tariffs were also imposed on nominally independent countries like Egypt, China, Iran, Thailand and Turkey, whose tariff powers were restricted by commercial treaties. In this respect the situation in Latin America was different. Brazil escaped from British dictation of its commercial policy in 1844 and imposed high and rising duties on textiles for revenue purposes which had a substantial protective effect. This was also true in Argentina and Mexico. India was able to develop a textile industry without tariff protection, and to build up exports to the unprotected markets of China and Japan. But it was only in the crudest products such as cotton yarn, that the Indian industry was able to withstand competition from Manchester, and from the 1890s onwards it started to lose ground steadily to Japan.

In the post-war period there has been a great acceleration in the economic growth of developing countries. Their GDP growth rate since 1950 has been close to the 5 per cent target of the United Nations for its Development Decade, and twice as high as the average for pre-war years. All the countries for which we have statistics, except Argentina and Malaya, have grown faster than ever in the past. Even such slow-growing countries as India and Pakistan have done three times as well as at any time in the preceding century.

There have been several reasons for this great leap forward. The external forces influencing the growth of developing countries have changed significantly. The colonial character of the relation with the developed world had largely disappeared by the end of the 1960s. Most countries are now politically independent. Instead of colonial exploitation there is now a substantial flow of foreign aid. The privileges, monopolies and restrictive practices of foreign enterprise have been largely eradicated, and royalty payments for natural resources have been greatly increased. The change required a great deal of pressure and struggle on the part of the developing world, but the readiness of imperial powers to make the change was due not only to their political weakness but also to the great improvement of opportunities for profitable investment and employment in the developed world. The cost of maintaining colonial-type pressures on developing countries now greatly outweighs the potential gain.

But the biggest change is that nearly all governments in developing countries now give development a high priority. Most of them have managed to mobilize resources for investment, education and other developmental expenditure on a much larger scale than in pre-war years. In this first phase of accelerated growth, resources have not been allocated very efficiently and rapid population growth has absorbed some of the gains in income, but there has been a willingness to experiment with a very wide range of policy instruments for development, and policies are becoming more sophisticated with experience. Belatedly, these countries are acting to develop their economies in the same way as the Japanese did a century ago. In the rest of this book we shall try to see why post-war growth has accelerated, what role policy has played and what scope there is for further acceleration of growth through through improved policy.

Any attempt to generalize about the post-war growth of developing countries is a risky business, given the poor quality of statistical information and the large number of countries involved. Some analysts have tried to cover all the countries for which any data are available, e.g. Irma Adelman and Cynthia Morris have recently subjected seventy-four countries to factor analysis using forty-one indicators of social and political development.[1] Professor Chenery and others have also built econometric models exploiting available data to the maximum which have been very useful for testing hypotheses. But the strategy of maximum statistical coverage means that

[1] See I. Adelman and C. T. Morris, *Society Politics and Economic Development*, Johns Hopkins, Baltimore, 1967.

the investigators (*a fortiori* a single investigator) are not able to analyse the quality of individual series, to reject data of poor quality or to make major adjustments for better comparability. The mathematical processing of data may well show up logical inconsistencies which lead some information to be rejected, but such an analysis will be uneven in coverage. One may find foreign trade and population figures for all countries, GDP figures for only half of them, and investment statistics for a quarter. In this situation the consistency of the analysis will suffer considerably. A more fundamental difficulty of this approach is that it does not permit qualitative judgement on economic policy because it involves too many countries for the investigator to cover even if he is a vigorous jet-setter who has devoted his life to it. For this reason serious attempts at aggregate qualitative appraisal are usually confined to international organizations with large staffs. But if they are left to do this without any outside competition there is a danger that their techniques of analysis will grow stale and will tend to be affected by political constraints or institutional bias.

We were therefore faced with the problem of choosing a sample select enough to permit consistent quantitative analysis, small enough for detailed analysis of policy, and big enough to allow conclusions of general validity. The requirement of reasonable statistical consistency immediately eliminates more than half of the 110 developing countries. One of the basic indicators we required was informaton on the growth of gross domestic product. But for the period we wanted to cover, figures were available for only forty-two countries.[1] We also wanted to make our own estimates of real income *levels*, as this information is of fundamental importance in studying problems of poverty, and figures at official exchange rates are misleading. In order to make real product estimates, information is needed on agricultural and industrial output, and employment in services. For agriculture, FAO publishes indices on thirty-six developing countries, but only twenty nine of these were countries for which figures are also available on GDP growth. Information on industrial output is less complete than for agriculture, so our choice of the sample coun-

1 See *National Accounts of Less Developed Countries 1950–1966*, Development Centre, OECD, July 1968. This publication gives information on a few more countries than the UN *Yearbook of National Accounts Statistics*. The US government publication, *Gross National Product: Growth Rates and Trend Data*, AID, Washington, April 1969, gives data for only thirty-two developing countries for the whole period since 1950.

tries was dictated to a great extent by statistical constraints. As a result we ended up with a sample of twenty-two countries.

In spite of statistical difficulties, our twenty-two-country sample covers two-thirds of the population of non-communist developing countries, and, apart from Africa, it does provide a reasonable geographic spread. In Africa statistics are usually poor, and we had to stretch our standards somewhat even to include Ghana and Egypt.

Our sample also includes most of the countries for which a comparison with pre-war performance is feasible.[1] But the question still arises as to whether our sample is representative of the situation in the developing world. As statistics are not available for all countries, we cannot really be sure how representative the sample is. International organizations publish aggregate indices on the growth of GDP, agriculture and industrial output in developing countries, but these are based on incomplete information and the country coverage of the different series varies a good deal. Most of the aggregate indices published by international agencies also have unsatisfactory weights. The UN has only recently undertaken a study of real incomes and still uses official exchange rates or very crudely adjusted figures as weights for its own aggregate GDP index. FAO uses different weights for each major region, and the industrial production weights suffer from the same defects as the national income series.

Another problem is that there is a variation in the definition of developing countries. For some purposes, UN agencies leave out southern Europe, which is included in OECD statistics. Our own feeling is that the OECD definition of developing countries is currently the most useful. Southern Europe (i.e. Greece, Spain, Turkey and Yugoslavia) consists of countries relatively well-off by Asian or African standards, but if we were to exclude them on these grounds (which may well be desirable in future) it would also be necessary to exclude some Latin American countries, Israel and the Middle East oil producers which are as prosperous as southern Europe.

The weighted aggregate index of GDP published by OECD, shows a growth rate of 4·9 per cent a year for all developing countries for the period 1950–66.[2] The weighted average for our twenty-two

[1] However, there are also estimates for Jamaica back to 1830; see G. Eisner, *Jamaica*, Manchester University Press, 1966.

[2] See *National Accounts of Less Developed Countries 1950–1966*, OECD Development Centre, Paris, July 1968, p. 22. This is a weighted average for all developing countries using official exchange rates to convert national currencies to a common unit.

countries is 5 per cent a year for the same period, so our sample does seem fairly representative at first sight.

However, as the purpose of our analysis is to judge the policy performance of *countries*, we have preferred to use unweighted averages. For the twenty-two country sample, the unweighted average growth was 5·6 per cent a year for 1950–68, compared with 4·9 per cent in the forty-two countries for which OECD provides information for the whole period since 1950. The sample therefore has an upward bias, because it includes a number of countries with rather high growth rates. We have tried to take cognizance of this bias in drawing our conclusions, but the possibility of analysing performance in some of the more successful countries is, of course, an advantage in a study which attempts to make recommendations for policy purposes.

With these reservations in mind we can now analyse growth experience since 1950

During the 1950s all countries except Argentina and Malaya grew much faster than ever before, and twelve of the countries grew faster in the 1960s than in the 1950s. However, the dispersion of growth experience has been very wide indeed.

Nine countries were in the high growth league, with their output growing at more than 6 per cent a year since 1950. These countries were Greece, Israel, Mexico, South Korea, Spain, Taiwan, Thailand, Venezuela and Yugoslavia. Six of these accelerated growth in the 1960s and only one, Venezuela, fell out of the group. One other country, Malaya, joined the group in the 1960s. Although our sample probably contains an 'unrepresentative' proportion of these high growth countries, it should be noted that their experience is not unique in the developing world. There are a number of other countries in this category which we have not studied, e.g. Iraq, Ivory Coast, Jamaica, Kuwait, Libya, Panama and Trinidad. As we shall see later in our analysis, most countries owed their membership in this group to specially favourable factors not available to the typical developing country. But several countries were in this group because of successful economic policy.

The second group is more typical of average developing country performance and includes countries where growth ranged from 4 to 6 per cent a year. Nine countries were in this group for 1950–68, and ten of them in the 1960s.

Our low-growth group included four countries in the period 1950–68, i.e. Argentina, Ceylon, Ghana and India. India was by far the biggest member of this group, and her slow growth is the major reason why the weighted average for our sample is so much lower than the unweighted average. However, Indian growth accelerated in the 1960s and she moved out of the low-growth group. Although our low growth sample did rather badly, they were by no means the worst performers in the developing world. Bolivia, Haiti, Indonesia and Uruguay had growth rates below 2 per cent a year, and the same is probably true of the Congo.

Although there are low-income countries (Korea and Thailand) in the high growth group, and one high-income country (Argentina) in the low growth group, there is nevertheless a tendency for the higher growth countries to be those with the higher income *levels*. The

Table I–2
Growth of Gross Domestic Product 1870–1968

	Annual average compound growth rates				
	1870–1913	1913–50	1950–60	1960–68	1950–68
Argentina	5·0	3·0	3·1	2·9	3·0
Brazil	—	4·6†	5·8	4·7	5·3
Ceylon	—	—	3·6	3·6	3·6
Chile	—	2·1	3·5	4·5	4·0
Colombia	—	3·7	4·6	4·5	4·6
Egypt	—	1·6	5·4	4·9¶	5·2¶
Ghana	—	3·8‡	4·8	2·8	3·9
Greece	—	1·1	5·7	7·3	6·4
India	1·1	1·2	3·7	4·0	3·8
Israel	—	—	11·5	8·3	10·1
Malaya	—	4·3	2·3	6·3	4·1
Mexico	2·6*	2·6§	6·1	6·4	6·2
Pakistan	(1·1)	(1·2)	2·7	5·8	4·1
Peru	—	3·2	5·1	5·7	5·4
Philippines	—	2·2	4·8	5·7	5·2
South Korea	—	—	6·1	8·4	7·1
Spain	—	0·6	6·6	7·7	7·1
Taiwan	—	2·7	7·7	10·1	8·7
Thailand	—	—	6·0	7·0	6·5
Turkey	—	—	5·8	5·2	5·5
Venezuela	—	—	7·6	4·7	6·3
Yugoslavia	—	1·5‖	6·9	6·7**	6·8**
Average	2·5	2·5	5·4	5·8	5·6

* 1877–1910; † 1920–50; ‡ 1911–50; § 1910–50; ‖ 1909/12–50;
¶ terminal year is 1966; ** terminal year is 1967.
Source: Appendix B.

average growth rate in the nine countries with per capita incomes above $500 a year in US prices was 6·3 per cent a year, whereas in the thirteen countries below this level, the growth rate was only 5·1 per cent for the period 1950–68. As we shall see later in our analysis, the poorer countries have greater difficulty in achieving high growth rates than the richer ones, and their slower growth is not necessarily a reflection of poorer policy.

In order to measure growth it is necessary to have data for reasonably long periods, so that trends are not obscured by temporary fluctuations. The analysis starts with 1950 because the immediate post-war years were dominated by recovery from wartime disturbance. However, in a few countries 1950 output per head was still below pre-war peaks and subsequent growth contained an element of recovery.

Output per head in 1950 in Greece, South Korea, Spain and Taiwan was still about a quarter below pre-war levels. It was also a little below pre-war peaks in India, Pakistan and the Philippines.[1] By contrast with these countries, Brazil's output per head in 1950 was 50 per cent above 1938, Mexico's 40 per cent higher.

It is obvious that the restoration of pre-war levels of income is not a normal process of economic growth. In an economy recovering from war damage and neglect, substantial gains in output can be secured by restoring inventories to normal, by repairs to equipment, roads, railways, ports and electric generating stations, which in other countries would require major new investment. The process of recovery will not be finished when pre-war output is regained. As long as labour productivity lags below previous peaks, some element of recovery is probably present; and pre-war output per head was not regained until 1954 in Spain and 1956 in Greece and Taiwan.

Recovery is therefore a special kind of growth which can be attained at smaller cost in terms of new inputs of capital, labour and skill, than can normal economic progress. It would be exaggerated to treat all of the growth which represents recovery as if it were a free bonus to the economy, but it must be discounted to some degree. It

[1] Israel was a special case. For the Jewish sector of the economy, output per head was higher in 1950 than in 1938 and the Jewish population had quadrupled. However, there had been a big outflow of Arab refugees, and some of the post-1950 growth involved elements of recovery, e.g. in the citrus industry, where 1947 export levels were not regained until 1957. See R. Shershevsky, *Essays on the Structure of the Jewish Economy in Palestine and Israel*, Falk Foundation, Jerusalem, 1968, for estimates of prewar GNP for the Jewish sector of the economy.

was therefore assumed that the recovery bonus was equivalent to half of the gap between 1950 and the pre-war peak in per capital income. The results can be seen for the individual countries in Table I–3. The GDP average growth rate for the twenty-two countries is reduced from 5·6 to 5·4 per cent when this recovery element is eliminated.

Table I–3

Impact of Recovery on Growth 1950–68

	Per cent growth required to move from 1950 level to pre-war peak in per capita income	Impact of recovery factor on annual percentage growth rate 1950–68	GDP growth adjusted to eliminate recovery bonus
Greece	44·0	1·00	5·40
India	5·1	0·15	3·65
Pakistan	5·1	0·15	3·95
Philippines	4·3	0·10	5·00
South Korea	31·3	0·75	6·35
Spain	39·0	0·95	6·15
Taiwan	31·3	0·75	7·95

Source: Appendix B. South Korea is assumed to be in the same position in 1950 as Taiwan, but in fact it was probably considerably worse compared with the pre-war peak.

The acceleration in output has been accompanied by a massive increase in population. This reflects an improvement in welfare, for it was due to a fall in mortality. But the reduced death rate will have to be matched by a reduction in fertility before the full income benefits of increased growth can be enjoyed.

On average, population grew by 2·6 per cent a year from 1950 to 1967 as compared with 1·6 per cent in pre-war years.[1] As population accelerated less than output, per capita income has accelerated more than output. From 1950 to 1967, per capita output grew by 2·8 per cent a year in the twenty-two countries, compared with a historical average of about 1 per cent a year. Output per head has therefore grown three times as fast as it has historically. However, the contrasting experience of countries in the high and low income groups is very marked. In the nine countries with a per capita income level of $500 and above, per capita income grew by 3·8 per cent a year,

[1] Population problems are analysed later in Chapter IX.

whereas in the other thirteen countries growth was only 2·2 per cent. It is clear therefore that the income gap has widened within the developing world, and it is obviously important that our later analysis should try to explain this.

The increase in per capita output has been higher than the rise in per capita consumption, because most countries have increased the share of resources going to investment and government and only part of this was financed by foreign aid. If we allow for this shift in resource allocation, the rise in per capita consumption in real terms was probably about 2·5 per cent a year, though some of the increased

Table I–4

Growth of Gross Domestic Product per Head of Population 1870–1967

Annual average compound growth rates

	1870–1913	1913–50	1950–67
Argentina	1·5	0·7	1·1
Brazil	—	2·4†	2·1
Ceylon	—	—	0·8
Chile	—	0·6	1·6
Colombia	—	1·4	1·3
Egypt	—	0·2	2·7
Ghana	—	1·2	1·3
Greece	—	−0·1	5·5
India	0·7	0·2	1·6
Israel	—	—	5·0
Malaya	—	2·2	0·8
Mexico	1·2*	1·2‡	2·8
Pakistan	(0·7)	(0·2)	1·5
Peru	—	1·5	2·9
Philippines	—	0·1	1·8
South Korea	—	—	3·8
Spain	—	−0·3	6·4
Taiwan	—	0·7	5·3
Thailand	—	—	3·2
Turkey	—	—	2·8
Venezuela	—	—	2·5
Yugoslavia	—	0·9§	5·6
Average	1·0	0·8	2·8

* 1877–1910; † 1920–50; ‡ 1910–50; § 1909/12–50.

Sources: Appendices B and C.

government share was devoted to expenditures on health and education which raised welfare considerably. In addition there was some income loss due to a deterioration in the terms of trade. In spite of the extensive theoretical literature on the terms of trade, the statistical data are, unfortunately, rather weak. On the evidence available, the terms of trade loss may have reduced real consumption by 0.1 points a year on average over the period as a whole.

Within developing countries, the gains of accelerated growth have been unevenly shared. Agricultural productivity has risen more slowly than that in the economy as a whole and the terms of trade for farmers have deteriorated in many countries. The farm population, which is the poorest group in each country, has received less of the fruits of progress than the rest of the community.

Having described the post-war acceleration in growth and the big variations in the experience of different countries, we will try in the next chapter to explain why the acceleration occurred and why performance was so varied.

Chapter II

Reasons for Accelerated Growth and Variations in Performance

Economic growth depends ultimately on the input of productive resources and the efficiency with which they are used. Resource input and efficiency are both affected (*a*) by the spontaneous action of private forces in the economy, (*b*) by government policy. In order to clarify their impact on growth it is useful to set out a simple model in which their relationship and relative importance is made explicit. Our model, like most others, is only a crude approximation to reality because on several important points the quantification is based on judgment rather than evidence, and in the real world there is a more complex interdependence between causal factors than we can hope to numerate. The novel feature of our model is the distinction between autonomous and policy-induced growth. Previous models of economic growth have not set out to do this for developing countries.

Historically, economists have considered land, labour and capital to be the important factors of production. But so much of environment is now man-made, that variations in natural resource endowment are more relevant in explaining the historical differences in level of income than in explaining current rates of growth. In Denison's major work on developed country growth, natural resources play no explanatory role.[1] In developing countries, where

[1] See E. F. Denison, *Why Growth Rates Differ*, Brookings Institution, Washington, 1967, and Allen & Unwin, London, 1968. Our own analysis in this chapter is heavily influenced by Denison's work, though the methodology is different on several important points. Denison's approach was first used in his book on the US economy, *The Sources of Economic Growth in the United States and the Alternatives Before Us*, Committee for Economic Development, New York, 1962. This has been subjected to detailed appraisal by M. Abramovitz, 'Economic Growth in the United States', *American Economic Review*, September 1962, pp. 762–82, by R. R. Nelson, 'Aggregate Production Functions and

man-made capital is scarcer, natural resource endowment looms larger as an explanatory variable, particularly in countries with mineral wealth.

In developed countries where productivity is high and labour scarce, no economist would now think of explaining growth without analysing the labour supply, but developing countries are often assumed to have such a surplus of labour that several quite respectable model-builders have tried to explain performance by models which leave labour out of account.[1] In our view, growth in labour supply has had a substantial influence on output, and it would be absurd to build a model which ignores the advantage to Israel of its 5·4 per cent annual growth in employment as compared with the low 0·7 per cent in Spain. There is also an enormous difference between the productivity of labour in agriculture and non-agriculture which makes it necessary to disaggregate the analysis of labour supply.

The third resource input which economists have considered important is capital. In fact, some growth models consider it the only important source of growth. This is an exaggerated view, but our own conclusion is that the acceleration in investment has been the most important engine of growth in the post-war developing world. We might also have treated research and technical progress explicitly as inputs which affect the quality of capital, but we did not do so as we have already given capital a rather big weight.[2]

Recent analysis of growth has emphasized the importance of non-conventional inputs, particularly education and research. We share the feeling that these have been important, and we treat improved education (and health) as resource inputs which increased the quality of labour.

In analysing the contribution of policy to resource mobilization we have made allowance for constraints imposed by income level. In this respect our model differs from most of those currently used. The result is a better performance rating for some of the low-income countries, e.g. India, than has lately been conventional.

Medium Range Growth Projections', *American Economic Review*, September 1964, and by a group of economists in J. Vaizey, ed. *The Residual Factor in Economic Growth*, OECD, Paris, 1965.

[1] See H. B. Chenery and A. M. Strout, *Foreign Assistance and Economic Development*, AID, Washington, 1965.

[2] See R. M. Solow, 'Technical Progress, Capital Formation, and Economic Growth', *American Economic Review, Proceedings*, May 1962, for a model of 'embodied' technical progress.

We have not treated balance of payments problems as an independent constraint, though they are the most publicized obstacle to faster growth. Developing countries generally do have specific balance of payments constraints because their exports are concentrated on primary products for which demand is sluggish, and some of their potential manufactured exports such as textiles are heavily protected in developed countries. Furthermore, in a period of rapidly rising investment they are heavily dependent on imports. However, balance of payments difficulties are also the reflection of other problems such as inadequate savings, overvalued exchange rates, excessive protection, neglect of agricultural development, etc. As these two sources of payments difficulty are difficult to disentangle in an *ex post* analysis, and as the first kind of problem—the structural one—is characteristic of most developing countries except those with large mineral resources, large-scale aid or tourist earnings, we felt entitled to build a model in which the payments constraint does not figure explicitly. However, the model does give substantial weight to the benefits derived from external finance and mineral resources, so it makes indirect allowance for factors which have affected the payments position of some countries favourably.

As later data are not available for some countries, the model is confined to explaining growth which occurred between 1950 and 1965. However, our other chapters include analysis of policy trends since 1965.

a. *Capital*

In most developing countries, it is only since the last war that investment has risen significantly above the level in Europe in the eighteenth century. The increase has been the biggest factor responsible for accelerated growth.

In the 1950s, economists gave major stress to the importance of high investment in achieving a 'take-off', i.e. in transforming a stagnant economy into a developing one. Arthur Lewis[1] and W. W. Rostow[2] suggested that the critical effort involved in the development process was to increase net investment from 5 to 10 per cent of national income. The argument for a 10 per cent net investment rate implies a target for gross investment, including allowance for replacement, of about 13 or 14 per cent of GDP. In fact, the Lewis–Rostow targets have actually been reached.

1 See *The Theory of Economic Growth*, Allen & Unwin, London, 1959.
2 See *The Stages of Economic Growth*, Cambridge, 1960.

Table II–1

Change in Non-Residential Gross Fixed Investment as Percentage of GDP at Current Market Prices 1950–66

	1950	1966	1950–66 average of annual ratios
Argentina	14·7	13·4	14·3
Brazil	11·3	10·9	12·5
Ceylon	7·1	11·0	10·0
Chile	9·6	10·3	11·7
Colombia	11·4	(12·1)	12·9
Egypt	10·2	(16·3)	11·5
Ghana	7·4	12·0	13·1
Greece	11·7	15·6	11·1
India	7·4	13·8	11·2
Israel	15·6	14·1	17·3
Malaya	5·0	(15·1)	10·3
Mexico	10·8	14·8	13·2
Pakistan	4·8	12·9	9·9
Peru	11·0	13·9	15·3
Philippines	7·4	16·5	10·7
South Korea	5·7	18·1	8·8
Spain	10·3	18·6	13·7
Taiwan	9·8	16·7	12·2
Thailand	11·9	(19·3)	13·9
Turkey	6·9	(10·4)	10·0
Venezuela	20·0	15·6	19·5
Yugoslavia	22·0	18·2	21·1
Average	10·5	14·5	12·9
France	13·6	15·5	14·1
Germany (FR)	14·3	19·9	17·6
Italy	14·8	12·3	15·1
Japan	15·7	(25·2)	23·0
UK	10·3	14·3	12·2
USA	13·7	14·6	13·3
Average	13·7	17·0	15·9

Source: Appendix D, for developing countries, developed countries from sources indicated in A. Maddison, *Economic Growth in Japan and the USSR*, Allen & Unwin, London, 1969, p. 39. Figures in brackets are for 1965. The figures exclude inventories for which data are poor or often not available.

For the twenty-two countries combined, gross fixed non-residential investment rose from 10·5 per cent of GDP in 1950 to 14·5 per cent in 1966. The biggest increases occurred in the poorer countries. In Africa and Asia (excluding Israel) the average rose from 7·6 in 1950 to 14·6 per cent in 1966. In Pakistan, Malaya and South Korea the rate has roughly trebled since 1950 and in India, the Philippines and Spain it doubled. In Ceylon, Egypt, Taiwan, Thailand and Turkey it rose by about half. In Latin America, Mexico and Peru made progress, but there were falls in Argentina, Brazil and Venezuela. The investment rate also fell in Israel and Yugoslavia, but in these countries the level was considerably higher than in Asia and Africa.

One difficulty in comparing investment rates is that the price of capital goods varies a good deal. Construction is generally cheaper than in the developed world, and equipment more expensive. The Economic Commission for Latin America found that overall, the relative price of capital goods was higher than in the USA.[1] But as the coverage of developing country estimates is often less complete, these two factors tend to be offsetting.

Figures on investment as a share of GDP show the current financial burden of capital formation. But to measure the effect of investment on output, it is more relevant to see how fast the capital *stock* was growing. Two countries may each devote the same share of GDP to investment, but if GDP is growing faster in one than in the other its capital stock will be rising more quickly. By cumulating the investment which took place between 1950 and 1964 we can arrive at a figure for the gross addition to the capital stock from beginning 1950 to beginning 1965, but to calculate the net increase in capital stock we need to know how much of the new capital formation went to replacement.

As information for 1950 was not generally available, we assumed that the 1950 non-residential capital stock of each of the countries was one and a half times as high as its GDP, i.e. an average initial capital-output ratio of 1·5,[2] and that half of the initial stock was

[1] See ECLA, *A Measurement of Price Levels and the Purchasing Power of Currencies in Latin America 1960–62*, E/CN. 12/653, Santiago, March 1963.

[2] It is necessary to make a uniform assumption as estimates are available only for a few countries. In Israel, the ratio was 1·3 in 1957; see A. L. Gaathon, *Capital Stock, Employment and Output in Israel, 1950–59*, Bank of Israel, Jerusalem, 1961, p. 95, for estimates of the Israeli capital stock. In Colombia the ratio was 1·6 in 1953 and in Yugoslavia 2·3 in 1953; see R. W. Goldsmith and C. Saunders, eds., *Income and Wealth Series VIII, The Measurement of*

replaced in the fifteen years 1950–64. This implies that assets have an average useful life of thirty years, and that their age structure was similar in the different countries in 1950. The assumed life for assets is a fairly standard one, and although the age and condition of the capital stock in fact varies a good deal in 1950, our assumption of similar age structures is the only one that can reasonably be made. Perhaps more questionable is the assumption that the average capital-output ratio was similar. The ratio tends to be bigger in countries which are relatively more advanced and have a more complex economic structure. Building requirements also vary for climatic reasons. The kind of building necessary for the rigorous winters of Yugoslavia is not needed in Egypt. With these caveats, we nevertheless assume that our estimates provide a crude idea of differences in the growth of the capital stock, and they are shown in Table II–2.

The estimates of the growth of the capital stock show big differences between the fast and the slower-growing countries. The Israeli stock grew 2·4 times as fast as that of India, although her investment ratio (non-residential) was only 50 per cent higher. On average, for the twenty-two countries, the capital stock grew by

Table II–2

Rates of Growth of the Non-Residential Fixed Capital Stock 1950–65

Annual average compound growth rates

Argentina	5·6	Pakistan	3·7
Brazil	6·1	Peru	6·8
Ceylon	4·0	Philippines	5·1
Chile	4·9	South Korea	4·4
Colombia	5·8	Spain	7·6
Egypt	5·6	Taiwan	7·0
Ghana	6·0	Thailand	6·8
Greece	5·7	Turkey	5·0
India	4·7	Venezuela	9·3
Israel	11·2	Yugoslavia	9·7
Malaya	3·6		
Mexico	6·4	Average	6·1

Source: Appendix D.

National Wealth, Bowes and Bowes, London, 1959, pp. 9 and 10. In the USA, the ratio in 1962 was 1·4 excluding government structures and roads; see E. F. Denison, *Why Growth Rates Differ*, Brookings, Washington DC, p. 415.

6·1 per cent a year. This was considerably faster than the increase in employment and led to rapid growth in capital per head. Unfortunately, data on pre-war investment rates are rare, but it seems likely that pre-war investment was generally below 1950 levels, and the capital stock may well be growing three times as fast as in prewar years.

Our analysis of investment excludes housing because its contribution to productive capacity is rather indirect. Although we would not suggest that the contribution of housing is so negligible that it should be ignored, we have chosen to do so in our model, mainly because data on the housing stock are non-existent for most developing countries, and the statistical coverage of current housing investment is very uneven, with some countries leaving out most of the rural sector.

For what they are worth, the figures on housing investment were as follows:

Table II–3

Average Level of Housing Investment as Percentage of GDP in Current Prices 1950–65

	Average of annual ratios		
Argentina	4·8	Pakistan	0·9
Brazil	2·2	Peru	4·3
Ceylon	2·9	Philippines	2·5
Chile	3·7	South Korea	1·7
Colombia	3·5	Spain	3·4
Egypt	2·6	Taiwan	1·6
Ghana	1·9	Thailand	1·7
Greece	5·8	Turkey	3·2
India	1·3	Venezuela	2·6
Israel	9·8	Yugoslavia	4·7
Malaya	1·8		
Mexico	1·3	Average	3·1

Source: Appendix D.

b. *Labour*

On average, employment has grown by about 2·1 per cent a year, which is quicker than in pre-war years, and considerably faster than in developed countries. In most cases, the labour force grew more slowly than population. There are two main reasons for this. The fall in death rates was concentrated on children, so there was a decline in the proportion of the population available for work. There were also big increases in school enrolment which reduced the activity rate.

In a few countries the labour force increased faster than population for special reasons. In both countries these special circumstances made the labour force grow considerably faster than population. In Greece the birth rate declined and in Israel there was large-scale immigration.

As we are concerned with growth potential, it might seem reasonable to use the labour force rather than employment as a measure of labour supply. However, unemployment in developing countries is usually due to lack of capital and not to failure of policy to maintain adequate demand. Most of the unemployed could not have been used and it is therefore legitimate to eliminate them in measuring output potential.

Our employment figures are rather rough, because few countries have an adequate statistical reporting system. Only Taiwan and South Korea measure unemployment by a regular sample survey similar to that used in the United States and they are the two countries with the highest recorded unemployment rates, 11·5 per cent for Taiwan and 7·4 per cent for Korea in 1965. It seems likely that several other countries would have had higher unemployment rates, if the figures had been properly recorded.[1]

In calculating the contribution of labour to output, we must take account of the highly dualistic character of these economies. Except in Argentina and Israel, productivity in agriculture is extremely low, on average is only a fifth of that in the rest of the economy (see Table II–4). This low productivity in agriculture is due partly to the fact that farm workers are not fully employed. Some economists argue that a substantial proportion of the agricultural population (30 per cent or more) could be removed without any loss of output. This is the position of Doreen Warriner who first tried to measure 'disguised unemployment' in her pre-war studies of peasant agriculture in eastern Europe. More recently, this view has been contested by writers who have argued that though heavy seasonal unemployment may exist, it is nevertheless impossible to remove

[1] The special ILO sample survey in Ceylon in 1959 found a 10·5 per cent unemployment rate, which is much higher than the unemployment recorded by the census. The figures we have used for Ceylon are based on the sample survey benchmark.

Table II–4

Level of Output per Person Engaged in Agriculture and Non-Agriculture in 1965 and 1950

Dollars at US 1965 relative prices

	1965 Agriculture	1965 Non-agriculture	1950 agriculture	1950 Non-agriculture
Argentina	2,226	3,665	2,001	2,846
Brazil	556	2,372	370	2,018
Ceylon	455	1,524	365	1,347
Chile	644	3,536	504	2,450
Colombia	434	2,004	337	1,503
Egypt	262	1,950	181	1,223
Ghana	211	1,178	n.a.	n.a.
Greece	493	2,629	223	1,470
India	90	1,205	75	1,341
Israel	1,877	3,812	846	1,778
Malaya	515	2,776	363	2,951
Mexico	332	2,401	208	1,828
Pakistan	133	1,381	138	1,148
Peru	550	2,055	373	1,150
Philippines	247	1,591	181	1,450
South Korea	164	1,560	59	1,382
Spain	596	3,574	320	1,582
Taiwan	461	2,551	204	1,103
Thailand	219	1,618	175	1,243
Turkey	240	1,756	161	1,247
Venezuela	599	5,454	301	4,385
Yugoslavia	303	3,179	140	1,751
Average	528	2,444	359	1,783

Source: Appendixes A and B.

any substantial fraction of labour from agriculture without some loss of output.[1]

The burden of modern evidence suggests that there is not a large amount of completely surplus labour in agriculture, but whether or

[1] See C. Clark and M. R. Haswell, *The Economics of Subsistence Agriculture*, Macmillan, London, 1964; A. A. Pepelasis, *Labour Shortages in Greek Agriculture, 1963–73*, Centre of Economic Research, Athens, 1963; and B. Hansen, 'Marginal Productivity Wage Theory and Subsistence Wage Theory in Egyptian Agriculture', *The Journal of Development Studies*, July 1966.

not we choose to accept the concept of disguised unemployment, it is quite uncontestable that the productivity of labour in agriculture is low and that additions to farm labour make little contribution to output.

In the past two decades, there has been an absolute increase in farm employment in most developing countries, but the relative share of agriculture has fallen everywhere. In all countries, therefore there has been some improvement in the effectiveness of labour because of this shift to higher productivity employment. However, the higher output per head of non-agriculture is due in part to the fact that it has more capital per head, and we therefore exaggerate somewhat by treating the whole gain from this structural shift as a contribution of labour.

We have divided the employment increase into two parts. The contribution of those entering agriculture is smaller than that of people lucky enough to find jobs in other sectors, and it was assumed that the difference in their 'effectiveness' could be measured in terms of the average productivity of labour in agriculture and non-agriculture.[1] In all countries, the effectiveness of labour increased to some degree and on average, the 'effective' labour supply grew by 3·2 per cent a year compared with an actual employment increase of 2·1 per cent (see Table II–5).

Apart from the improved sectoral distribution of labour there were other improvements in quality which had a significant positive effect on productivity. Rising health standards increased physical working capacity, and probably mental alertness as well. The improvement was particularly important in Asia, where malaria was greatly reduced, thanks to DDT,[2] and the incidence of dysentery declined because of better sanitation. These two illnesses are probably the most debilitating in terms of working efficiency, but there are many others whose impact has faded.[3] Improved nutrition also made

1 The formula was as follows for the last column of Table II–5:
$\frac{E_1^a p_0^a + E_1^e p_0^e}{E_0^a p_0^a + E_0^e p_0^e}$, where E is employment; a is agriculture; e is non-agriculture; and p is labour productivity.

2 Malaria eradication has proceeded furthest in Ceylon, where 57 per cent of the population had the disease in 1940, 8 per cent in 1950; in 1960 there were only 460 cases in a population of nearly 10 million. See D. R. Snodgrass, *Ceylon: An Export Economy in Transition*, Irwin, Illinois, 1966, p. 87. In Pakistan, malaria still killed 100,000 people a year in 1965.

3 In East Pakistan there were 79,000 cases of small-pox in 1958 and only fifty in 1964 after the whole population was vaccinated. See *Third Five Year Plan*, Planning Commission, Pakistan, p. 244.

Table II–5

Increase in Actual and in 'Effective' Employment 1950–65

Annual average compound growth rates

	Agriculture	Non-agriculture	Actual total	'Effective' total
Argentina	−1·0	2·1	1·4	1·6
Brazil	1·6	4·3	2·9	3·8
Ceylon	0·7	3·0	1·6	2·3
Chile	0·3	1·6	1·3	1·5
Colombia	1·2	3·3	2·3	2·9
Egypt	0·7	2·8	1·5	2·4
Ghana	n.a.	n.a.	n.a.	n.a.
Greece	0·1	2·6	1·2	2·2
India	1·3	4·4	2·2	3·9
Israel	3·8	5·6	5·4	5·5
Malaya	0·0	4·1	1·7	3·5
Mexico	2·2	4·2	3·1	4·0
Pakistan	2·2	3·0	2·4	2·8
Peru	0·1	2·5	1·3	1·9
Philippines	0·7	4·9	2·2	4·1
South Korea	−0·1	5·3	1·8	4·9
Spain	−1·6	2·4	0·7	1·9
Taiwan	0·2	3·0	1·7	2·6
Thailand	2·3	5·6	3·1	4·5
Turkey	1·3	3·3	1·8	2·7
Venezuela	0·9	5·2	3·6	5·1
Yugoslavia	−0·5	3·3	1·0	2·8
Average	0·8	3·6	2·1	3·2
France	−3·2	1·5	0·3	—
Germany (FR)	−3·5	2·8	1·7	—
Italy	−2·5	2·7	0·9	—
Japan	—2·3	4·4	1·9	—
UK	−2·4	0·8	0·7	—
USA	−3·4	1·7	1·3	—
Average	−2·9	2·3	1·1	—

Source: Appendix C for developing countries, developed countries derived from sources described in A. Maddison, *Growth in Japan and the USSR*, Allen & Unwin, London, 1969.

a contribution in some countries, although there was little significant change in the two poorest countries, India and Pakistan.

It is not easy to quantify the impact of better health and nutrition on working efficiency. In the poorest countries, the improvements must have had some effect, and it was therefore assumed that better physical well-being raised the working efficiency of the labour force in Ceylon, Egypt, Ghana, India, Pakistan, the Philippines, South Korea, Thailand, and Turkey by 3 per cent over the fifteen years under review. In the other countries (where per capita income is above $300 a year) the initial level of health and nutrition was probably high enough to secure reasonable working efficiency. The improvement in standards added to welfare but not to economic potential.

The quality of labour has been improved substantially in terms of education. Table 11–6 gives some rough indicators of the educational attainments of the different countries in 1965. The picture is encouraging, thanks to the vigorous efforts of the past few years. On average, over 70 per cent of the labour force is now literate, and the average employee has 5·4 years of schooling. This is very much better than the record of today's developed countries when they were at similar income levels. The countries with the lowest educational standards were Egypt, Ghana, India, Pakistan, Thailand and Turkey, and those with the highest achievements were Argentina, Chile, Greece and Israel. Educational achievement is positively correlated with the level of income, though there are some low-income countries like South Korea and the Philippines with relatively high standards.

In the 1960s, education received considerable credit as a source of economic growth, and it is now usual to consider it as an 'investment in human resources' as well as an element of communal consumption. In the first flush of enthusiasm for education it was even suggested that it is a more important source of economic growth than investment in physical capital, though most of these claims were not based on a direct identification of its role as a propulsive force, but gave it credit for most of the growth not specifically attributable to other causes.[1] Our own estimates of the role of education are more modest, but they suggest that it added

[1] See R. Solow, 'Technical Change and the Aggregate Production Function', *The Review of Economics and Statistics*, August 1957; O. Aukrust, 'Investment and Economic Growth', *Productivity Measurement Review*, No. 16, OEEC, Paris, 1959.

Table II–6

Educational Qualifications of the Labour Force 1965

	Per cent literate	Per cent with high level technical training	Average number of years of primary and secondary education per member of the labour force
Argentina	93·1	0·8	6·9
Brazil	67·3	0·4	3·9
Ceylon	76·0	n.a.	7·5
Chile	86·1	n.a.	6·9
Colombia	65·5	n.a.	3·8
Egypt	36·1	0·3	3·2
Ghana	n.a.	0·05	3·3
Greece	90·1	0·9	7·4
India	35·4	0·35	3·2
Israel	89·3	1·3	8·5
Malaya	64·7	n.a.	5·1
Mexico	70·7	0·3	4·9
Pakistan	27·0	0·08	2·5
Peru	73·0	n.a.	4·9
Philippines	75·6	0·7	7·8
South Korea	82·5	0·9	6·5
Spain	92·1	0·9	5·9
Taiwan	78·9	0·9	5·7
Thailand	74·9	0·1	5·5
Turkey	46·1	0·3	3·7
Venezuela	70·6	n.a.	5·4
Yugoslavia	84·3	0·7	6·0
Average	70·4	n.a.	5·4

Source: Literacy rates for labour force aged 15 to 64 estimated with help of data on literacy by age and sex, data on age structure and activity rates in UNESCO, *Statistical Yearbook* 1965, Paris, 1967, *Yearbook of Labour Statistics*, 1967, ILO, Geneva, 1968, and *Demographic Yearbook* 1966, UN, New York, 1967. Second column refers to scientists and engineers, doctors, dentists and veterinarians. Data derived from A. Maddison, *Foreign Skills and Technical Assistance in Economic Development*, OECD Development Centre, Paris, 1965, F. Harbison and C. A. Myers, *Education, Manpower and Economic Growth*, McGraw Hill, New York, 1964, and data supplied by Mr Jan Auerhan of UNESCO. Years of schooling were calculated from historical data on enrolments as given by UNESCO.

0·3 percentage points to the growth rate of the twenty-two countries, which is a sixth of the policy-induced growth.

Almost all countries made big increases in their educational effort. In 1950 just over a third of the children aged 5 to 19 were going to school, and by 1965 the ratio was well over half (see Table II–7). The rise was biggest in Africa. In Ghana enrolments rose from one-seventh to over half of the population of school age.

Table II–7

Ratio of Enrolments in Primary and Secondary Education to Population aged 5 to 19

	1950	1964		1950	1964
Argentina	51	60	Peru	34	50
Brazil	22	46	Philippines	59	57‡
Ceylon*	54	65	South Korea	43	63
Chile	50	63	Spain*	43	59
Colombia	22	45	Taiwan	38	64
Egypt	20	41	Thailand	38	48
Ghana	14	57	Turkey	24	40
Greece	56	60	Venezuela	30	61
India	19	38†	Yugoslavia	44	68
Israel	58	66			
Malaya	35	50	Average	36	54
Mexico	30	52			
Pakistan	16	25	USA	80	84

* Includes pre-school enrolments; † 1963; ‡ seems to exclude private schools.
Source: *Statistical Yearbook*, 1964 and 1966 editions, UNESCO, Paris, 1966 and 1968.

Secondary and higher education expanded much faster than primary, so that the average quality of education may have risen. We have made no allowance for this, as the calculation would be quite complex, and there were offsetting losses in quality due to overcrowded schools and the inadequate supply of teachers. The curricula have remained similar to those in the colonial period and emphasis on scientific and technical training is often inadequate.

Enrolment data of past years enable us to make rough estimates of the change in the educational qualifications between 1950 and 1965. There was a rise of about a quarter in the years of education which an average employee had received (see Table II–8). The problem now is to decide what economic impact this was likely to have had.

Table II–8

Change in Educational Qualifications per Employee 1950–65

	Years of education per employee 1950	Years of education per new employee 1950–65	Proportion of 1950–65 entrants to 1965 employment	Years of education per employee 1965	Difference in years of education per employee 1950–65
Argentina	6·12	8·37	35·5	6·92	0·80
Brazil	2·64	5·22	47·7	3·87	1·23
Ceylon	6·48	8·99	37·4	7·42	0·94
Chile	6·00	8·55	33·6	6·86	0·86
Colombia	2·64	5·15	42·8	3·71	1·07
Egypt	2·40	4·68	36·0	3·22	0·82
Ghana	1·68	5·55	40·6	3·25	1·57
Greece	6·72	8·72	32·7	7·37	0·65
India	2·28	4·47	41·6	3·19	0·91
Israel	6·96	9·35	63·4*	8·48	1·52
Malaya	4·20	6·45	41·3	5·13	0·93
Mexico	3·60	6·27	49·9	4·93	1·33
Pakistan	1·92	3·12	44·1	2·45	0·53
Peru	4·08	6·39	33·3	4·85	0·77
Philippines	7·08	8·70	42·0	7·76	0·68
South Korea	5·16	8·06	38·6	6·28	1·12
Spain	5·16	7·74	28·4	5·89	0·73
Taiwan	4·56	7·79	37·6	5·77	1·21
Thailand	4·56	6·51	49·1	5·52	0·96
Turkey	2·88	4·89	38·9	3·66	0·78
Venezuela	3·60	6·99	53·1	5·40	1·80
Yugoslavia	5·28	7·73	30·9	6·04	0·76
Average	4·36	6·80	40·8	5·36	1·00

* In Israel there was a large influx of immigrants from Asia and Africa with low levels of education, so we may have overstated the increase in the average level of education.

Source: Enrolments are shown in Table II–7 for 1950 and 1965 as a percentage of the population aged 5 to 19. It was assumed that the schooling which had been obtained by the average member of the labour force in 1950 was 80 per cent of the level being provided in 1950, e.g. the 1950 enrolment ratio for Argentina was 51 per cent or 7·65 years of education. 80 per cent of this is 6·12 years. It was assumed that 20 per cent of the labour force of 1950 had retired by 1965, and that the new entrants to the labour force for 1950–65 had a level of schooling equivalent to the average provided in 1950 and 1965.

The best guide to the economic returns from education is information on the earnings of people with varying qualifications.[1] Earnings are heavily influenced by intelligence and social position and it is difficult to segregate the impact of these from that of education.[2] The earnings structure will also vary over time because of changing demand-supply relations and institutional conventions. In newly independent countries like Ghana where educated people were very scarce and were usually expatriates until very recently, the returns on education have been much higher to those possessing it than in Israel. Ideally therefore we need information on the stock of people with different skills and their relative income for each country. In the absence of such information, we simply assumed that an extra year of schooling added 10 per cent to the quality of the labour force in each country. This is a slightly higher return than Denison obtained for European countries, but the salary differentials for educated people in developing countries are higher than in Europe.[3]

Many of the skills most helpful to efficiency are acquired by on-the-job training and experience. The provisions for practical training are much better in some countries than in others. They are excellent in Brazil and almost non-existent in Pakistan. Work experience—'learning by doing'—is very important in the early stages of industrialization and was significant in all the countries under review. Unfortunately, we have no comparable statistical information on practical training, but the impact of on-the-job training and experience is partially reflected in our earlier adjustment for changes in the sectoral composition of employment.

Table II–9 shows the increase in total human resource inputs from 1950 to 1965 after allowing for improvements in quality due to better industrial composition, better health and education. On average, human resources grew by 3·9 per cent a year or considerably faster than in the developed countries.

[1] See T. W. Schultz, 'Investment in Human Capital', *American Economic Review*, March 1961, and T. W. Schultz, *The Economic Value of Education*, Columbia, New York, 1963. Interestingly enough, Professor Strumilin, the father of Soviet planning, produced estimates similar to those of Schultz in the early 1920s to help justify the Soviet educational effort.

[2] Denison assumed that in Europe and the USA, three-fifths of earnings differentials were due to education and two-fifths to characteristics such as intelligence, social position of parents, etc. See E. F. Denison, *op. cit.*, pp. 83 and 85.

[3] See Denison, *op. cit.*, pp. 103 and 107.

Table II–9

Increase in Total 'Human Resource' Inputs 1950–65

Annual average compound growth rates

Argentina	2·1	Pakistan	3·4
Brazil	4·7	Peru	2·4
Ceylon	3·2	Philippines	4·8
Chile	2·1	South Korea	5·8
Colombia	3·6	Spain	2·4
Egypt	3·1	Taiwan	3·4
Ghana	n.a.	Thailand	5·4
Greece	2·6	Turkey	3·5
India	4·7	Venezuela	6·2
Israel	6·4	Yugoslavia	3·4
Malaya	4·1		
Mexico	4·9	Average	3·9

Source: Derived from Tables II–5 and II–7 with adjustment for health and nutrition.

c. *Natural Resources*

There are big differences in the natural resource endowment of countries. The most important are land, climate and minerals. Table II–10 shows the land-labour ratio for agriculture.

Differences in natural resource endowment are obviously a major historical reason for the high output of farmers in Argentina and for low output in India. Most of the effects of these differences had already made themselves felt before 1950 and there were few significant *changes* in known natural resource endowment in these countries between 1950 and 1965. However, we assumed that countries with less than 1·5 hectares of land per agricultural worker were at a disadvantage, and that this reduced their agricultural growth *potential* by 1 per cent a year. The impact of this drag on growth varies with the importance of agriculture in the economy. Thus a country where agriculture was a third of total output would suffer a reduction in its total growth potential by 0·3 percentage points a year. The countries affected by natural disadvantage were Ceylon, Egypt, India, Pakistan, South Korea, Taiwan and Thailand. In the case of Chile and Venezuela, copper and oil provided government with large revenues from corporate taxation. These two countries were therefore credited with special growth benefits deriving from their mineral endowment. It was assumed that

Table II–10

The Land-Labour Ratio in Agriculture in 1965

	Hectares per person engaged		Hectares per person engaged
Argentina	91·6	Mexico	14·8
Brazil	11·0	Pakistan	0·9
Ceylon	0·8	Peru	18·8
Chile	21·1	Philippines	1·9
Colombia	8·0	South Korea	0·5
Egypt	0·5	Spain	8·3
Ghana	1·4	Taiwan	0·4
Greece	4·6	Thailand	1·2
India	1·2	Turkey	5·2
Israel	9·8	Venezuela	27·3
Malaya	1·6	Yugoslavia	3·1

Source: *Production Yearbook* 1966, FAO, Rome, 1967, for land area. Appendix B for employment. We have simply added together all agricultural land without adjustment for quality, and this understates the endowment of Egypt and Taiwan where a good deal of land can produce three crops a year, but the differences in land availability are so enormous, that there can be no doubt as to the balance of advantage.

government tax revenue from foreign corporations (2·5 per cent of GDP in Chile and 7 per cent in Venezuela) was a rough measure of this and could be regarded as an external source of finance for capital formation.

GROWTH 'EXPLAINED'

We are now in a position to summarize the contribution of the different influences on the growth of output. We know how the supply of capital and human resources changed, and we need to give each one a weight in order to measure their aggregate impact. In this study of growth in developed countries, Edward Denison[1] has made a composite index of factor inputs, giving each one a weight equivalent to its share in natural income in the country concerned. He assumes that income shares reflect the importance of each factor's contribution to output. Thus, for the USA, he gives labour a weight of 79 per cent, and capital (of all kinds) gets a weight of 21 per cent. For Italy, labour's share is lower at 72 per

[1] See E. F. Denison, *Why Growth Rates Differ*, Brookings, Washington DC, 1967.

cent. A recent study on the same lines gives labour a weight from 50 to 60 per cent in Latin American countries.[1] Information on factor shares in developing countries is scarce but there is a definite tendency for labour's share to be lower. In these countries this is to be expected as labour is abundant and capital scarcer than in the developed world.

In any case, factor rewards are likely to under-state capital's contribution to output. Technical progress is exploited mainly by being embodied in capital, but the benefits are not monopolized by capitalists. It is only if the capitalist has secret technical knowledge that he can keep the whole benefit for himself. His profits are a reward for enterprise and thrift and not for exploiting techniques which are, for the most part, freely available to any other capitalist. Therefore, his income is not an adequate reflection of the contribution of capital to the production potential of the economy, unless we are willing to assume that technical progress is a separate factor of production which casts its blessings on an economy irrespective of the investment effort. For these reasons we have given capital a much greater weight (50 per cent) than in the Denison model.

Table II–11 shows the weighted contribution of factor inputs and efficiency to economic growth. The first column shows the contribution of human resources (i.e. figures of Table II–9 with 50 per cent weight) and the second column the contribution of capital (i.e. figures of Table II–2 with 50 per cent weight). The fourth column shows the growth of GDP and the fifth column shows the residual change in efficiency (i.e. the difference between GDP growth and the growth explained by the increase in factor inputs). In this, and in subsequent tables, the presence of two decimal points should not be taken to imply a high degree of accuracy. It is necessary simply because some influences are very small.

From Table II–11, we can see that Israel, for example, with a growth in labour supply of 6·4 per cent a year and of capital stock by 11·2 per cent, increased its total factor input by 8·8 per cent a year. Labour contributed 3·2 percentage points to the growth rate (50 per cent of 6·4) and capital 5·6 points (50 per cent of 11·2). The remaining 1·9 per cent a year of Israeli growth was due to increased efficiency in resource allocation.[2] Efficiency gains arise

[1] See H. J. Bruton, 'Productivity Growth in Latin America', *American Economic Review*, December 1967.

[2] If we had used factor income weights labour would have probably been 70 per cent of the total and non-residential capital about 30 per cent. This

Table II–11

Contribution of Factor Inputs and Increased Efficiency to Economic Growth 1950–65

	Percentage point contribution to annual average compound growth rate of GDP				
	Human resources	Non-residential capital	Labour and non-residential capital combined	GDP growth rate	Growth due to changes in efficiency
Argentina	1·05	2·80	3·85	3·20	−0·65
Brazil	2·35	3·05	5·40	5·20	−0·20
Ceylon	1·60	2·00	3·60	3·40	−0·20
Chile	1·05	2·45	3·50	4·00	0·50
Colombia	1·80	2·90	4·70	4·60	−0·10
Egypt	1·55	2·80	4·35	5·50	1·15
Ghana	(1·50)	3·00	4·50	4·20	−0·30
Greece	1·30	2·85	4·15	6·40	2·25
India	2·35	2·35	4·70	3·50	−1·20
Israel	3·20	5·60	8·80	10·70	1·90
Malaya	2·05	1·80	3·85	3·50	−0·35
Mexico	2·45	3·20	5·65	6·10	0·45
Pakistan	1·70	1·85	3·55	3·70	0·15
Peru	1·20	3·40	4·60	5·60	1·00
Philippines	2·40	2·55	4·95	5·00	0·05
South Korea	2·90	2·20	5·10	6·20	1·10
Spain	1·20	3·80	5·00	7·50	2·50
Taiwan	1·70	3·50	5·20	8·50	3·30
Thailand	2·70	3·40	6·10	6·30	0·20
Turkey	1·75	2·50	4·25	5·20	0·95
Venezuela	3·10	4·65	7·75	6·70	−1·05
Yugoslavia	1·70	4·85	6·55	7·10	0·55
Average	1·94	3·07	5·00	5·55	0·55

Source: First column derived from Table II–9, second column from Table II–2, both weighted by 50 per cent. Third column is the sum of first and second columns. The fourth column is derived from Table I–1. The fifth column is a residual after deducting third column from fourth column.

would mean, e.g. for Israel, that the labour supply would contribute 4·5 points to the annual growth rate and capital 3·4 points, i.e. a total factor input of 7·9. The residual which we have attributed to efficiency would then be bigger (2·8 points). This is true of most of the countries because capital inputs were generally growing faster than human resource inputs.

from several sources. Normally an economy will benefit from economies of scale as production increases. There will be technical improvements which arise independently of expenditure on capital, health and education which we have already accounted for. On the other hand, there may be losses in efficiency if the price system is distorted by inflation, if capacity if left idle by recessions, if inefficient industries are created through excessive tariff protection, or if the balance of payments becomes a bottleneck because of domestic policy mistakes. Thus in some countries, such as Argentina or India, there was an efficiency loss rather than the normal gain.

AUTONOMOUS AND POLICY-INDUCED GROWTH

For our purpose, it is necessary to separate the growth due to policy from that which would have occurred spontaneously. There are, in fact, several growth influences which had little direct connection with government policy in the period under examination. The growth in the labour supply was autonomous, because it was determined by demographic events in an earlier period and could not have been substantially influenced by population policy in the period under review. (Improvements in health and education were due to government policy.) Similarly, a good deal of capital formation was financed from spontaneous private savings or by foreign funds and was not primarily attributable to government domestic policy.

All the countries, except Malaya and Venezuela, were able to draw on external capital. Economic aid and private investment were dominant, but there were also reparations, private gifts (e.g. Jewish community donations to Israel), short-term commercial credit, drawings on exchange reserves, transactions with the IMF, private gold hoarding, and military aid. Some of these were gifts, others were loans which may ultimately have to be repaid, but they were all additions to the resources which the country itself produced within the period.

On average, these resources were equal to 2·8 per cent of GDP.[1]

[1] It should be stressed that our figures (in Table II–12) refer to the net contribution of foreign capital in a national accounting sense, i.e. the balance on trade in goods and services and the balance on factor payments to abroad. Typically a developing country will use external resources both to finance a deficit on goods and services and to pay interest and dividends on foreign capital. Nearly all developing countries are in deficit on 'factor payments' except lucky ones like Greece which have relatively large receipts from emigrants' remittances.

But the benefits were very heavily concentrated. In Israel, they were equal to nearly a fifth of GDP, in South Korea 8·3 per cent, in Greece 7·6 per cent and in Taiwan 5·4 per cent. The contribution of these resources was relatively small in Latin America. In India, they were only 1·9 per cent of GDP. In Malaya, there was actually a

Table II–12

External Finance as a Percentage of GDP and Investment 1950–65

Average of annual ratios

	Per cent of GDP	Percentage contribution to non-residential investment		Per cent of GDP	Percentage contribution to non-residential investment
Argentina	0·9	6·3	Pakistan	2·4	24·2
Brazil	1·1	8·8	Peru	3·0	19·6
Ceylon	0·3	3·0	Philippines	2·2	20·6
Chile	1·9	16·2	South Korea	8·3*	94·3
Colombia	1·4	10·9	Spain	1·0	7·3
Egypt	3·4	29·6	Taiwan	5·4	44·3
Ghana	0·4	3·1	Thailand	1·4	10·1
Greece	7·6	68·5	Turkey	2·4	24·0
India	1·9	17·0	Venezuela	−0·2	0·0
Israel	19·1	100·0	Yugoslavia	2·9	13·7
Malaya	−6·5	0·0			
Mexico	1·6	12·1	Average	2·8	24·3

* 1953–65.

Source: First column from Appendix D. The figures are equivalent to the deficit in the balance on trade in goods and services and the deficit on factor payments to abroad. Second column derived from first column of this table and from Appendix D.

large outflow due to repatriation of British capital, and to the traditionally high Chinese remittances.

External resources did not all go to investment. Some were used for military purposes and others went to meet pressing consumption needs. But if they had not been available, domestic investment

For some purposes, however, it is useful to analyse the impact of external resources on a completely net basis and to deduct factor payments. If this is done we get the figures in Table II–13 which some authors describe as the 'net transfer of resources'. On average these transfers were only 1·7 per cent of GDP.

would have been the main sufferer. Foreign resources not only financed investment, but also had indirect beneficial effects. They greatly eased balance of payments constraints and the domestic adjustments which would otherwise have been necessary when demand exceeded domestic resources. They provided governments with additional revenue and made it easier to promote development without squeezing consumption and inhibiting production incentives. They enabled countries to be more open to international trade, and thus contributed to the productivity benefits of increased specialization. Considering the importance of these indirect effects it does not seem exaggerated to treat the whole of external resources as a contribution to capital formation.

We must also make some allowance for investment which would have been carried out by the private sector even if there were no government policy for economic growth. We assumed that this autonomous investment would vary directly with the level of per capita income of each country within a range from 4 per cent of GDP in the poorest country to 8 per cent in the richest,[1] and that all domestically financed non-residential investment beyond this level was induced by government policy.

This assumption that poor countries are at a disadvantage in resource mobilization is, curiously enough, not now generally accepted. At one time, it was widely held that the spontaneous propensity to save tends to increase as income rises, and this was the view held by Keynes in his general theory. Since then, however, this idea has been challenged as far as developed countries are concerned,[2] and even for developing countries, many writers assume that the policy problem involved in raising savings or taxation does not depend on the level of income so much as on its distribution. Our own view is therefore an old-fashioned one.

[1] The upper limit of 8 per cent corresponds with the average rate of non-residential fixed investment which prevailed in west European countries before 1913 when there were no significant government policies to stimulate growth, and the lower limit corresponds with the situation in low income Asian countries before their governments started to pursue active growth policies. The actual post-war relation of savings to income does not provide a guide to spontaneous propensities, because the savings ratios are heavily influenced by policy.

[2] See J. S. Duesenberry, *Income, Saving and the Theory of Consumer Behavior*, Harvard, 1949, p. 57, 'According to our hypothesis, the savings rate is independent of the absolute level of income'. Duesenberry's conclusion was based entirely on evidence for the United States. Similarly in Professor Kaldor's writings on taxation it is sometimes suggested that poor countries have just as great a taxation potential as rich ones (see our Chapter III below).

Table II–13

Net Transfer of Resources as Percentage of GDP 1950–65

Average of annual ratios

Argentina	0·9	Pakistan	2·3
Brazil	0·3	Peru	1·2
Ceylon	–0·5	Philippines	1·2
Chile	0·3	South Korea	9·1*
Colombia	0·2	Spain	0·9
Egypt	2·9	Taiwan	5·3
Ghana	–1·2	Thailand	1·1
Greece	9·3	Turkey	2·1
India	1·6	Venezuela	–9·8
Israel	18·3	Yugoslavia	2·7
Malaya	–11·9		
Mexico	0·4	Average	1·7

* 1953–65.

Source: Appendix D. The figures are equivalent to the deficit on trade in goods and services.

Finally, we must make some allowance for those gains in efficiency which arise from the normal operation of economic forces and which are not due to any special action on the part of government. We assumed that these are 10 per cent of the growth attributable to autonomous factor inputs.

Table II–14 shows the growth which would have been achieved without any policy effort. For the twenty-two countries, growth would have averaged about 3·5 per cent a year if there had been no domestic policy measures to stimulate growth. This is higher than the 2·5 per cent growth average of pre-war years, but in 1950–65 there were recovery factors, a faster growth in labour supply, and two-thirds of external finance consisted of government aid which did not exist in pre-war years.

Autonomous growth varied very widely between countries. In Ceylon, Ghana, India and Malaya it was well under 2.5 per cent a year, whereas in Greece, Israel, South Korea, Taiwan and Venezuela it ranged from 4 to 9 per cent! The wide range of autonomous growth shows that judgements on policy performance will be very misleading if based on crude comparisons of GDP growthrates.

We are now in a position to see how much of growth was due to domestic policy. This is shown in Table II–15. Policy measures

Table II–14

Contribution of Autonomous Growth Influences 1950–65

	Percentage point contribution to annual average compound growth rate of GDP					
	Total GDP growth due to autonomous forces	Contribution of autonomous growth in labour supply	Contribution of external finance	Contribution of autonomous domestic investment	Contribution of natural resources	Autonomous growth in efficiency
Argentina	2·64	0·70	0·18	1·52	0·00	0·24
Brazil	3·26	1·45	0·27	1·24	0·00	0·30
Ceylon	1·58	0·80	0·06	0·88	−0·30	0·14
Chile	3·20	0·65	0·40	1·34	0·52	0·29
Colombia	2·79	1·15	0·32	1·07	0·00	0·25
Egypt	2·71	0·75	0·83	1·09	−0·21	0·25
Ghana	2·29	(1·00)	0·09	0·99	0·00	0·21
Greece	5·05	0·60	1·95	0·90	0·00	1·60*
India	2·26	1·10	0·40	0·86	−0·17	0·07*†
Israel	9·13	2·70	5·60	0·00	0·00	0·83
Malaya	1·91	0·85	0·00	0·89	0·00	0·17
Mexico	3·43	1·55	0·39	1·18	0·00	0·31
Pakistan	2·48	1·20	0·45	0·75	−0·28	0·36*
Peru	2·62	0·65	0·67	1·06	0·00	0·24
Philippines	2·82	1·10	0·53	0·80	0·00	0·39*
South Korea	4·20	0·90	2·07	0·13	−0·10	1·20*
Spain	3·86	0·35	0·28	1·88	0·00	1·35*
Taiwan	5·25	0·85	1·55	1·55	0·00	1·30*
Thailand	3·05	1·55	0·34	1·05	−0·17	0·28
Turkey	2·88	0·90	0·60	1·12	0·00	0·26
Venezuela	5·84	1·80	0·00	1·84	1·67	0·53
Yugoslavia	2·81	0·50	0·66	1·39	0·00	0·26
Average	3·46	1·05	0·80	1·07	0·04	0·49

* Includes impact of recovery bonus as shown in Table I–3, calculated for 1950–65.

† India is the only country in which our measure of output is distorted by the choice of an end-year in which output was below peak. We must make allowance for this, just as we did under (*a*) above for initial years below peak. We have therefore assumed that the fall in output from 1964 to 1965 reduced Indian growth from 3·8 to 3·5 per cent a year for 1950–65, i.e. imposed an efficiency loss equivalent to 0·3 per cent a year prorated over the whole period.

were responsible on average for 2·0 per cent a year of economic growth, with a range from 0.6 per cent in Argentina to 4.3 per cent in Yugoslavia. On average, all the policy-induced growth was due to increased factor inputs, i.e. increases in investment induced by government and improvements in the quality of the labour force because of better structural allocation of labour, and programmes for education and health. In most countries, the government effort at resource mobilization was very impressive by any historical

Table II–15

Economic Growth Attributable to Domestic Policy 1950–65

Percentage point contribution to annual average compound growth rates

	Total GDP growth due to domestic policy	GDP growth due to policy-induced factor inputs	GDP growth due to policy-induced changes in efficiency
Argentina	0·56	1·45	−0·89
Brazil	1·94	2·44	−0·50
Ceylon	1·82	1·86	−0·04
Chile	0·80	0·59	0·21
Colombia	1·81	2·16	−0·35
Egypt	2·79	1·68	1·11
Ghana	1·91	2·42	−0·51
Greece	1·35	0·70	0·65
India	1·24	2·34	−1·10
Israel	1·57	0·50	1·07
Malaya	1·59	2·11	−0·52
Mexico	2·67	2·53	0·14
Pakistan	0·91	1·15	−0·24
Peru	2·98	2·22	0·76
Philippines	2·18	2·52	−0·34
South Korea	2·00	2·00	0·00
Spain	3·64	2·49	1·15
Taiwan	3·25	1·25	2·00
Thailand	3·25	3·16	−0·09
Turkey	2·32	1·63	0·69
Venezuela	0·86	2·44	−1·58
Yugoslavia	4·29	4·00	0·29
Average	2·08	1·98	0·09

Source: Derived from Tables II–11 and II–14.

standards, and particularly high in Yugoslavia. In Greece, Israel, Korea and Taiwan, external finance was so large that governments did not need to make the effort to increase savings. In fact, they reduced private savings below their normal 'autonomous' level and devoted the resources instead to large military programmes.

The government contribution to economic efficiency was very uneven. In Taiwan, policy was particularly conducive to efficiency and accounted for two points a year of the GDP growth. A good deal of this gain was due to active policies of agrarian improvement through extension work and research, and to vigorous efforts to improve industrial efficiency and promote manufactured exports. The efficiency record was also good in Israel and Spain, but on the whole the record was poor and in half the countries there were actually losses due to government policy, the biggest being in Argentina, India, and Venezuela. In Argentina this was due to the deleterious effects of instability and inflation (demand-induced and cost-induced with a strongly entrenched spiral process), to neglect of agriculture, and heavy protection for inefficient industries. In India, the inefficiency was due to excessive use of direct controls, poor agricultural incentives, premature expansion of heavy industry, and badly administered state enterprises. In Venezuela, the efficiency loss seems to have been due primarily to lavish use of capital on massive investment projects which have been slow to produce their yield.

It should be remembered that our efficiency measure is a residual and will be affected by significant errors in the figures for GDP. There is a possibility that GDP growth may be overstated in Ceylon, Egypt and Peru and the efficiency record for these countries may well be worse than Table II–14 indicates.

One objection which may be raised in criticism of our model is that it makes no explicit allowance for balance of payments constraints. Many developing countries are faced with 'structural' payments difficulties because their exports are concentrated on foodstuffs and raw materials for which demand is growing slowly. Prices for their exports have been weak and they have fluctuated a good deal. As they have rather small capital goods industries, the effort to accelerate development usually involves an upsurge in imports of capital goods which is difficult to finance. Most developing countries are faced with these difficulties to a much more serious extent than developed countries, and if our model were trying to compare development and developing countries, it might be worth quantifying these payments constraints. Within the developing world there are also important variations in the stringency of payments problems, but we have already made indirect allowance for most of these. We treated the whole of external finance as if it contributed directly to capital formation, whereas we know that some of it was not used for these purposes. In this way we hoped to cover crudely some of the indirect benefits of foreign aid, including its contribution to alleviating payments contraints. Similarly, we have treated Chile and Venezuela as deriving special benefits from their favourable mineral resources, and there would be double counting if we were to attribute payments benefits in addition. However, Mexico and Spain were favoured by particularly high tourist receipts (which were encouraged by policy, but were possible because of geographic and climatic reasons) which eased payments constraints and helped their growth, and we may therefore have given them somewhat higher marks for policy-induced growth than they deserve.

Taking the overall impact of government policy measures (first column of Table II–15) the countries with the best record are Mexico, Peru, Spain, Taiwan, Thailand and Yugoslavia. Those where policy contributed least were Argentina, Chile, India, Pakistan and Venezuela. In the succeeding analysis therefore we must look to the first group of countries for examples worth imitating and to the latter group for most of the illustrations of errors to be avoided. However, the rating of some countries would be changed by using data for a more recent period. This is particularly true of Pakistan which did much better in the 1960s than in the 1950s. The Pakistani case is, in fact, a rather drastic demonstration of the effectiveness and importance of improving development policies.

In any study of performance, the question naturally arises as to how much faster growth might have been if policy had been better. If every country had mobilized domestic resources on the Yugoslav scale and increased efficiency as fast as Taiwan, the policy induced growth would have been 6·0 per cent a year, and total growth would have been 9·5 per cent per annum. This probably represents the upper limit of feasible growth for countries with the political will and competence to reach their maximum potential, but it is not a realistic target as an average for the group. If we were setting targets for this group of countries for the 1970s, a 6·5 per cent rate would seem a reasonable figure to aim at. This would involve an average policy-induced growth of 3 per cent, 1 per cent growth due to external finance, and 2·5 per cent due to spontaneous growth forces of the kind which operated in prewar years. However, we know that our sample has an upward bias of about 0·7 points, so that 6 per cent growth would probably be a reasonable target for developing countries as a whole.

We should note, finally, that the growth capacity of some of the poorer countries such as India will remain below 6 per cent a year because of the smaller size of spontaneous savings, lower taxable capacity and inferior natural resources. This handicap in the spontaneous growth potential of the poorer countries is of fundamental importance in any judgement of past performance, in target setting for the future, and in decisions on aid allocation.

fundamental instruments by which governments can exert leverage on the economy.

The treatment of the plan document as holy writ was carried furthest in India. This is reflected in Nehru's comment:

'(Planning) for industrial development is generally accepted as a matter of mathematical formula. (Men) of science, planners, experts, who approach our problems from a purely scientific point of view (rather than an ideological one) agree, broadly, that given certain preconditions of development, industrialization and all that, certain exact conclusions follow almost as a matter of course.'[1]

Nehru's attachment to the plan document was based on misjudgement of the reasons for rapid growth in communist countries. Soviet growth was rapid because of a massive effort of resource mobilization. In fact, the practice of *detailed* resource allocation through the plan has led to considerable inefficiency and most communist countries are now moving gradually towards greater reliance on markets and less centralized control.

In India, the failure of the third plan (when output grew by one-sixth instead of one-third) has shattered confidence in the usefulness of planning even though two wars and two bad harvests explain a lot of the shortfall. The 'crisis of planning' has induced a wave of pessimism and has created disturbing and disorienting uncertainty about methods of formulating future strategy.[2] The gloom was deepened by the death of Nehru, and the subsequent political changes which strengthened the power of the states and led business circles to be more vocal in their criticism of *dirigiste* methods. As a result the fourth plan was unveiled with a three-year delay and its political significance has been perfunctory compared with the status its predecessors enjoyed.

[1] Quoted from G. Rosen *Democracy and Economic Change in India*, University of California Press, Berkeley, 1966, p. 105.

[2] The climate in India is described in detail in P. Streeten and M. Lipton, *The Crisis in Indian Planning*, Oxford University Press, London, 1968. On p. 5 it is summarized as follows: 'Optimists view it as a short-run crisis. They point to the Third Plan's bad luck in two droughts and two wars. Pessimists see the failure of the Third Plan as marking the virtual collapse of political authority over India's economy. They see federalism rampant as non-Congress states abolish taxes, Congress weak at the centre and defeated or faction ridden in the States, and over-optimistic projections by planners who are unable to raise taxes or aid (or to improve the efficiency with which they are used) to anything like the extent their plans require'.

The earlier view of planning as a panacea for development was too euphoric, and it will be healthier in the long run to take a more modest view of its functions. This should lead to a more realistic and better rounded view of the other instruments of development policy.

Now that the importance of the plan as a political symbol has faded, it should be easier to produce targets which are realistic. In the past it was not sufficiently realized that substantial exaggeration of the growth potential can do more harm to resource allocation and the phasing of public investment than no plan at all. There is no point in making plans which governments do not have the political will or technical capacity to implement.

Although a plan is mainly concerned with public expenditure, it should also take an articulate view of likely developments in the private sector. In most countries this is by far the largest part of the economy. However, information on savings and investment behaviour, the structure of domestic markets, demand elasticities, and income distribution is still remarkably poor. Consultation with the private sector in plan formulation is often desultory. It is weaker in India and Pakistan than it was, e.g. in Brazil during the formulation of the programme for the Kubitschek régime.

If the plan is consistent, realistic and looks at the economy as a whole, it can be a valuable instrument of policy. But the plan itself will simply provide an outline of strategy. The implementation will depend on the efficacy of government in mobilizing resources through taxation, borrowing and foreign aid, in preparing public investment projects carefully, and in infusing dynamism in the private sector.

The most appropriate model for planning in a developing economy with a substantial public sector is Mexico rather than India. Mexico has had some kind of macro-economic plan since the 1930s, but it was not given symbolic importance. Sixteen different government agencies were successively responsible for planning but none had any great political weight. Hence the government avoided embarrassing public commitments, but always had a basis for reasonable judgement of what was economically feasible. Furthermore, Mexico has built up an extremely strong cadre of economists, bankers and engineers in the public service who can apply sophisticated techniques to analyse the feasibility of particular projects. Micro-economic planning is stronger technically than in any other developing country. Finally, the execution of plans has been supervised by three powerful agencies of government, the President's Office, Nacional Financiera and the Bank of Mexico. There has been close co-ordination of public, private and foreign investment, reasonable financial equilibrium and external balance. As a result there has been thirty years of very substantial economic growth.[1]

Only three other countries, i.e. Egypt, Pakistan and Turkey, have given planning anything like the elevated status it enjoyed in India. In most of the countries where growth has been rapid, its status has been modest. In Israel, there was no attempt to set up a comprehensive plan until 1962, and the first plan (for 1965–70) was not officially adopted by the government. There has, of course, been careful preparation of individual projects, and detailed planning of agricultural settlement by the Jewish agency. In Greece, formal planning has been largely decorative and has had little effect on resource allocation. In Taiwan, the plan contained only broad indications for the private sector. In Yugoslavia, the central planning authorities have not played a very important role. In all of these countries, however, the fiscal and monetary authorities have strong statistical and economic staffs capable of taking a sophisticated analytical view of the general economic prospects and of developing carefully documented schemes for public investment.

The tasks of a fully-rounded growth strategy are now quite complex, but we can usefully divide the problem into six main components for analysis here and in subsequent chapters:

(*a*) The primary production factors are investment, labour, skills, and natural resources, but to activate these the government must increase its own revenue, encourage the private sector to increase its savings, and persuade foreigners to provide finance and technical help. Most governments have seen this need clearly and we shall analyse their record in this chapter.

(*b*) A significant part of economic growth can be derived from increases in efficiency. But there is often a conflict between efficiency and other goals. In several countries, the efficiency record has been poor. We shall try to see why in this chapter as well as in Chapters IV to VII.

(*c*) The most elementary task of policy is to maintain an adequate level of home demand, so that resources are not wasted for lack of markets. In the post-war period, most governments have overfulfilled their responsibilities in this respect. As a result inflation has distorted

[1] See R. J. Shafer, *Mexico, Mutual Adjustment Planning*, Syracuse, 1966, for an excellent description of the Mexican system.

resource allocation and created payments difficulties. The problems of demand management are analysed at length in Chapter IV.

(*d*) In developing countries resources are not flexible enough or market forces strong enough to bring about the desired degree of structural change. Governments must therefore intervene to promote industrialization and modernize agriculture. We have examined policy under these headings in Chapters V and VI.

(*e*) Governments must take steps to keep their balance of payments in reasonable equilibrium, otherwise growth will be interrupted by lack of essential imports, or the country's policy options will be determined by foreign creditors. We have analysed the problems of import substitution, export promotion and external finance in Chapters VI, VII and VIII.

(*f*) In order to ensure that the sacrifices of resource mobilization bear their fruits in the form of higher per capita income, most governments need to take active measures to reduce the rate of population growth (this problem is discussed in Chapter IX).

In addition to these primary tasks of growth policy, governments have other economic objectives. Most countries in Asia and Africa took measures to decolonialize their economies and free them from foreign tutelage. Some of these measures have hindered economic growth in the short term and may seem irrational to outside observers. However, these actions were a political necessity and their long run economic benefits may well be large. Mexico, for instance, has emerged from a period of profound xenophobia with strengthened national pride and capacity for imaginative policy. It has also been able to attract more private foreign investment than any other developing country, because foreigners know that Mexican policy is now based on mature and pragmatic considerations of self interest.

Another important economic problem is the great inequality between different regions and groups in the community. In most countries this 'dualism' has been accepted rather fatalistically as an inevitable feature of economic development. Unfortunately, we have not been able to analyse this problem adequately because the statistical information is poor and the problems of each country are very different.

RESOURCE MOBILIZATION

The Soviet experience of the 1930s dramatized the contribution which increased resource mobilization could make to economic growth, and the importance of capital formation and government spending has been heavily stressed in post-war policy. On average, about 30 per cent of GNP now goes to investment and government services compared with about 20 per cent in pre-war years, and consumption has been correspondingly squeezed. None of the countries in our sample has attempted to cut the absolute level of per capita consumption, but in most cases the share of consumption has declined since 1950.

The effort to mobilize domestic financial resources has two main components; (i) the increase in private savings; (ii) the increase in government revenue, and we shall discuss each one separately. The contribution of external finance is discussed in Chapter VIII.

(i) *Private Savings*

Governments have promoted private saving mainly by creating favourable profit opportunities for new capitalists. The fastest growing sector has been industry. Inflation and protection against foreign competition created booming markets for local industrial products. Industrial profits were helped by favourable access to government credit at low interest rates, and by low tariffs or favourable exchange rates for imported capital goods. The light burden of direct taxes and the absence of capital gains taxes made it easy to save. And some countries created tax holidays in new lines of enterprise and high depreciation allowances which increased the incentive to invest. To some extent these new opportunities for industrial capitalists were an unintended by-product of protection and payments restrictions. This was certainly true in India. But in practically all cases, industrial capital has been treated more favourably than in the developed world. Even in countries where government enterprise has been greatly extended, local entrepreneurs seldom complained, because state enterprise has usually taken on projects they would not have wanted for themselves and has often sold its products at subsidized prices to private business. The hostility of many governments to foreign private capital has hindered growth by restricting the supply of funds and technical knowledge, but it has also strengthened the position of local entrepreneurs who have generally welcomed policies hostile to foreign capital.

One factor which has increased income inequality is the existence of surplus labour. The wage for unskilled urban labour is usually determined by the alternative income available as a family dependent in agriculture. This is low and has been rising slowly. In Israel,

Chile, and Argentina, the situation is different and there are powerful trade unions. In most countries, however, the bargaining power of labour is weak and is likely to remain so until population pressure is cut substantially. Government action to promote minimum wage and social security legislation has not been effective enough to modify the position very much. As a result workers have a much lower share in industrial output than they do in developed countries. It is usually well under half of value added compared with over two-thirds in developed countries.

It is not possible to get very reliable evidence on income distribution in developing countries, but it is generally more unequal than in the developed world,[1] and inequalities have probably been increasing. There are some exceptions. Egypt and Yugoslavia are socialist countries without really large-scale capitalists; Israel has greater income equality than any other non-communist country; Argentina has a more equal distribution of income than France or Italy;[2] in Ghana, most people are peasant proprietors and income distribution is fairly equal; and in Ceylon government policy has redistributed income in favour of the lower income groups mainly by providing a free rice ration to the whole population.[3]

The increased relative importance of industrial capitalists has produced some changes in consumption patterns amongst the rich. Maharajahs have lost out to industrial tycoons in India, and coffee planters have lost ground to bankers and industrialists in Sao Paulo. The new men set the fashion, and although they are far from frugal, they probably have a higher propensity to save than the older class of property owners.

Most governments have neglected small savers. A good deal needs to be done if they are to get a fair deal. They often get a negative real return on their savings because of the low level of official interest rates. Governments could increase the flow of private saving and improve its allocation by strengthening local capital markets and financial institutions.

The basic situation for private savings in most developing countries is

1 See S. Kuznets, 'Distribution of Income by Size', *Economic Development and Cultural Change*, January 1963, gives evidence for India, Ceylon, Colombia, Mexico and developed countries.

2 Argentine income distribution is markedly more even than that of Brazil or Mexico, *Estudios Sobre la Distribucion del Ingreso en America Latina*, ECLA, March 1967, (E/CN. 12/770 mimeographed).

3 See G. Corea, 'Ceylon', in C. Onslow, *Asian Economic Development*, Weidenfeld & Nicolson, London, 1965, p. 30.

somewhat like that in the UK in the earlyday s of the industrial revolution. It is socially unjust but favourable to capital formation. There has been little intrusion on private property rights either through nationalization or expropriation, except to a minor extent under land reform schemes.

The only cases of large-scale expropriation of private property have been in Egypt and Yugoslavia. Egypt is an interesting case of the strategy of gradual expropriation. Most industrial activity, banking and large scale commerce is now government-owned, and big landowners have been eliminated, though the existing upper limit on land holding is generous enough to yield quite high incomes. The takeover of private property was apparently achieved without a major set-back to production, and the reduction in consumption of the rich and in foreign dividend payments helped the government to raise the savings rate considerably. To some extent the transition was eased by the fact that much of the property belonged to foreigners, and government action was supported by strong nationalist feeling. Resistance was also lowered by the payment of partial compensation.

(ii) *Government Revenue*

Government revenue from domestic sources varies from a third of GNP in Israel to 12 per cent in Korea. The capacity to raise revenue depends on the average level of income and its distribution, on the political strength and ambition of government and the efficiency of tax administration. It is also affected by fortuitous circumstances such as the presence of large foreign corporations, or of large export earnings from staple crops which make it politically easier to levy taxes. These differences in taxation potential make it difficult to use absolute levels of revenue as an indicator of performance in resource mobilization, but the important thing is that all governments except Yugoslavia have increased their revenue in relation to GNP. On average revenue rose by about a third from 1950 to 1965, and now represents about a fifth of GNP.

There are several ways in which governments mobilize revenue or exercise effective command of resources. They do this through:

(*a*) taxes and levies;

(*b*) profits of public enterprise;

(*c*) savings forced out of the private sector by increased monetisation or inflation;

(*d*) voluntary labour contributed to public investment projects.

Table III–1

Total Government Current Revenue from Domestic Sources as a Proportion of GNP in 1950 and 1965

	1950	1965		1950	1965
Argentina	19·2	19·7*	Thailand	8·4	13·6
Brazil	19·6	23·8	Turkey	n.a.	20·0
Ceylon	19·0	22·7	Venezuela	21·8¶	23·5
Chile	16·4	24·6	Yugoslavia	28·6**	28·0
Colombia	9·9	12·7			
Egypt	16·7	19·3†	Average of all countries	n.a.	19·9
Ghana‡	15·8§	16·8			
Greece	18·4	22·4	Average of 20 countries	14·8	19·4
India	7·9	14·8			
Israel	17·8§	33·0			
Malaya	12·1	22·6	France	28·6	36·6
Mexico	n.a.	30·0	Germany (FR)	31·6	36·4
Pakistan	8·4	12·8	Italy	26·6§	32·4
Peru	13·2§	16·2	Japan	22·9	21·7
Philippines	7·7	13·3	UK	32·7	32·8
South Korea	5·5§	12·3	USA	24·3	35·3
Spain	13·0‖	15·5			
Taiwan	16·5§	19·6	Average	27·8	32·5

* 1961; † 1962–63; ‡ central government only; § 1953; ‖ 1955; ¶ 1960; ** 1956.

Source: *Yearbook of National Accounts Statistics*, UN, New York, 1966 and 1964 editions, and national sources; the figures exclude government receipts from foreign grants and loans.

DIRECT TAXATION

In most countries, direct tax yields are relatively small. On average, they are only a third of those in developed countries. However, we should remember that in the USA as recently as 1929, direct taxation was only 3 per cent of GNP, which is lower than in any developing country in our sample except Pakistan, Taiwan, and Thailand.

Table III–2

Government Revenue from Direct Taxation and Social Security Levies as a Percentage of GNP in 1965

Country	%	Country	%
Argentina	8·3	Taiwan	1·7
Brazil	6·3	Thailand	1·4
Ceylon	4·0	Turkey	4·4
Chile	13·4	Venezuela	16·9
Colombia	4·8	Yugoslavia	8·2
Egypt	3·1		
Ghana	3·7	Average	5·9
Greece	7·7		
India	3·2		
Israel	11·0	France	20·9
Malaya	5·8	Germany (FR)	20·1
Mexico	4·1	Italy	17·1
Pakistan	2·0	Japan	11·9
Peru	5·0	UK	16·1
Philippines	3·7	USA	18·0
South Korea	3·2		
Spain	7·3	Average	17·4

Source: *Yearbook of National Accounts Statistics 1966*, UN, New York, 1967 and national sources.

Where most of the population is engaged in agriculture or small family business, income tax is hard to assess and collect. Its yield may not be worth the cost of collection because the average taxpayer can contribute only small amounts. In Mexico in 1960 less than 50,000 of the six million farmers paid income tax.[1] In India, only 1 million people were assessed for income tax in 1956, and only half of these paid tax, out of 200 million in the labour force. In Pakistan, income tax is paid by only one-tenth of 1 per cent of the total population.[2] In the UK, by contrast, 16 million out of 23 million earners pay income tax. Arthur Lewis has suggested that the typical developing country collects income tax from only 3 per cent of the occupied population compared with 50 per cent in the

[1] See I. M. de Navarrete, 'Agricultural and Land Taxation', in A. T. Peacock and G. Hauser, *Government Finance and Economic Development*, OECD, Paris, 1965.

[2] See N. Kaldor, *Indian Tax Reform*, Ministry of Planning, New Delhi, 1956, and M. Haq, *The Strategy of Economic Planning*, Oxford University Press, Karachi, 1966, p. 24.

developed world.[1] He suggests that simpler forms of personal tax assessment might be an economic source of revenue in rural areas, particularly if they are earmarked for local expenditure. In African countries, where income distribution is fairly even, poll taxes may be appropriate, but in most countries there has to be some allowance for differences in capacity to pay, and if this is decided on a rough and ready basis by local authorities there will be danger of injustice and exploitation.

In most developing countries corporate tax rates are almost as high as in the developed world. They are a major source of revenue in Chile and Venezuela where they are mainly collected from foreigners. This kind of tax is rather easy to collect, and will grow in size as industry expands. The main drawback at the moment is that the privileges and tax holidays granted to new companies are probably too generous.

It has been argued by Professor Kaldor that the 'taxation-potential' of many developing countries is 'fully as large as that of the highly developed countries'. He argues that the disadvantage of a lower average level of income is offset by greater inequality, and that the income and consumption of the rich represent a bigger share of GNP than is normal in the developed world. Rich people in developing countries almost invariably pay less of their income in taxation than those in developed countries, and their capital gains are usually untaxed. As most luxury goods, particularly housing and servants, are relatively cheap, they also spend more of their income and save less. It seems doubtful whether this untapped source of revenue is as large as Kaldor suggests, but it certainly does exist. The main problem is that most developing countries still have an oligarchic society in which the rich have great political influence, even in countries ruled by a bureaucratic or military *élite*, so that what is economically desirable is not politically feasible.

Another major difference between developed and developing countries is in taxes levied for social security. In developed countries these are sometimes bigger than personal income tax. In France they are over 14 per cent of GNP. In developing countries, it would be impossible to levy these taxes in agriculture, and if the burden were concentrated on industry it would discourage the use of labour intensive techniques. For these reasons, social security taxes are usually an important source of revenue only in countries at a

[1] See W. A. Lewis, *Development Planning*, Harper & Row, New York, 1966.

reasonably advanced stage of development, such as Argentina, Chile or Israel.

There is one area of direct taxation which most developing countries could usefully cultivate to a greater degree. They collect very little direct revenue from farmers. Instead they squeeze their income by export levies and by keeping domestic food prices at a low level. This has had a harmful effect on production incentives, even though the apparent tax burden on farmers may appear to be low. The best way to raise revenue from farmers is by a land tax based on the potential output of their land. This will not only produce revenue on a significant scale in countries where most people are farmers, but will improve production incentives and resource allocation by penalizing inefficient farmers and rewarding efficient ones. If the tax is progressive it can also be used to change the agrarian structure and improve the market in land.[1] Land taxation in Meiji Japan captured a third of farm income for government, provided three-quarters of its revenue, and was the major financial instrument in Japanese modernization. The initial cost of assessment for land tax is high because a detailed cadastral survey is required, but this kind of survey is needed only once in a generation. However, there is very strong political resistance to direct taxation in agriculture and few economists have been able to persuade governments to do this, e.g. the whole Turkish Planning Office resigned on this issue in 1962, but did not succeed in changing policy.

Revenue from income tax is low in developing countries partly because of low absolute income levels and the high cost of collecting income tax in small amounts. But direct tax collections are also low because corruption is significant, evasion is easy, and accounting procedures are lax. If people met their *legal* tax obligations, the revenue situation would often be transformed. What is needed is a more rigorous collection procedure, better paid tax officials and perhaps some reduction in *nominal* tax obligations. Because of the very high theoretical incidence of Indian income tax (90 per cent is the highest marginal rate), about half of the tax due is lost by evasion. But Indian tax morality is much better than that in Latin

[1] A scheme for progressive land taxation in India is outlined by I. M. D. Little 'Tax Policy and the Third Plan', in P. N. Rosenstein-Rodan, *Pricing and Fiscal Policies*, MIT, Cambridge, 1964. Little states, 'It is certain that wealthy individuals whose income is derived largely from the land escape much more lightly than those whose income is derived from other sources'.

America. In Brazil, the successful attempt of the Castelo Branco government to collect income taxes earned it great unpopularity. It reinforced the tax collection mechanism in 1964, and used some of the crosschecks on income assessment that are used in France, i.e. external signs of wealth, such as cars, yachts, servants and secondary residences. But the Costa y Silva government dismissed the tax chief under political pressure in 1967.

Tax collection is not simply a matter of administrative efficiency but of the law and attitudes to it. In the USA income tax delinquents are subject to criminal penalties, income is deducted at source and privacy in financial matters is not very highly regarded. The big increases in direct taxation were made in wartime, and would hardly have been politically acceptable otherwise. In most other countries, the state has less power to enforce sanctions for non-compliance, individuals have more privacy, and less respect for state power.

In developed countries, tax revenue tends automatically to rise faster than GNP without the need for increases in tax rates. This happens because the tax structure is progressive. But when progressive income taxes are a small part of total revenue, as is the case in most developing countries, the income of government tends to rise more slowly than GNP. Because of the low 'elasticity' of revenue, tax *rates* have to be raised fairly often to keep up with the needs of government. In India, for instance, the tax structure in the early 1950s was such that the 'automatic' increase in government revenue (i.e. the revenue forthcoming with unchanged tax rates) was only 0·83 per cent for each 1 per cent increase in GNP.[1] The situation in Pakistan seems to have been similar.[2] In Western Europe and the USA, revenue elasticity calculated in the same way would be about 1·2, i.e. government revenue tends to increase faster than GNP.[3] The responsiveness of revenue to income changes would also be improved by introduction of PAYE (pay as you earn) tax deductions at source. In many developing countries taxes are paid in arrears and this reduces the tax burden considerably in countries

[1] See G. S. Sahota, *Indian Tax Structure and Economic Development*, Asia Publishing House, New York, 1961. Sahota's estimates were for the period 1951–7 and showed that the central government had an even lower 'revenue elasticity' than state and local governments. The central government's 'revenue elasticity', was only 0·6 as compared with 0·83 for all levels of government combined.

[2] See M. Haq, *The Strategy of Economic Planning*, Oxford, Karachi, 1966, p. 24.

[3] Information supplied by Professor Bent Hansen; see W. Heller, *et al.*, *Fiscal Policy for a Balanced Economy*, OECD, Paris, December 1968.

with rapid inflation. Delay in tax payments also means that taxes may exaggerate cyclical fluctuations in income.

INDIRECT TAXATION

In most developing countries a large part of revenue is derived from import and export duties, or from profits of marketing boards which are equivalent to export taxes. These are the taxes which are easiest to levy, and developing countries with a large foreign trade will usually have a higher tax potential than those which do not.[1] However, heavy dependence on these sources of revenue usually has regressive effects on income distribution and may distort resource allocation. Brazil, Ceylon, Chile, India and Venezuela have all discouraged their exporters by levying very high taxes.

In theory, variable export taxes can be useful as an economic stabilizer. Increases in tax rates can absorb windfall gains during periods of high prices and tax reductions can cushion the impact of falling prices. In this way governments can modify fluctuations in demand and absorb some of the impact of fluctuations by allowing their exchange reserves to vary countercyclically. Unfortunately most governments have not operated export taxes or used their marketing boards in this way.

In the post-war period there has been a bigger increase in import and export duties in Asian and African countries than in Latin America where these were already highly developed. In some cases, however, and notably in India and Pakistan, revenue has been lost by the widespread use of licences which are issued by administrative priority whereas they could be sold by auction, or allocated through a system of differential exchange rates. The Indian licensing system has been violently attacked by Professor Shenoy of Ahmedabad University, who is perhaps the most outspoken domestic critic of Indian planning:

'We regulate imports by the issue of import licences. Foreign exchange to pay for the imports is provided by the Reserve Bank to the holders of import licences. The price charged for the exchange

1 See S. R. Lewis, 'Government Revenue from Foreign Trade: an International Comparison', *Manchester School*, January 1963, for a more refined statement of this point. Lewis has also provided an excellent survey of the whole literature on public finance in developing countries in his contribution to H. M. Southworth and B. F. Johnston, eds., *Agricultural Development and Economic Growth*, Cornell, 1967.

is based on the official price, which, as we have seen, is unconscionably lower than free market prices. But the imported goods are sold at the domestic free-market prices, which are phenomenally higher than the landed costs of the imports. The difference (varying from 30 per cent to over 500 per cent or more, depending on commodities), which is a windfall, accrues to the participants in the import activity—the traffickers in import licences and the dealers in import goods. This is a free gift of statism to the privileged recipients of the import licences disbursed twice a year; its magnitude may be of the order of Rs. 460 crores annually. If the import licences were sold by auction, like treasury bills and liquor licences, the bulk or whole of this difference might have accrued to the Union Revenues, converting budget deficits into budget surpluses. It might have removed, too, a potent instrument of corruption and a source of heavy antisocial income shifts. Instead, we have preferred to cover budget deficits by inflation and distribute the licences free to favourites among others, thus keeping alive corruption and undermining progress towards the national objective of a socialist pattern of society.'[1]

There is considerable scope for improvement in sales and excise duties in developing countries. Collections of sales tax will increase with the growth of the urban sector and the spread of modern accounting practices in retail outlets. Excise duties can also be made to fall more heavily on luxuries, so that they will discourage consumption of the rich and compensate to some extent for their low direct tax burdens. As administration improves there will also be scope for more sophisticated devices such as the value added tax which do not distort resource allocation and do not hinder exports in the way which often happens with existing sales taxes.

INCOME FROM PUBLIC ENTERPRISE

Many developing countries have substantial public enterprises which are operated with low profit margins. On average, public enterprise profits are only 2·4 per cent of GNP. In India, the average profit rate of state-owned enterprises in the 1960s was 2 per cent a year com-

[1] See B. R. Shenoy, *Indian Planning and Economic Development*, Asia Publishing House, Bombay, 1963, pp. 8–9. The sum of Rs. 460 crores mentioned by Shenoy was equivalent to $966 million at the official exchange rate. Shenoy is a tendentious critic and his estimate may well be an exaggeration. Nevertheless, it is obvious from Brazilian experience in selling licences that his point is perfectly valid and that the revenue foregone by government was very large.

pared with 11 or 12 per cent expected by the planners. To some extent this is due to managerial inefficiency, but it is also a reflection of poor pricing policy. Projects were designed initially with an artificially low interest rate in mind, and some products have been sold at prices well below what the market could have stood. Steel was sold at the same price all over India, irrespective of transport costs, and the black market price of steel products ranged from 15 to 100 per cent higher than official prices. In Argentina and Ghana the record of the public sector is even worse. In Mexico and Egypt, on the other hand, public sector profits have been much bigger and have contributed substantially to government revenue.

Table III–3

Government Revenue from Property and Entrepreneurship as a Percentage of GNP in 1965

Argentina	0·2	Pakistan	3·6
Brazil	2·9	Peru	n.a.
Ceylon	2·9	Philippines	0·4
Chile	0·8	South Korea	2·3
Colombia	0·8	Spain	1·1
Egypt	6·6	Taiwan	3·8
Ghana	0·3	Thailand	1·2
Greece	1·2	Turkey	0·5
India	1·9	Venezuela	0·9
Israel	2·0	Yugoslavia	n.a.
Malaya	3·1		
Mexico	10·5	Average	2·4

Source: *Yearbook of National Accounts Statistics 1966*, UN, New York, 1967 and national sources.

In some countries, the profits of public enterprise could be raised by eliminating redundant personnel and this is particularly true in Argentina, where the Peron régime cultivated political support by creating thousands of useless jobs. However, it is not easy to fire such people whether they work in Argentine railways or the US Post Office, and many politicians have been thrown into perpetual limbo for trying to do it.

INCREASED MONETIZATION

Government income from increased 'monetization' of the economy is a legitimate source of development finance. As a country becomes more developed and more transactions enter the market, the money holdings of the population will gradually rise in relation to GNP. As the government provides a good deal of the money supply by printing banknotes, increased monetization provides it with a legitimate source of revenue. However, it is a rather small source of income and most governments have gone well beyond the bounds of normal monetization in running budget deficits.

INFLATION

Some governments have tried to finance their deficit by inflation, i.e. by forced saving. For a time it may be possible to raise extra resources in this way, because prices rise faster than wages and workers are cheated of part of their real income to the benefit of the government. Private investors may also gain from inflation and some of the less competent capitalists will lose out to smarter ones. But if the inflation is serious or prolonged, it will no longer have this effect. The people who were being cheated will find devices to protect themselves, the inflation will simply generate a useless price spiral, it will reduce private savings, and will involve an unplanned accumulation of some of the worst kinds of external debt, i.e. short-term, high-interest trade credits. We examine these problems in detail in Chapter IV below.

VOLUNTARY LABOUR

Where there is a large amount of idle agricultural labour, there may appear to be opportunities for converting it into capital by using voluntary workers on labour-intensive projects. Examples of this have been cited in the Indian context, 'contour bunding, terracing and levelling, drainage, irrigation ditches and minor canals, digging wells, fencing, making local roads and other constructions from indigenous materials which can, again, be got with shovels and baskets'.[1] Some success has been achieved in Pakistan with a works programme using very cheap labour, but unfortunately the organizational powers of governments have not been great enough to mobilize much *voluntary* labour. It seems unlikely that labour can be mobilized in significant amounts without some form of payment, if only because the additional work will require bigger food consumption by

[1] See I. M. D. Little, 'The Strategy of Indian Development', *Economic Review*, National Institute of Economic and Social Research, London, May 1960.

labourers. The problem is therefore really one of ensuring that the technologies used take proper account of the ready availability of unskilled labour. But more attention should be given to the possibility of designing really low-cost housing units which people can build for themselves. Even very poor people will work harder or scrape up savings to improve their housing. No government has faced this problem squarely, and one of the worst aspects of poverty in developing countries is the universal prevalence of massive urban slums. When public housing has been provided on a large scale, e.g. in Mexico, the projects have usually been too costly for poor people and have really catered for the lower middle class.

POSSIBILITIES FOR RETRENCHMENT OF UNPRODUCTIVE EXPENDITURE

Some governments have been able to increase the development effort by cutting the share of military expenditure and devoting the resources to development. In the period 1950–65 only a few countries did this, e.g. Greece, Turkey and Yugoslavia. Unfortunately, the military burden has risen in several other cases and has absorbed resources which might have gone to development. In India, military spending took 2 per cent of GDP before the Chinese attack in 1962 and has more than doubled since then. In Egypt, Israel, and Taiwan it takes a bigger share of resources than in most developed countries.

Table III–4

Government Expenditure on Military Goods and Services as a Percentage of GNP in 1965

Country	%	Country	%
Argentina	1·7	Pakistan	5·4
Brazil	3·6	Peru	2·9
Ceylon	0·8	Philippines	1·5
Chile	2·4	South Korea	3·9
Colombia	2·0	Spain	2·7
Egypt	8·0	Taiwan	11·3
Ghana	1·6	Thailand	2·2
Greece	4·1	Turkey	5·2
India	4·2	Venezuela	2·3
Israel	8·8	Yugoslavia	4·2
Malaya	3·1		
Mexico	0·8	Average	3·8

Source: *World-wide Military Expenditures and Related Data*, Research Report 67–6, US Arms Control and Disarmament Agency, Washington DC, 1967.

To some degree, the problem has been alleviated by military aid, which has provided modern armaments on a large scale. This aid may be indirectly helpful to development if one assumes that the countries concerned would have proceeded with the military effort in any case. But it may simply escalate the military preparedness of neighbouring countries and the sophistication of the weapons which the generals and admirals demand. Agreement amongst developed countries to cut down military aid, and to limit commercial shipments of sophisticated arms might well help to divert substantial resources to development. But there seems little prospect that this will happen.

As far as non-military spending is concerned, it is difficult to get enough detail to know whether economies could reasonably be made. In education, on which there is most evidence, there is certainly some waste, but this arises from spreading resources too thinly over ambitious programmes, rather than from spending too much. One suspects that this is true in several fields, such as agricultural extension, technical training and research. However, there are cases such as Brazil with its swollen bureaucracy, and Ghana with its expensive string of foreign embassies in which there is clearly some scope for economy. There are also a few countries, e.g. Chile and Ceylon, with quite high expenditures on subsidies which might well be cut in favour of spending on development.

The record of most developing countries in mobilizing resources for economic growth has been encouraging. They have in fact achieved what the take-off theorists suggested. Both the rate of investment and the share captured by government have been higher than they were in most developed countries in pre-war years. In 1929, government revenue in the USA was only 10·9 per cent of GNP, which is only about half of that in developing countries now.

It is easy to see how more resources could be mobilized by bolder fiscal policy. But further taxation might well reduce the rate of private investment and distort resource allocation, and experience has shown that governments are pressing close to the politically feasible limits. Many have run into payments difficulties and inflation from pushing ahead too fast. Professor Kaldor has described the political constraints in detail in the countries which he has advised, i.e. Ceylon, Ghana, Guyana, India, Mexico and Turkey.[1] There are many cases

[1] See N. Kaldor, *Essays on Economic Policy*, vol. 1, Duckworth, London, 1964, pp. xviii–xx.

where a major increase in tax rates is likely to spark off riots or revolution rather than increase revenue.

It is not possible to postulate an optimum level of revenue because the welfare and military ambitions of governments vary a good deal and so does the role of public enterprise. Government responsibilities are also affected by differences in the age structure of populations. However, Japanese government revenue is only a little above the present average for developing countries, and one might query the need for going much further. It would certainly seem inappropriate to assume that developing countries should aim for revenue on the same scale as the UK, USA or Germany. Developed countries now have a tax structure which gives governments a rising share of GNP, and this fiscal buoyancy encourages them to expand their spending continuously. The automatic fiscal leverage was usually acquired inadvertently, and the phenomenon is by no means an unmixed blessing.

We saw in Table II–1 that the average rate of non-residential fixed capital formation in 1966 was 14·5 per cent of GNP in our twenty-two countries, whereas in six western countries it averaged 17 per cent. The difference is not large, and it should be quite feasible to match the investment rate of the developed world in future. But Japanese investment is almost twice as high as in developing countries, and they should perhaps be thinking of emulating this example if they want to narrow the income gap between themselves and the developed world.

However, it is illuminating to note that Israel, Yugoslavia and Venezuela, which might well have managed to save more, have now cut their rate of investment below previous peaks. Our model in Chapter II suggests that many countries have probably pressed their resource mobilization near the limits of 'absorptive capacity'.[1] In order for higher rates of investment to be worth while, they will first have to increase the efficiency with which resources are currently being used. We shall now examine the reasons why resource allocation has been inefficient since 1950.

[1] For an analysis of the concept of absorptive capacity, see J. H. Adler, *Absorptive Capacity: The Concept and its Determinants*, Brookings Institution, Washington DC, June 1965. The limit of absorptive capacity is not a point where capacity for further investment is saturated in the sense that further effort would yield a zero or negative return, but the point at which the yield is uneconomically low.

EFFICIENCY IN RESOURCE ALLOCATION

When economic policy in developing countries is condemned as inefficient, it is often implied that there is waste because of corruption, or foolish decision-making. It is true that these exist in the developing world and they may be somewhat more common than in developed countries, but to our mind they are not the major causes of waste, and indeed the corruption is sometimes a corrective to foolish decisions.

The kind of inefficiency which is significant in developing countries is not the result of moral or mental delinquency, but comes from operating the economy under great strain and trying to push it to the limit of capacity. In this situation four types of inefficiency are important.

The first kind of inefficiency is due to strain on human resources. The pace of expansion requires more technical competence than is available. This problem is most urgent in Africa, of medium importance in Asia, and not significant in the parts of Latin America we have studied.

The other three main sources of inefficiency are due to inflation, excessive protection and *dirigisme*. Again we cannot assume that these mistakes derive simply from incompetence or ideological prejudice. Because they are trying to change the structure of their economies, most countries run into payments difficulties or find it difficult to achieve their goals by relying on the private sector or by market incentives alone. Similarly, the politically feasible ways of mobilizing resources are often ones which will do some harm to resource allocation. Governments therefore impose controls which put their administrative capacity under strain and lead to waste. They usually know that this is likely to happen, but they are willing to take the risk of inefficiency if resources can thereby be mobilized on a larger scale. In nearly all countries the political odds are in favour of ambition rather than caution.

The problem for developing countries therefore has some resemblance to that of developed countries in the 1930s when they accepted the allocative inefficiency of protectionism in an effort to promote higher levels of employment. It also resembles the problem of the Soviet economy, which has reached a high level of resource mobilization by a command system which is rigid and bureaucratic in allocation decisions. In many developing countries the degree of protectionism is worse than in the 1930s, but the degree of *dirigisme* is substantially less than in the Soviet economy.

A fifth apparent source of inefficiency derives from the instability of developing economies. However, as we argue in our next chapter, a good deal of the instability is due to force of circumstance so that the resulting waste is often not remediable even by efficient policy.

The following chapters devote a good deal of attention to the problems of efficiency. Chapter IV deals with short-term demand management and the inefficiency caused by inflation and recessions. Chapter V deals at length with agricultural incentives. Chapter VI is a detailed examination of the costs and benefits of industrialization and import substitution, and Chapter VII deals with problems of export promotion. However, it is perhaps useful to comment in this more general chapter on the problem of *dirigisme*.

Because of the inadequacies of fiscal policy, the tendency to inflation, weakness in the balance of payments, and the need to make structural change in the economy, developing countries have made considerable use of direct controls. As temporary or emergency measures, these can be useful, but when they become quasi-permanent, they can do great damage to efficient resource allocation. In general, controls and permits are administered on a crude priority basis, and are often based on 'repeat licensing' which reflects past allocation needs. In countries undergoing rapid change this will be stifling to new enterprise.

The consequence of over-reliance on controls is vividly described as follows by the chief Pakistan planner:

'Once direct controls were introduced, they bred like mushrooms. In order to control the final price of cotton cloth, the Government started controlling the price of raw cotton, the dealer's margin, the manufacturer's costs, the distributor's profits and a whole lot of related activities. And as the direct controls started replacing the market, the pyramid kept on building, till the government officials sitting on top of it did not know any longer what on earth they were controlling.'[1]

The problem in making controls effective is that they make heavy demands on high quality administrative manpower, which is one of the scarcest resources in developing countries. In economies where government assumes a large role in development it is essential to create an administration equal to the tasks it sets itself, or at least to make this a long run aim of policy. In the past, some of the

[1] M. ul Haq, *op. cit.*, p. 51.

countries most committed to direct controls assumed that they could be administered without cost.

Reliance on controls has been greatest in India, which had licences for all imports, controls on exports, permits for new construction and entry into business, price fixing, allocations of steel and industrial materials, and internal trade zones for food grains. At the same time, the exchange rate was left overvalued, and interest rates were kept low. The big Indian business concerns were not worried by controls as they helped to consolidate their monopolist position, and the administration was pretty firmly convinced of its own capacity for decision making.[1] In general, controls were operated in favour of the urban middle class and the bureaucracy itself. In the Planning Commission, there was a tendency to discount the role of the price mechanism, to identify the planning process with direct controls, and to believe that acknowledged price distortions could be offset by using 'shadow prices' in calculating the return on big investment projects. 'Shadow pricing' involves the use of hypothetical (equilibrium) prices for foreign exchange, interest rates, and wages. It is a useful device in making decisions on government projects, but the private sector will base its decisions on actual and expected prices and not on hypothetical shadow prices.

In the past few years, there has been a considerable revision of Indian optimism about controls, and several government committees have pointed out their defects.[2] The rupee has been devalued, and the system has been considerably modified, but much of this has been done under foreign pressure, and there is still a strong political and bureaucratic preference for controls.

The most successful developing countries, e.g. Israel and Taiwan, have tended to make a positive use of the price mechanism rather than rely heavily on direct controls or shadow prices. The important prices in this context are the interest rate, the exchange rate, the

[1] In India, controls have been enforced more rigorously than in other countries. Professor E. S. Mason, *Economic Development in India and Pakistan*, Centre for International Affairs, Harvard, 1966, p. 15, concludes: 'controls were less effective in Pakistan with the result that markets, black, grey, and off-white, intruded more effectively than in India to redress some of the more distorting effects of controls'.

[2] The *Report on Steel Control* (Raj Committee), Ministry of Steel and Heavy Industries, Delhi, October 1963, pointed out the extensive licence applications by bogus importers. There have also been extensive delays in getting import licences for small firms. The Mathur Committee in 1965 cited cases of 1½ year delays, see *Report of the Study Team on Import and Export Trade Control Organization*, Government of India, New Delhi, 1965.

internal terms of trade between agriculture and industry, the structure of wages, and export incentives. In all these fields the government must ensure that market forces tend to push resources in the desired direction.

CONCLUSION

In the past two decades most countries have made considerable progress towards effective growth strategies and this is reflected in growth rates much higher than in pre-war years. Their biggest achievement has been in resource mobilization and their failings have been mainly in resource allocation and in population policy. We shall analyse the policy weapons used and the scope for further improvement in detail in subsequent chapters. However, it is perhaps useful to comment here on the role of institutional obstacles to economic development, because their importance is so often exaggerated.

The fact that developing countries were 'late starters' in terms of modern economic growth was due in large measure to institutional differences between their societies and those of Western Europe. When Japan set out to catch up with the developed world, she initiated the process by carrying out fundamental institutional change. For this reason, some writers on development attach great importance to contemporary social or religious obstacles to change,[1] and claim that basic institutional reform is a 'precondition' of accelerated growth. However, the evidence for this is not very convincing. The desire for material improvement is now overwhelmingly strong in poor countries and the motivation is powerful enough to reduce the importance of barriers which kept them back in the past. Anachronistic social arrangements still hamper growth, but there are no cases where they have stopped it from occurring. Muslims, Jews, Animists, Buddhists, Confucians, Catholics, and Orthodox Christians have shown as much eagerness for material progress as the earlier disciples of the Protestant ethic. Rapid growth has occurred in countries with widely varied social systems.

We do not suggest that institutional obstacles have disappeared,

[1] See G. Myrdal, *Asian Drama*, Twentieth Century Fund, New York, 1968, and E. E. Hagen, *On the Theory of Social Change*, Dorsey Press, Illinois, 1962. Latin American pessimism about the possibilities of growth without institutional reform is reflected in C. Veliz, ed., *Obstacles to Change in Latin America*, Oxford, 1965.

but simply that they are not much greater now than those in the developed world. The Alliance for Progress has given great stress to land reform as a means to promote economic growth in Latin America, but we shall argue in our chapter on agriculture that differences in land tenure systems are only a partial explanation of differences in agricultural performance. Amongst the countries we have selected, the institutional and religious constraints are probably greatest in India. The pervasive influence of caste reduces Indian social and occupational mobility. The attitude to animals lowers the efficiency of livestock husbandry and inhibits the suppression of rodent and insect pests. Even so, India has managed to increase agricultural output by 2.5 per cent a year since 1950, after a half century of almost complete stagnation.

Considering the difficulty of the United States in getting tax changes through its complex political system, and British difficulties with restrictive trade union practices, one cannot really complain that institutional constraints are a monopoly of developing countries. One of the biggest obstacles to more rational policy is religious prejudice against birth control, but this is now important only in catholic countries, and could probably be reduced fairly quickly if it was not for the policy of the Vatican.

Most of the countries which we have analysed have not made basic institutional reforms in the post-war period. South Korea and Taiwan had far-reaching land reforms, but only Egypt and Yugoslavia have undergone institutional change that could be considered fundamental. And in both these countries the reforms were inspired by ideology rather than economic efficiency. There has been a widespread consciousness of the fact that institutional change involves costs as well as benefits. As economic growth involves continual adaptation, most institutions are provisional in any case, and there is little point in seeking perfection. Instead, most countries have tried to buy off interest groups which might have opposed change, and have hoped that their resistance would gradually wither away. There has been more pragmatism than experimentation on a grand scale. But at least there have been no spectacular failures like Soviet collectivization or the Great Leap Forward in China. Some of the worst problems arise in countries where there is an alleged policy for social change and an incapacity to achieve it. This has happened with the Indian aim of a socialist society, and the Chilean aim of land reform. These countries have borne some of the costs of social change without the benefits. In Mexico, by contrast, the mythology of revolution exaggerated the changes already accomplished and mitigated some of the strains which its extreme social inequality might otherwise have produced.

Most governments have conceived of economic development partly as a means of asserting their new-found national identity and independence. They have had to take measures to decolonialize their economies and free them from foreign tutelage. They have had to reconcile various tribal, racial, linguistic, caste, regional, social, class or religious groups. There have therefore been conflicts of interest in which the policy adopted has been only second or third best in terms of economic growth criteria alone. The strong nationalist feeling has had distinct drawbacks in the approach to some economic issues such as commercial policy. But there have been certain compensations. There has been a reasonably broad view of national welfare. Political power has usually resided in a technocratic *élite* of bureaucrats, either civilian or military, and they have been successful in implanting an enthusiasm for growth, for 'desarrollo', 'desenvolvimento', the 'plan', etc. Feudal elements and agrarian interests have not been as important in holding back growth as one might have expected. In most countries, economic growth has been given priority over distributive justice.

Political stability and clarity of purpose have been important in the success achieved by Taiwan, Israel, Mexico and Yugoslavia. In Taiwan, and Israel, military spending conflicted in an important degree with growth objectives, but the fact that survival as a state also depended on economic success helped greatly to make policy effective. Other countries were not so fortunate. Political change sometimes involved major switches in economic policy which interrupted growth. This was true in Brazil, Ceylon, Pakistan, Turkey and Venezuela, and the instability was probably at its worst in Argentina, where there were four quite distinct economic régimes and quite bitter social conflicts in the period under review.

Governments have had varying social or ideological objectives, but in practice, the role of the state in economic activity has been decided on fairly pragmatic grounds. Where there was a clash between the state and private capital, it was directed against foreign interests. Conflicts with the local business community were unimportant except in Egypt and Yugoslavia, where large private entrepreneurs have been eliminated. The other countries are all basically capitalist with varying degrees of state ownership. None of them has been wholly dedicated to private enterprise or to *laissez-faire*. Even in Taiwan, where public enterprise was sold off to the private sector, there was elaborate regulation of private business activity. In India there has been a professed ambition to create a socialist society, but there has been very little nationalization of existing private property. The state simply reserved major new ventures in certain fields for itself. Although public investment is very large, its relative size is not much different from that in Pakistan which has given more emphasis to the role of private enterprise.

Chapter IV

The Reasons for Instability

A major responsibility of any modern government is to ensure that the level of demand in the economy is kept in line with its production potential. Demand must not be allowed to wilt to the point where resources are left idle unnecessarily, and it should not be so excessive that their allocation is seriously distorted. A fully-rounded growth strategy must include proper attention to these short-run stabilization problems, but the precise level of demand which is appropriate for a developing country is difficult to judge both because statistical information is weak and because it is likely that there will be significant unemployment even if policy is successful in achieving the full growth potential. Given these difficulties and the ambitious goals for growth, it is not surprising that developing countries have leaned towards inflation. The average price increase for the twenty-two countries was around 9 per cent a year for 1950–65. This is much more extreme than the record of developed countries and has led to considerable inefficiency, but in some situations inflation has been a useful instrument of development policy.

Instability has also been reflected in a high incidence of recession. Half of our twenty-two countries have had recessions since 1950, and in most cases they were much more serious than in the developed world. Developing countries are at an earlier phase in business cycle history than developed countries are now, because agriculture plays a much greater part in their economies and their exports. We must therefore interpret their experience in the light not only of modern Keynesian analysis but also take cognizance of older theories no longer relevant for developed countries. Most of their recessions were not due to failures of policy, but to exogenous causes, so the recession record is not as bad as it looks.

The causes of instability in developing countries are extremely complex and one cannot hope to provide any simple general theory to explain their experience. Nor can we hope to judge the efficiency of policy by simply looking at indices of prices or the fluctuations in aggregate output. We must rather look in some detail at different types of instability. We will look first at different types of inflation.

INFLATION

In Latin America, inflation has a long history. Latin American governments have rarely been practitioners of orthodox finance, and only in the 1960s did a general awareness of the dangers of inflation emerge. In Asia and Africa, however, the high level of post-war demand is a significant change from the cautious policy of the old colonial régimes, which usually had balanced budgets, massive exchange reserves and deflationary monetary policies. In the early 1950s, when Ghana was a colony, its fiscal policy was cautious, commodity stabilization funds piled up large surpluses, and exchange reserves rose well above reasonable requirements. Similarly, Indian development ambitions were very modest in the first few years of independence when policy was dominated by the rather conservative finance ministry. In the first five year plan (1951–56), the target was a GNP growth of only 2 per cent a year, and India's huge exchange reserves were run down very gradually. Since the mid-1950s, however, demand has generally been more than adequate in most developing countries. Governments have leaned towards excess demand and set themselves low goals in terms of price stability. The imposition of exchange controls and the availability of substantial aid enabled them to do this, which would not have been possible if they had remained as open to the outside world as in the colonial period.

To some extent inflation in developing countries has been due to lumpiness of individual investment projects, e.g. the High Dam in Egypt, or to sudden military commitments unrelated to development. In most cases, however, inflation occurred because governments deliberately promoted levels of demand in excess of domestic production capacity. In the early post-war years, there was strong emphasis on the need to initiate the development process by a 'big push', i.e. an effort to stimulate development in many branches of the economy simultaneously, because of the complementary character of different industries. By expanding together, industries would provide each other with markets and technical economies of scale. It was thought that a gradual approach to development would not work because the economy was too stagnant to respond to a limited

Table IV–1

Percentage Change in the Domestic Price Level 1950–65

Annual average compound rate of change

	1950–55	1955–60	1960–65	1950–65
Argentina	17·0	37·0	23·0	25·0
Brazil	15·7	21·0	60·0	31·0
Ceylon	0·7	−0·8	0·0	−0·1
Chile	42·0	31·0	28·0	33·0
Colombia	5·3	10·4	12·3	9·3
Egypt	0·8	1·6	2·5	1·6
Ghana	8·5	1·4	7·4	5·7
Greece	10·4	2·2	2·6	5·0
India	−2·4	3·2	6·4	2·3
Israel	20·0	6·1	8·1	11·3
Malaya	2·9	0·4	0·9	1·4
Mexico	9·8	5·6	3·3	6·2
Pakistan	−0·1	5·3	1·9	2·3
Peru	6·9	9·2	8·4	8·2
Philippines	−1·2	2·2	4·6	1·8
South Korea	46·0*	11·6	18·7	19·8*
Spain	5·0	6·1	6·1	5·7
Taiwan	−0·2†	15·8	2·2	6·6†
Thailand	2·0‡	2·1	0·9	1·6‡
Turkey	8·3	12·5	3·9	8·2
Venezuela	−0·1	0·8	2·8	1·2
Yugoslavia	−2·5	3·7	14·3	4·9
Average	8·6	8·6	9·9	8·7

* beginning in 1953; † beginning in 1952; ‡ beginning in 1951.

Sources: GNP or GDP deflator derived from sources cited in Appendix B.

stimulus.[1] It was recognized that such a policy would be inflationary, but this was accepted as an inevitable and creative process.

Excess demand was not always due to developmental ambitions. Some countries created it for distributive reasons, i.e. they attempted to bribe certain parts of the community by subsidies and tax favours

[1] See P. N. Rosenstein-Rodan, 'Problems of Industrialization of Eastern and South-Eastern Europe', *Economic Journal*, June–September 1943, and his paper on the 'big push' in H. S. Ellis, ed. *Economic Development for Latin America*, Macmillan, London, 1962. Similar views were held by R. Nurkse, *Problems of Capital Formation in Underdeveloped Countries*, Oxford, 1953.

which they could not really afford to finance. And a few countries had excess demand for demonstrative purposes, i.e. to build useless or marginally useful monuments. In most developing countries, inflation due to an independent wage push was not important because trade unions are too weak, but some countries let inflation develop to the point where an independent wage-price spiral was generated. This is the most difficult kind of inflation to combat, and the most dangerous in its effect on the economy. Inflation is not therefore a simple phenomenon, and it is useful to look at a few examples of the leading species.

Several countries have gone through a period of sharp inflationary pressure which turned out to be a useful phase of development, and was then brought under control. This happened in Greece, Israel, Mexico and Taiwan, and some idea of their experience can be gained from Table IV–1 which shows the price history of the fifteen years 1950–65, broken down into five year intervals. From an initially weak fiscal position the governments of these four countries steadily built up their tax revenues, their monetary policy kept interest rates and exchange rates at realistic levels, and active steps were taken to create local capital markets. In all of these four countries, there was a substantial increase in the domestic savings rate between 1950 and 1965. The case for creative inflation as a *temporary* phase of development policy is well made by the leading Mexican economist and development banker, Alfredo Navarrete:

'the policy of forced savings through inflation should not be condemned as inappropriate or "inefficient" during the first stages of development of a backward economy, because it must be judged in the light of real and possible alternatives under the historical circumstances. At the outset of its economic development, Mexico could not easily have resorted to a modern system of voluntary savings or an efficient tax system. For the same reason, inflation cannot now be considered the best method of promoting Mexico's economic development. National savings are being generated in satisfactory amounts and can be collected by existing mechanisms that should be improved (taxes, securities market, and the profits of state enterprises).'[1]

In fact Navarrete is perhaps putting the matter too cautiously, for it may be reasonable for a country to have more than one period

[1] See A. Navarrete, 'The Financing of Economic Development', in E. Perez Lopez *et al.*, *Mexico's Recent Economic Growth*, Texas, 1967, p. 129.

of 'planned' or creative inflation in the course of its economic development. As long as the process is checked before the wage-price spiral gets deeply imbedded, the effects may be beneficial. What is really dangerous is the assumption, sometimes made in Latin America in the 1950s, that inflation could be a *permanent* instrument of development policy.[1] One suspects that some of the advocates of this policy were really supporting it because it might lead to revolution rather than economic development. In fact, it has usually led to rather repressive military dictatorships.

Brazil is a country where inflation was carried far beyond the 'creative' stage and where the motivation was mixed—being both developmental and demonstrative. The big push in Brazil was the expansion programme of 1956 to 1961. It included the simultaneous development of electricity, transport, steel, cement, fertilizers, shipbuilding, heavy electrical plant, and the creation of a large automobile industry more or less from scratch. The technical preparation of the investment decisions required close consultation between ministries, development banks and private industry, both home and foreign. The execution of the projects was carried out with remarkable efficiency and involved a well planned extension of industry which added enormously to the range of Brazil's productive capacity.[2] The automobile programme was somewhat premature but better planned than that of Argentina and Mexico.

If one simply looks at the industrial component of the Kubitschek programme, it represents an enlightened example of developmentally-inspired inflation and had a considerable creative impact. However, Kubitschek also built a new capital in a completely empty area

[1] Some Latin American economists have considered inflation to be an inevitable feature of effective growth policies because of 'structural' bottlenecks (i.e. rigidity of supply of farm products and inelasticity of exports). However, the bottlenecks which they stress are to a large extent a by-product of inflation rather than independent causes and they can be broken by specific measures such as land reform and export promotion rather than by excess demand. For an outline of the structuralist case, see O. Sunkel, 'Chilian Inflation: An Unorthodox Approach', *International Economic Papers*, vol. X, 1960. For a critique, see the essay by Roberto Campos in A. O. Hirschman, *Latin American Issues*, Twentieth Century Fund, New York, 1961.

[2] The projects had required intensive preparation both by the Brazilian-American Joint Commission which had started work in the early 1950s in the expectation of large-scale US aid, and the 'programa de metas' prepared by the National Development Bank. For a detailed description of the programme, see 'Fifteen Years of Economic Policy in Brazil', *Economic Bulletin for Latin America*, November 1964.

which required 7,000 kilometres of access roads. Some of the roads were useful, but Brasilia was a very dubious investment. It was costly to build because of the haste of construction and the use of air transport to bring in materials. It is still not used by most ministries. Many people who work there have to commute from the rest of the country, it is expensive to supply such an isolated area with food, and it was so designed that automobiles are more or less essential for urban transport. The cost of Brasilia was disguised by extensive use of social security funds and public resources originally destined for other purposes. The Vargas Foundation estimated that the annual construction costs amounted to about 2·5 per cent of GNP over a six-year period. Building Brasilia in such a hurry was an example of demonstrative populism of a type which has also characterized Ghana and Indonesia and which is one of the least fruitful kinds of inflation.

During the Kubitschek boom, publicly-controlled investment rose from a third to half of the total, and the government budget deficit from 0·5 per cent to 5 per cent of GNP in spite of an increase in government revenues. There was an acceleration in the rate of price increase and a very large accumulation of foreign debt of a short-term character. Because of price controls on utilities, bottlenecks developed in power and communications. Inflation created major social tensions, and extreme balance of payments disequilibrium. The three following years were ones of weak government in which the inflationary spiral process gathered momentum, and successful wage demands from embittered trade unions began to add an independent element of cost-push inflation to the already complex situation. As a result, Brazil acquired a military regime, and spent the three years from 1964 to 1967 in relative stagnation while it was implementing its stabilization programme. This was one of the indirect results of the Kubitschek period.

In Turkey and Argentina, governments deliberately generated excess demand in an attempt to gain popularity. In both cases, the inflation was originally motivated by an attempt to bribe one section of the population by boosting their incomes. Turkish farmers were the main beneficiaries of Menderes. Industrial workers and government servants were the beneficiaries of Peron.

The Argentine experience is probably the most complicated case of inflation within our group of countries. In the 1890s, Argentina had a big surge of inflation by the standards of those times, which led to the Baring crisis and a major collapse in the London capital market. In this century it had rather mild inflation until the access to power of Juan Peron. The Peronist regime was not old-fashioned *caudillismo* but was populist and nationalist, and had to appeal to new classes to strengthen its power against the old oligarchy of ranchers and commercial interests. Peron therefore built up the power of trade unions and pushed up real wages. He also increased the number of government workers and those in state enterprises to a high level of redundancy. Most of the wartime accumulation of foreign exchange reserves was used to buy out foreign investors. Exports were retarded by unfavourable exchange rates for farm products. Government purchasing agencies sold beef domestically below cost to lower the cost of living. As a result, investment in agriculture came to a halt and exports fell. Peron was finally evicted in 1955 by a military government, and ever since then successive governments have been struggling unsuccessfully to fight inflation against the extreme social tensions created under Peron. There have been three stabilisation programmes which on average reduced GNP by nearly 6 per cent, and each time they failed to beat the inbuilt spiral process. Tensions were further complicated by the peculiar social structure of Argentina which has a large population of recent immigrants (60 per cent of Buenos Aires were immigrants in the 1930s) with no very clear process of assimilation. Even in the third generation, Argentines of British origin consider themselves Anglo-Argentines and retain British passports. It was therefore very difficult to mobilize national support for any stabilization programme.

In the post-Peron period, the IMF has participated in stabilization loans for Argentina, together with a group of European creditors who have arranged rollovers for indebtedness. The IMF has been bitterly attacked by nationalists and apostles of permanent inflation. To some extent the criticism is justified because IMF analysis of the causes of inflation was too superficial. But the real trouble was that the size of foreign credits which would have been required to tide Argentina over its difficulties and give the government adequate breathing space was too big. Within the country, consumption demand was much bigger than resources available. As a result inadequate stabilisation policies checked growth rather than inflation. Once a country is in as deep a mess as Argentina, the only real possibilities for breaking inflationary expectations and the spiral process are: (*a*) policies of extreme deflation; (*b*) to let the monetary system collapse completely in the hope of subsequently inducing the kind of sharp psychological reaction against inflation which has occurred in Germany. Both of these courses are obviously extremely unpleasant. Instead Argentina has had fifteen years of sub-explosive inflation and slow growth.

In some cases governments have followed inflationary policies partly in order to induce a bigger flow of foreign aid.

In the mid-1950s, when serious discussion started on the need for substantial aid to finance development, the most influential contributions were those by Millikan and Rostow.[1] They argued that development involved a break from a stagnant economy to one with quite different characteristics in which growth becomes 'more or less automatic', or 'self-sustained'. To move from one stage to the other, a 'take-off' is needed. This requires a sudden burst of effort, in which the rate of investment is raised from 5 to 10 per cent of national income. After this is achieved, per capita income will no longer stagnate but grow steadily. A new political, social and institutional framework will emerge which will give growth 'an on-going character'. It would be beyond the domestic resources of most countries to achieve this sudden burst of effort, but they could do it with the help of foreign aid, 'in a decade or two'.

The emphasis on the need for a 'take-off' as a brief once-for-all phase is difficult to accept as a general proposition.[2] Not all of the countries concerned were stagnant economies. Many of them had already had substantial growth in per capita income and the best method of accelerating it in these cases (e.g. Latin America) was not a short burst of effort but a more gradual process. Amongst the twenty-two countries, it was only in India and Pakistan that the previous long-run record was one of almost completely static per capita income. Secondly, the definition of the ultimate scope of development policy was too restrictive. It was assumed that a

[1] See M. F. Millikan and W. W. Rostow, *A Proposal: Key to an Effective Foreign Policy*, Harper, New York, 1957. See also W. W. Rostow, 'Take-off into self-sustained Growth', *Economic Journal*, March 1956. At about the same time H. Leibenstein produced his theory of the 'critical minimum effort', which is much less ambitious as a general theory of development but involves a rather similar policy prescription; see his *Economic Backwardness and Economic Growth*, Wiley, New York, 1957.

[2] The 'take-off' theory of Rostow is not simply a prescription for future action, but was also intended to be an interpretation of the historical experience of developed countries. It has been widely attacked as historical analysis, but this is not a point which concerns us here. For a self-edited critique see W. W. Rostow, ed., *The Economics of Take-off into Sustained Growth*, Macmillan, London, 1965.

successful take-off would lead to a situation of 'self-sustaining' growth where the spontaneous private forces in the economy would be powerful enough to provide an adequate momentum, and the need for deliberate policy action would presumably wither away. This ignores the fact that government policy is nowadays continuously active in promoting growth in developed countries. For this reason the distinction between the policy tasks of countries at different stages of development was exaggerated. The process of raising the investment rate may well continue for several decades requiring several successive surges and going much further than Rostow and Millikan suggested.

However, the emphasis on the short and decisive character of the take-off arose mainly because of the need to assure aid donors that they were not undertaking an open-ended commitment to support the poor countries. From this point of view the theory was useful. It did help influence the US Congress to increase aid,[1] and it also provided substantial intellectual encouragement and support to the more ambitious strategists in countries where a sharp initial breakthrough was essential to the development process, i.e. India and Pakistan.

The take-off theory undoubtedly encouraged India to generate excess demand, but the problem was that India was not sure how much aid she would get. For instance, the Indian government and the US Ambassador to India, Professor Galbraith, both anticipated US government finance for the state steel-mill at Bokaro, but the Kennedy administration was not able to get this aid from Congress.[2] Indian inflation and payments difficulties were successful in inducing a bigger supply of aid, but there would have been less distortion in resource allocation if India had been a little less ambitious. The second five-year plan was too optimistic about capital output ratios, import requirements and aid, and also had a residual savings deficit. The third plan was also too ambitious, and its inflationary impact was enhanced by delays in getting the public steel plants into operation, by rearmament and harvest failures.

[1] The Rostow Millikan thesis was an important part of the evidence presented to the US Congress in the 1957 aid hearings. See US Senate, Special Committee o Study the Foreign Aid Program, *The Foreign Aid Program: Compilation of Studies and Surveys*, US Government Printing Office, Washington, 1957.

[2] Similarly, in the early 1950s, the investment programme devised for Brazil by the Joint Brazil-United States Commission could not be carried out because the Eisenhower government did not provide the expected finance.

BENEFITS AND COSTS OF INFLATION

We can now try to draw up a balance sheet of the benefits and costs of inflation. Inflation may, in some circumstances, serve as a useful instrument of development policy. When the economy is emerging from the colonial phase, entrepreneurial initiative and investment incentives may well need the stimulus of a slightly excessive level of demand before they can be properly mobilized. Inflation and the accompanying balance of payments crises may help induce foreign aid. A short burst of inflation may be deliberately planned as the easiest method to get a once-for-all shift of resources in favour of government and investment. It can squeeze consumption to the benefit of profits, bankrupt the less enterprising property owners in favour of new entrepeneurs, and shift resources from agriculture to industry. In African countries, inflation may be the only politically acceptable way of reducing the exaggeratedly high real incomes of civil servants, which are often still based on expatriate scales. For a time it may be possible to finance a government budget deficit by forced savings. Prices rise faster than wages and workers are cheated of part of their real income to the benefit of the government. Real wages will suffer and profits will rise, although the government may squeeze profits in less favoured sectors by price controls and some of the less competent capitalists will lose out to smarter ones.

But if inflation is serious or prolonged, it can produce very dangerous effects. It is not easy to measure the damage in quantitative terms and the relative impact cannot be judged simply by looking at the overall rate of price increase. Some countries may suppress inflation by controls which impede the growth of the economy severely, whereas others with bigger price increases may suffer less distortion in resource allocation.

If inflation is prolonged, the people who were being cheated will find devices to protect themselves, the inflation will simply generate a useless wage-price spiral, it will reduce private savings, and will involve the unplanned accumulation of some of the worst kinds of external debt, i.e. short-term high-interest trade credits. When these complications are fully evolved, there will be increasing distortions in the economy and growth will eventually be brought to a grinding halt. It is noteworthy that both Brazil and Argentina experienced a fall in the savings rate from 1950 to 1965, and the Indian inflationary experience in the mid-1960s also reduced the savings rate.

The deliberate pursuit of policies of excess demand will also create a balance of payments bottleneck which both impedes growth and reduces the range of policy options by making governments dependent on foreign creditors, who will often insist on changes which seriously affect the development objectives of the recipient government. Inflation discourages exports and increases imports, reduces foreign exchange reserves and builds up foreign debt. At some stage, foreign creditors will refuse to carry the process further and the country will be forced to readjust. This will usually involve a sudden sharp reduction in domestic demand to release resources for exports and reduce imports, but the squeeze will need to be bigger than the payments deficit, so that some parts of the economy will be working below capacity, and investment may fall whilst resources are being reoriented. The exchange rate which is needed to secure payments equilibrium in this situation may involve much worse terms of trade for the country than its long-run potential would warrant.

Even if a foreign exchange crisis is avoided, this is often achieved only by a complex apparatus of import controls which has harmful effects on the efficiency of the economy because it creates an incentive for import-substituting industrialization in every industry where imports are controlled, and provides those who get import licences with windfall profits.

It the tax structure were progressive, rising prices and incomes would automatically increase tax revenues and the initial budget deficit might in time be self-correcting. But developing countries do not have this kind of tax structure, and the checks to inflation which are enforceable are usually price controls, particularly those on commodities which affect the cost of living directly, such as foodstuffs. These will reduce profits and incentives in agriculture, slow down growth in that sector and reduce the availability of traditional agricultural products for export.

Inflation will push resources into highly speculative outlets which offer a quick profit but which do not promote development. It will swell the size of the financial and banking sector unnecessarily,[1] and make rational decision-making difficult in every kind of business. In particular, it will introduce major new elements of risk into

[1] Over-investment in luxury housing is usually considered one of the effects of inflation, but in fact it is often held in check by rent control and the absence of mortgage facilities. There is more evidence of this phenomenon in Mexico and Greece than there is in Brazil where inflation has been more severe.

capital budgeting and make it impossible to calculate depreciation properly.

In Brazil, price controls on transport, gas, electricity, and telephones left these enterprises without profits or depreciation funds. This caused constant breakdowns in utilities which affected the quality of urban life adversely. The poor quality of the telephone and transport services was a direct check to industrial efficiency and intermittent failure of the electric supply to industrial plants was a common occurrence. The government limited the worst consequences of these price-control policies by itself investing heavily in public utilities and taking these over from the private sector. To a large extent, this extension of the Brazilian public sector was an unintended by-product of inflation.

The primary inflation due to excess demand may generate an independent spiral process if it is carried too far, and it may antagonize trade unions to such a degree that they will not co-operate in government incomes policies in periods of stabilization. The growth of corruption, social tension, and political disenchantment with the normal process of government has in several cases led to the installation of political dictatorship.

For these reasons it is clear that the initial advantages of inflation are easily outrun, and once the spiral process becomes strong, it will have negative effects on growth. This has certainly been the case in Brazil, Chile and Argentina. However, we should stress again that the damage done by inflation was not the same in each country. Although Chile, Argentina, and Brazil have had a similar average price experience, the inflation has probably done less damage to the economy in Brazil than in Argentina and Chile. India, in spite of its rather modest price increases, has suffered a good deal from suppressed inflation, because of the distorting effect of controls on resource allocation and exports.

The major problem of inflation is its political character. Governments may know quite well that their policies will be harmful in the long-run, but they usually like to be popular in the short-run and hope the ultimate burden will fall on others. They have the philosophy 'Grow now, pay later'. The Kubitschek boom was one of very rapid growth for the Brazilian economy, and Kubitschek still retains great popularity because of this. There is similar nostalgia for Menderes in Turkey and Peron in Argentina. The successor government, which has to carry out the balance of payments adjustment and remove the distortions of inflation, is usually unpopular.

However, as experience in development policy accumulates, and the public realizes that it will be a problem for decades and cannot be solved in one presidential term, there may well be a more sophisticated appreciation of the real cost of too big a push.

RECESSIONS

Thus far we have been discussing the level of demand as if it were entirely within government control, but there have also been disturbances of an accidental kind which were not foreseen or controllable by development policy. These accidental factors have in fact been the predominant cause of recessions.

Since 1950, Argentina, Ceylon, Ghana, India, Malaya, Philippines, South Korea, Turkey and Yugoslavia have had recessions of an amplitude well beyond that experienced in the developed world since the 1930s. All of these were big enough to have a major damaging effect on the confidence of investors, and to bring big reductions in real income to most people in the economy. The most severe declines in output occurred fairly early in the period and were generally associated with the collapse of the Korean war commodity boom.

In Ceylon, Ghana, and Malaya most of the fluctuation was due to violent changes in world market conditions for rubber, tin, and cocoa, and, in Malaya, there was the added complication of guerrilla warfare. In India, Turkey and Yugoslavia the fluctuations were due to harvest failures, and in South Korea, to war. Only in Argentina were the recessions largely due to failures of domestic stabilization policy.

Table IV–2 shows the situation in all countries where GDP fell by more than 1 per cent in any of the fifteen years covered. In all these countries except Israel and Spain, instability has been much worse than in the USA, and per capita income instability has been worse still.

In the early 1950s, which were strongly affected by the Korean war, there was heavy stress in United Nations literature on the instability problems of developing countries, particularly the instability of their exports.[1] To some extent the UN studies may have overstated the problem by concentrating on fluctuations in export proceeds from particular commodities rather than countries.

[1] See UN *Instability in Export Markets of Underdeveloped Countries*, New York, 1952.

Table IV–2

Incidence of Recession 1950–65

	Number of recessions	Average per cent fall in GDP from peak to trough		Number of recessions	Average per cent fall in GDP from peak to trough
Argentina	3	5·8	Philippines	1	3·5
Ceylon	1	5·3	South Korea	1	7·7
Ghana	3	3·3	Spain	2	1·1
India	1	4·3	Turkey	2	5·3
Israel	1	1·3	Yugoslavia	1	8·1
Malaya	1	6·3*			

* This is the fall in GNP. The fall in GDP was 22·3 per cent, but this was cushioned by a massive reduction in profits remitted abroad.

Source: See Appendix B for annual data on GDP from which the table was calculated. In some cases, the volatility of the economy may be exaggerated for statistical reasons, because the GDP data contain a rather high degree of error for measuring short term movements, particularly when changes in the direction of growth are involved.

However, in recent years academic analysts have tended to lean in the opposite direction and have understated the instability problem. In a recent study, Alasdair MacBean has suggested that developing countries' export proceeds are not much more unstable than those of developed countries.[1] In fact MacBean measures fluctuation after eliminating trend, so that he is really measuring volatility rather than the incidence of recession. German or Japanese exports may be just as 'volatile' as those of developing countries but an inflection in the upward growth of Japanese or German exports obviously poses smaller policy problems than an absolute decline in the exports of developing countries which have a slower growth trend. If we measure cyclical variations in exports by the classic techniques developed by the National Bureau of Economic Research, export instability of developing countries is notably bigger than that of developed countries, as is clear from Table IV–3. We do not mean to imply from this that export instability is the only major cause of

[1] See A. I. MacBean, *Export Instability and Economic Development*, Allen & Unwin, London, 1966. Similar conclusions, with similar analysis were reached by J. D. Coppock, *International Economic Instability*, McGraw Hill, New York, 1962.

instability in developing countries, but our strong disagreement with MacBean's conclusions is important because MacBean's evidence has misled some distinguished economists to underrate the instability problem of developing countries.[1]

In a few countries the internal consequences of export instability are cushioned by the fact that the most volatile incomes are the profits of foreign corporations, as in Malaya. In booms the big increase in income takes the form of increased remittances, and in recessions these are reduced. For this reason Malayan GNP has been more stable than GDP. However, where the fluctuations primarily affect domestic incomes one would expect them to induce instability in spending, and the instability might also be expected to lower the long-term incentive to invest. For governments in most developing countries, export instability poses worse problems than it would in the developed world, because their tax revenue from exports is a much bigger proportion of their total income. During export booms, government revenue is swollen and expenditures tend to expand, and it is difficult to contract spending quickly in recessions when revenue falls.[2] A better tax structure and a more prudent attitude to 'windfall' gains in revenue during booms would be helpful, but it has been very difficult for most developing countries to break away from this kind of tax system, and it is never easy to decide whether an increase in export receipts is going to be a 'windfall' or the beginning of a new trend.

It is difficult to quantify the influences which recessions have had on the growth trend. Four of the countries which have experienced recessions have had GDP growth rates of 4 per cent or less, but recessions have also occurred in three countries with average growth (Malaya, Philippines and Turkey) and in four countries with fast growth. Generally the recessions lasted a couple of years and were followed by a sharp recovery which carried the economy beyond previous peaks. The ease with which recovery from these short-term disturbances occurred suggests that in several cases they have not

[1] See E. S. Mason in the preface to MacBean's book: 'In the course of this investigation it became clear that the less developed countries are little if any more subject to fluctuations of export earnings than the developed countries.' See A. I. MacBean, *op. cit.*, p. 9. H. G. Johnson has made similar references to Macbean's results in his *Economic Policies Towards Less Developed Countries*, Brookings, Washington DC, 1967, p. 143.

[2] For a detailed exposition of the problem as it has arisen in Chile, see G. Maynard, *Economic Development and the Price Level*, Macmillan, London, 1963, pp. 266–75.

had a serious long-term impact on growth. It may well be the case that people in developing countries are psychologically better attuned to the 'accidental' character of their fluctuations[1] than investors in developed countries were to their pre-war type of business cycle. This may dampen the influence of harvest fluctuations and a cycle in export proceeds. The most damaging recessions have been those which were associated with severe payments difficulties, and these have undoubtedly hindered growth in Argentina, Ghana and India.

Given the difficulty of defining the appropriate level of demand, the lack of finesse in the major domestic policy instruments, the uncertainty about the size of external resources, and the proneness to external shocks or harvest fluctuations, the post-war record of demand management is not too discouraging for developing countries as a whole. Some of the biggest countries, Argentina, Brazil and India, had chronic difficulties, but many of the others tackled their inflationary recessionary or balance of payments problems by effective stabilization policies and experienced only temporary disturbances. This is true of Greece, Mexico, Peru, South Korea, Spain, Taiwan, Thailand, and Yugoslavia, where the record of effective policy action is just as good as in any of the developed countries.

POLICIES FOR STABILITY

In so far as instability has been caused by excess demand, it is obvious that improvements can be achieved by a better phasing of public expenditure and a more realistic effort to match development ambitions with the capacity for resource mobilization. The scope for improvement lies fundamentally in a better mix of fiscal and monetary policy.

[1] This point has been argued by Sir Sydney Caine, 'Private individuals living in primary producing countries are naturally not unaware that prices fluctuate, and they are perhaps more prudent than economic theorists give them credit for, so that they do not spend the whole of the higher incomes received in good times as soon as they are received. They do in fact put a certain amount away, as shown by the evidence of bank deposits and other forms of short-term saving, and they draw on these reserves in periods of lower prices, so maintaining a good deal more stability of consumption and expenditure than crude figures of income might suggest.' See Caine as cited by Macbean, *op. cit.*, p. 125. However Caine was referring to the situation in Malaya in the colonial period when prices were stable, and the same consumer behaviour could not be expected in inflationary conditions in Latin America, nor does it seem to be characteristic of government reactions in countries which are politically independent.

Table IV–3

Fluctuations in the Dollar Value of Exports 1950–67

	Number of years in which exports below previous peak within the period	Maximum fall from peak to trough or minimum annual rise in exports within the period (per cent)
Argentina	13	49·5
Brazil	16	31·0
Ceylon	14	21·0
Chile	9	28·5
Colombia	13	33·8
Egypt	14	33·1
Ghana	14	24·2
Greece	3	12·5
India	15	32·2
Israel	2	6·4
Malaya	16	52·7
Mexico	7	17·4
Pakistan	16	60·4
Peru	6	12·2
Philippines	7	19·0
South Korea	8	57·5
Spain	6	8·3
Taiwan	4	28·5
Thailand	10	22·9
Turkey	10	37·6
Venezuela	4	1·9
Yugoslavia	2	24·7
Average	9·5	28·0
France	3	7·4
Germany (FR)	0	+4·5
Italy	3	15·8
Japan	2	6·1
UK	4	1·9
USA	5	15·5
Average	2·8	7·0

Source: *Yearbook of International Trade Statistics*, UN, New York, 1959 and 1966 editions, and *Monthly Bulletin of Statistics*, UN, New York, March 1969.

a. *Fiscal policy*
Fiscal policy is the major instrument for mobilizing and allocating resources and for affecting the incentives of the private sector, but budgetary procedures are usually too crude to permit any finesse in compensating demand movements in the private sector, and variations in government spending have themselves set off major fluctuations in economic activity. Revenue estimates tend to be made in a very perfunctory fashion, and many expenditures do not come under proper scrutiny. The information given to legislatures is often small and there is little possibility of informed public discussion. In many countries there are important autonomous agencies whose accounting does not enter the official budget. These agencies are useful in breaking bureaucratic bottlenecks but when they account for a substantial proportion of expenditure, the usefulness of the budget for allocating financial resources is greatly reduced. We have already examined the substantial scope for improvement in fiscal policy in Chapter III and there is no point in repeating our conclusions here.

b. *Better Economic Indicators*
One factor which reduces the efficiency of short-term economic policy a good deal is the lack of adequate and up-to-date economic intelligence. Usually the only statistical indicators which the government receives quickly are those for foreign trade and the price level in the capital city. In Brazil the industrial production index is usually available with a lag of about two years, and even the banking statistics take about three months to process. Statistical offices are usually very weak, because the type of person required to produce good economic indicators can find more exciting positions elsewhere in government. This is an area where foreign technical assistance can help a good deal in filling the gap in domestic skills, but it has not been used very extensively. There are a few countries like Israel, Taiwan and Greece where short-term economic indicators are well developed, but these are rare exceptions, and only in Israel is the full range of indicators available on a seasonally adjusted basis.

c. *Monetary Policy*
In most developing countries, monetary policy is a powerful weapon of short-term economic management because business is heavily dependent on bank credit and on government financial institutions for its funds. Capital markets are relatively weak, and as domestic

public debt is small the government is not inhibited by efforts to stabilize this market. Foreign exchange operations are usually tightly controlled so that domestic monetary policies can be isolated from those abroad much more easily than in the developed world. Very often, the government itself is engaged in commercial banking on a large scale. The Banco do Brasil is a government bank which does 35 per cent of the country's commercial banking. In Argentina all bank deposits were nationalized in 1946, and although the system has now changed, the public sector still makes two-thirds of the loans and has half of commercial bank deposits.

In spite of the powerful potential leverage of monetary policy, the central bank itself is usually subordinate to the fiscal authorities, and its policy is generally a reflection of the government's fiscal difficulties rather than an instrument for managing the economy efficiently.[1] Monetary policy in many Latin American countries has often exacerbated the problem of inflation, and in periods of deflation, it has been used to put a very sharp break on the private sector when the government was not making an adequate effort to cut public expenditure. In Greece, Mexico, and Thailand, however, there are powerful and well-staffed central banks which have played an effective independent role in development strategy, and have been mainly responsible for ending inflation and avoiding payments difficulties in these countries.[2]

The main instruments of monetary policy are usually direct quantitative controls on the allocation of credit, advance deposits on imports and the imposition of varying reserve ratios which the commercial banks must maintain against their liabilities. In some countries, and particularly in Latin America there has been a rapid growth of non-bank financial intermediaries, particularly those which were able to devise ways of evading statutory regulation over

[1] Developing countries have had less experience with central banks than developed countries. In Japan, the central bank was created in 1882 more or less at the beginning of its efforts at modern economic growth. In Mexico and Chile the central banks were created in 1925, India in 1934, Argentina 1936, Thailand 1942, the Philippines 1949, Ceylon 1950, Israel in 1954, Ghana in 1957 and Malaya in 1959. Brazil has had three central banks and acquired its latest one in 1965; in theory it was to be strongly independent, but it had three governors in its first three years.

[2] See X. Zolotas, *Monetary Equilibrium and Economic Development*, Princeton, 1965, for a description of Greek policy by the governor of the bank. D. Brothers and L. Solis, *Mexican Finacial Development*, Univ. of Texas, Austin, 1966; and the article by Dr Puey, Governor of the Bank of Thailand in C. Onslow, ed., *Asian Economic Development*, Weidenfeld & Nicolson, London, 1965.

interest rates in conditions of rapid inflation. These institutions are sometimes outside the control of the monetary authorities, but it is not a difficult matter to extend the powers of central banks to cover their activities as has been done in Mexico.

One of the weaknesses of financial policy in developing countries has been the maintenance of artificially low interest rates, partly to reduce the apparent costs of the government's own investment. However, this practice leads to misallocation of capital and is inflationary. In several countries, the rate of interest has been well below the rate of price increase, so that the real rate of interest to lenders has been negative, and borrowers have been subsidized. Brazil, India and Pakistan are cases where artificially low interest rates have probably led to misallocation of public investment and to use of too capital-intensive a technology, whereas Greece, Mexico, Peru, South Korea and Taiwan have all had realistically high rates of interest.

In countries emerging recently from a colonial situation, the power of monetary policy is limited.[1] This is particularly true of Ghana, where a large part of the banking system is owned by foreign banks which have access to very large funds abroad. Until exchange control was imposed, the leverage of domestic monetary policy was negligible, and even then it was weakened by the fact that most of the banks were branches of foreign enterprises. Furthermore, it is clear from Nigerian experience that an attempt to build up domestic banks too quickly can lead to large scale failures.

Whilst fiscal and monetary policy are the major instruments for bringing inflation under control, there is a whole range of other weapons for mitigating its impact. It is very useful if the exchange rate is adjusted frequently to prevent a worsening of the balance of payments due to uncompetitive exports. Domestic price controls should be kept as temporary as possible. Attempts should be made to keep movements in housing investment in tune with the overall needs of the economy. In countries where trade unions are important it is useful for governments to have an incomes policy on the lines adopted (admittedly without much success) in developed countries. In all of these respects the measures used to deal with short run stabilization problems should also be fashioned in the light of longer-term development needs.

[1] For a description of the scope for monetary policy in a colonial-type situation, see H. A. de S. Gunasekera, *From Dependent Currency to Central Banking in Ceylon*, G. Bell, London, 1962.

d. *Commodity Price Stabilization*

However, there are two aspects of the stabilization problem which deserve special attention and which require international co-operation. One of the major causes of instability in developing countries is the relatively large role of agriculture in their domestic economy and their heavy dependence on exports of a few agricultural products. For this reason their exports are more unstable than those of developed countries, and this in turn is one of the reasons why their economies are more unstable.

There are several reasons for this greater instability. In the first place, agricultural output is subject to instability because of weather variations. Secondly, for several important commercial commodities such as coffee, cocoa and rubber, supply is very sensitive to price changes but there is a considerable lag before new trees yield a crop. As a result the long run equilibrium is unstable. There is a long-term (cobweb) cycle in which the supply response to increased prices is delayed and exaggerated, so that when the increased output comes on the market, it depresses prices which in turn induces a lagged decline in output. This kind of cycle has taken place in coffee over the past sixty years and is also characteristic of other crops. On the demand side, we no longer have the major fluctuations induced by large business cycle movements in developed countries. But the demand situation is strongly affected by speculation on likely supply movements, inventory movements are higher relative to output than in the case of industrial commodities, and there have been a number of special factors such as the Korean war boom, US stockpiling policy, etc., which have induced demand instability.

One way in which these problems can be mitigated is by industrialization, which reduces the relative importance of agriculture in the economy. Diversification of exports is also useful so that the country does not depend too heavily on one commodity. However, neither of these measures is likely to do more than mitigate the problem for countries with a strong comparative advantage in a particular product.

For this reason, there have been many attempts to achieve greater stability by schemes aimed directly to affect the market for particular commodities. Another motive for such action is the effort to get higher export earnings by raising prices permanently higher than would be the case on a free market. This will be possible only if demand for the product is rather insensitive to its price—which happens to be the case for coffee.

A country cannot hope to influence the market for a commodity by its own action unless it holds a semi-monopoly position, as was the case in Brazil with coffee. Brazil has experimented with coffee marketing schemes since 1906, but, partly as a result of its own actions in withholding coffee and raising prices, other producers have now gained 70 per cent of the market, whereas in 1900 they only had 30 per cent. Coffee stabilization must now be carried out by international agreements between a number of countries, like that for other commodities. Negotiation of these agreements is always difficult because the interests of different countries will vary. New producers with a small share of the market will have to be offered some scope for increasing sales at the expense of older established producers. It is also usually necessary that the main consumer countries co-operate or at least remain relatively benign towards such agreements. The interests of consumers and producers in the schemes will be different at different phases of the commodity cycle. When prices are high, producers will be reluctant to enter agreements, but when they are low, consumer countries will not want to participate. These agreements also require government intervention in each of the national markets because it will often be necessary to pay producers less than the government selling price, to impose production quotas, restrict acreage, introduce diversification schemes, etc. Governments running such schemes will also have to make a realistic assessment of likely long-run demand and price trends.

Given the difficulties involved, it is not surprising that many of the schemes have been failures in the past. Brazilian coffee schemes led to massive overproduction in the 1930s and in the 1960s.The West African cocoa boards stabilized farm prices but destabilized earnings and made mistakes in assessing price trends. The possibilities for international co-operation until the late 1950s were limited by the opposition of the USA to stabilization schemes.

The present outlook is somewhat more favourable for international stabilization schemes because US policy has changed, and the developing countries have also shown greater willingness to co-operate and to carry out the domestic policies to restrict and diversify domestic production which are necessary to success. Nevertheless, the only schemes which are currently functioning are the buffer stock for tin (which has in the past run out of funds and out of tin), the international coffee agreement which relies on export quotas, and the new international sugar agreement whose successful negotiation by Raoul Prebisch was a real *tour de force* in view of the enormous difficulties.

These schemes are likely to make a modest contribution to export stability in future, and they may well help to secure somewhat better terms of trade for primary products like coffee for which demand is relatively insensitive to price.[1] However, many of the instability problems will not be curable by commodity stabilization schemes, and developing economies will remain more vulnerable to fluctuation than the developed world. It is for this reason that they require favourable treatment from developed countries in the provision of international liquidity if they are to have a reasonable chance of mitigating the effects of instability on growth.

e. *Foreign Exchange Reserves and International Liquidity*

One of the major instruments of stabilization policy is foreign exchange reserves. In times of payments difficulty they can help cushion the impact of deficits until corrective measures take effect, and they are particularly necessary in countries where export earnings are subject to violent fluctuation.

In 1937, the exchange reserves of the twenty-two countries were about $2·5 billion,[2] and there were no international organizations to provide credit. This meant that remedies for payments difficulties were usually highly deflationary. During the war, reserves rose considerably, particularly in Latin America and in India, Egypt and Palestine. The increase for all developing countries was about $14 billion ($10 billion in sterling and about $4 billion in gold and dollars) and for our twenty-two countries about $8 billion. This large increase in reserves together with a reduction in indebtedness ($8 billion for all developing countries) was the major reason why there was no apparent need for aid in the early post-war period. The Latin American countries ran down their reserves quickly, but in India and Pakistan the process of using up excess reserves lasted until the mid-1950s, and in Ghana until the 1960s.

By 1965, the only developing countries which might be considered to have excessive reserves were Greece, Israel, Spain, Thailand and

[1] There is very considerable scope for increasing primary producer income from higher prices. This is demonstrated by the fact that, in 1962, developed countries collected over $7 billion from revenue duties and internal fiscal changes on commodities imported from developing countries. Most of it was raised on petroleum and tobacco (some $5·9 billion); coffee and sugar yielded about $450 million each.

[2] See *International Reserves and Liquidity*, IMF, Washington DC, 1958, p. 100.

Venezuela. In most other countries, reserves were inadequate. Net reserves of the twenty-two countries had been \$10·5 billion in 1945, \$7·6 billion in 1950 and \$6 billion in 1965. The real value of the 1965 reserves was only about 30 per cent of those in 1945, and was back to something like the real 1937 level.

The major post-war innovation in the field of international liquidity was the IMF, but in 1950 the IMF was not a very important source of finance for developing countries. Only three of our twenty-two had borrowed from the Fund, and six of them were not even members. Conditions for drawings were more strict than now, and IMF quotas amounted to only 15 per cent of their net foreign exchange reserves. By 1965, the net exchange reserves had declined but IMF quotas had risen two and a half times, and the 1963 compensatory financing facility enabled them to make additional drawings of 25 per cent of their quota when export earnings fell for reasons beyond their control. IMF facilities in 1965 were more than 50 per cent of net reserves, and eleven of the twenty-two countries had outstanding borrowings from the IMF.

The IMF has therefore played an increasingly important role in the stabilization policies of these countries, but on several occasions IMF resources have proved inadequate to prevent major doses of deflation.

In the 1950s, there was a strong feeling that the IMF was unsympathetic to the development ambitions of developing countries, and was too conservative in the lending conditions it imposed.[1]

The IMF was unfortunate in that its first major experience of stabilization policy occurred in Latin American countries where inflationary problems were most acute, i.e. Chile and Argentina. Chile's inflationary record since the 1880s is worse than that of any other country and Argentina's record has also been bad.

In both Argentina and Chile inflation had reached the stage where inbuilt spiral processes were very strong, and where competition between social groups was particularly bitter. In both countries governments were politically weak and there was no significant element of government planning to offset the chaos in the price

[1] See A. Shonfield, *The Attack on World Poverty*, London, 1958, for an unfavourable contrast of IMF and IBRD attitudes to developing countries in the 1950s. This unfavourable view of the IMF is expressed in its most extreme form in E. Eshag and R. Thorp, 'Economic and Social Consequences of Orthodox Economic Policies in Argentina in the Post-War Years', *Bulletin of the Oxford University Institute of Economics and Statistics*, February 1965. However, the authors do not suggest what alternative policies the IMF might have followed.

Table IV–4

Exchange Reserves and IMF Quotas 1950 and 1965

$ million end year

	End 1950		End 1965		
	Reserves	IMF quota	Reserves	Reserves minus IMF drawings	IMF quota plus compensatory financing facility
Argentina	655	0	236	90	350
Brazil	666	150	505	346	350
Ceylon	191	15	73	35	81
Chile	55	50	138	13	125
Colombia	101	50	130	46	125
Egypt	979	60	193	193	150
Ghana	302	0	131	122	69
Greece	83	40	235	235	75
India	2,000	400	599	274	750
Israel	31	0	631	631	63
Malaya	298	0	482	482	73
Mexico	297	90	483	483	225
Pakistan	506	100	224	170	188
Peru	54	25	165	165	48
Philippines	296	15	185	171	94
South Korea	27	0	141	141	24
Spain	134*	0	1,268	1,268	188
Taiwan	39	†	300	300	†
Thailand	289	13	720	720	95
Turkey	195	43	141	101	108
Venezuela	373	15	805	805	188
Yugoslavia	21	60	104	−6	150
Total	7,592	1,126	7,889	6,785	3,519

* 1952.

† Taiwan is only a token member of IMF as it has paid only a tiny portion of its subscription. The effective quota was $0·1 million in 1950 and $0·5 million in 1965.

Source: *International Financial Statistics*, IMF, Washington DC.

mechanism. In spite of IMF-supported stabilization programmes, Chile continued to have very high inflation and slow growth, and Argentina experienced three major recessions as well as continued price increases. The only real achievement of stabilization programmes was to prevent the currencies from collapsing completely. In both countries IMF advice seems[1] to have involved pretty comprehensive recommendations. These included cuts in government spending, increased taxes, wage restraint, and reduction in public employment. However, somewhat greater emphasis seems to have been placed on the need for sharp credit restraint, devaluation and simplification of exchange rates,[2] freeing of imports and removal of domestic price controls, etc. As such programmes are always painful, governments always welcome outside advice which takes the burden of responsibility off their own shoulders, and the IMF naturally became something of a scapegoat. It also tended to be identified with *laissez-faire* solutions and a monetarist or quantity theory approach to economic policy.

The association of the IMF with these views first occurred in 1950 when Chile asked both the United Nations and the IMF to send advisory missions. The UN report was milder than that of the IMF and leaned in the direction of quantitative controls, whereas the Fund report placed emphasis on stringent credit restrictions. Neither of the reports was implemented or associated with any IMF action, but they were both published and widely discussed. Later in 1956, a Fund loan to Chile became identified with the conservative views of the Klein-Saks mission.[3] In fact, the mission was not sent by the

[1] In fact, details of IMF recommendations are usually confidential, so we cannot be sure what exactly was recommended.

[2] At that time the Fund was rather firmly opposed to multiple exchange rates although these can often serve a useful purpose if properly used. See N. Kaldor, 'Dual Exchange Rates and Economic Development', *Economic Bulletin for Latin America*, November 1964. Multiple exchange rates have been used extensively for protectionist purposes in Latin America, and like quantitative restrictions, were originally introduced for balance of payments reasons in the 1930s. They have also been used in Taiwan, Thailand, the Philippines, Yugoslavia and Spain. The case usually made for multiple exchange rates is they can stimulate new exports with low rates without lowering receipts for exports of traditional primary products for which demand is not price sensitive. It is a way of obtaining a partial devaluation without worsening the terms of trade unnecessarily. But in order to make such a system work effectively and prevent fraud, it is usually necessary to have a state trading agency for the basic export products, and if such an agency exists, it can, in any case, fix its selling price independently of the exchange rate. In practice, the system has not usually been used to promote new exports, but mainly as a device to collect a tax on traditional exports, and as a substitute for tariff protection by imposing different rates for different categories of imports.

[3] See A. O. Hirschmann, *Journeys Toward Progress*, Twentieth Century Fund, New York, 1963.

IMF, but was a group of private bankers invited by the Chilean government.

The Fund was also involved in an unsuccessful stabilization programme in Turkey in the 1950s. The Menderes regime failed to carry out Fund suggestions, and relations with Turkey became so bad that the IMF representative had to leave the country.

The worst point in the IMF relations with developing countries was reached in 1958, when Brazil rejected the terms of IMF aid as incompatible with its development programme. As a result, the Kubitschek expansion programme was driven into heavy dependence on suppliers' credits, which cost 8 per cent a year or more and were only available for short maturities. The eventual stabilization programme involved a massive debt-rescheduling exercise (about $2 billion), which was well beyond the resources of the IMF.

The basic difficulty of the Fund in these situations was that it was tackling inflation of a very deep and persistent kind, and the governments concerned were following populist policies with little concern for the future. At that time, there were still economists of some influence in Latin America who believed that growth could be achieved mainly by inflation. The Fund's stabilization policies were not integrated with any clear long run development strategy; its policies of exchange liberalization generally clashed with protectionist efforts to promote industrialization, and its advocacy of demand restraint took inadequate account of the pressing investment needs of certain sectors.[1] However, in the case of Argentina and Chile, there was no long-term strategy into which the Fund's policies could be

[1] See R. Campos, 'Economic Development and Inflation, with Special Reference to Latin America', in *Development Plans and Programmes*, OECD Development Centre, Paris, 1964. Until recently at least, the absorbing preoccupation of the Fund's programmes was the cutting of overall excess demand, with but little effort to distinguish between consumption and investment expenditures and to identify bottleneck sectors, in which investment would have to be maintained or even accelerated, by an expansion, if needed, of foreign financing. The Fund's formalistic attitude of passing over the investment problem on the ground that its statutory function is confined to balance of payments problems is not helpful; in several cases, if stabilization may turn out to be realistic the Fund must take the initiative of co-ordinating with other investment agencies the provision of non-inflatory financial resources for (*a*) the short-term correction of certain strategic bottlenecks; (*b*) offsetting unemployment effects arising from the contraction of non-priority or inflated investment sectors.' Campos stresses the deep-rooted political problem of ending inflation in countries like Argentina, Chile and Brazil and the need to allow for complexities in timing of the different corrective measures.

fitted, and it was not within the Fund's mandate to lay down long-term goals. They were dealing with economies with neither a plan or a price mechanism. In view of the political constraints involved and the complexity of the problems, the governments would in any case have needed very much bigger external resources than the Fund was able to provide.

Since 1958, the IMF has had much greater success. It engaged in successful stabilization programmes in Peru, Spain and Yugoslavia. It has ceased to take such a strongly conservative and *laissez-faire* line, and the era of populist economic policy in developing countries has gradually faded away. There is, therefore, much more possibility of dialogue within a common analytical framework between the IMF and developing countries than there was in the days of confrontation between Kubitschek and Jacobsen. There has been an appreciable rise in the flow of long-term aid, which has taken some of the weight off the IMF. In its operations to help Argentina, Brazil, Chile, India, Peru, Turkey and Yugoslavia, the Fund was able to mobilize bilateral lending to support its own actions. Its own resources were increased by the general increase in quotas in 1959 and 1966, and by the 1963 decision on compensatory financing. In fact, although the IMF incurred its unpopularity of earlier years in part through its own mistaken judgments, its views were often more sensible than those of the governments which rejected its advice. Its efforts to criticize policies it felt to be incorrect, to impose sanctions, and its willingness to face unpopularity have, in fact, earned respect, particularly now that its criteria for judgment take more account of the specific problems of development. There is, therefore, a strong case for strengthening IMF resources further, and for giving it greater flexibility in the size of its loans and their maturity.

There is also a case for strengthening the liquidity position of developing countries by creating regional institutions for clearing, and payments arrangements designed primarily to stimulate regional trade liberalization but also to stimulate confrontation and mutual surveillance of economic policy. The EPU played a major role in improving the efficiency of economic policy in the early post-war years in Europe, even though the amount of aid involved in its creation was relatively modest. Developed countries have also had EMA, BIS and a whole network of central bank swap facilities to supplement IMF facilities. There is therefore no reason to think that provision of supplementary international liquidity through regional institutions would diminish the role of the IMZ. They would, in fact, powerfully reinforce its objectives and would help create a dialogue between developing countries themselves on matters of stabilization policy, which is something the IMF can hardly hope to do.

CONCLUSIONS

The stabilization problems of developing countries are extremely complex and are much more difficult than those of most developed countries. A great many of them are due to the internal structure of these economies and the structure of their exports. Many of them are due to weaknesses in fiscal and monetary instruments which are partly technical, partly political and institutional, and solutions to the latter kind of problem are not easy. Given the fact that these problems are likely to continue, it would seem that the most obvious scope for mitigating their impact on growth is through more flexible exchange-rate policy, improvement in economic statistics so that at least the problems can be more clearly analysed, and a greater willingness on the part of developed countries to strengthen international and regional liquidity arrangements.

Chapter V
Has Agriculture been Neglected?

GROWTH IN OUTPUT

Agriculture shared in the general acceleration of post-war growth. From 1950, output grew faster than ever before in all our countries except Argentina and Colombia. Average growth was twice as high as in the pre-war period, and per capita growth three times as fast.

On average, farm output grew by 3·7 per cent a year in our sample of countries, but the increase was slow in Argentina, India and Pakistan which account for half the output, so the weighted average shows only 2·5 per cent growth. We prefer to use unweighted averages because we want to judge the success of national policies, and for this purpose we must count each country equally. Use of a weighted average gives an overly pessimistic view of policy performance, and is one of the reasons why some observers accuse developing countries generally of neglecting agriculture, when the serious neglect has really been concentrated on a few big countries. However, the acceleration in post-war growth shows up equally well on a weighted basis. Both India and Pakistan have grown much faster than they did in the past.

There has been a wide range of performance. In ten countries output grew annually by 4 per cent or more. There was an element of recovery in Korea, Taiwan and Israel which makes their achievement smaller than appears at first sight, but, in all of the ten countries, growth was impressive by any historical standards. The fastest growth was attained by Israel, Mexico, Venezuela and Taiwan. At the other end of the scale, we find Argentina where output was completely stagnant, and six other countries where output grew by 2·5 per cent a year or less.

WHY GROWTH DIFFERED

In explaining aggregate economic performance in Chapter II, we were able to provide a detailed quantitative analysis of the reasons

Table V–1

Growth in Physical Volume of Gross Agricultural Output 1911–66

Annual average compound growth rates

	1911–15 to pre-war	Pre-war to 1949–51	1949–51 to 1964–66
Argentina	2·3	0·1	0·1
Brazil	3·4	1·3	4·0
Ceylon	n.a.	2·0	2·5
Chile	n.a.	1·8	2·0
Colombia	n.a.	4·1	2·4
Egypt	0·8	1·0	3·1
Ghana	n.a.	n.a.	4·8*
Greece	n.a.	0·9	4·7
India	0·4	−0·1	2·5
Israel	n.a.	n.a.	9·3
Malaya	n.a.	2·3	2·6
Mexico	0·0	3·6	5·6
Pakistan	(0·4)	0·4	1·9
Peru	n.a.	2·1	2·9
Philippines	n.a.	1·1	3·1
South Korea	3·0	−2·1	5·0
Spain	n.a.	−0·3	2·1
Taiwan	3·6	−0·4	5·3
Thailand	n.a.	2·7	4·5
Turkey	n.a.	1·7	4·4
Venezuela	n.a.	n.a.	5·4
Yugoslavia	n.a.	−0·1	3·9
Average	1·7	1·2	3·7

* 1954/6 to 1964/6.

Source: 1911–15 to pre-war, Argentina from *El Desarrollo Economico de la Argentina*, ECLA, Santiago, 1959, mimeographed annex; Brazil (1920–38) information supplied by Vargas Institute, Rio de Janeiro; Egypt (1917–37) from B. Hansen and G. A. Marzouk, *Development and Economic Policy in the UAR (Egypt)*, North-Holland, Amsterdam, 1965, pp. 47 and 61; India from S. Sivasubramonian, *National Income of India 1900–1 to 1946–7*, Delhi School of Economics, 1965; Mexico from *La Economia Mexicana en Cifras*, Nacional Financiera, Mexico, 1966; South Korea (1910–38 rice only) from UN Korean Reconstruction Agency, *Rehabilitation and Development of Agriculture, Forestry and Fisheries in South Korea*, New York, 1954; Taiwan from Yhi-Min Ho, *Agricultural Development of Taiwan 1903–60*, Vanderbilt, 1966, p. 17. Pre-war to 1949/50 from *Production Yearbook*, F.A.O., Rome, 1952 edition; 1950/1 and 1951/2 from 1954 edition, 1964/6 from 1967 edition. Israel 1949/52 from

for variations in growth rates. There is not enough information to permit an equally rigorous analysis for agriculture[1] but we can get a rough idea of the reasons.

New inputs of fertilizers, insecticides and better seeds can be important contributors to increased output and are the major instrument for transforming traditional agriculture. They played an important role in Greece, Israel, Mexico, Taiwan and Korea, and, until recently, were neglected in India, Pakistan and Argentina.

Variations in labour supply also explain some of the differences. In all the countries, the proportion of people employed on farms dropped, and in some cases the absolute number fell, as in Argentina and Spain. But in Israel the farm population rose by 3·8 per cent a year and in other counties too there was a substantial absolute increase. On average, labour productivity grew by 2·9 per cent a year with a range from —0.3 in Pakistan to 5.3 in Israel. The two top performers in terms of productivity were Israel and Taiwan. Mexico, which held second place in terms of output, holds eighth place in terms of labour productivity. The worst performances in labour productivity came from Argentina and Pakistan. In the other countries, productivity growth was modest, but respectable.

Agricultural investment generally received lower priority than that in industry, but there was a good deal more farm investment in the post-war period than there was historically. This included irrigation, power supplies, roads, and, to a small extent, mechanization. Unfortunately it is not possible to quantify the investment, but we do know that some of the faster growing countries were able to afford it on rather a large scale. Israel and Taiwan were able to do this because they had large foreign aid, Venezuela because it had large financial resources from oil.

Difference in land endowment has obviously been a major historical reason for the high level of productivity in the USA and

[1] The nearest approach to this kind of quantitative comparative analysis is to be found in *Changes in Agriculture in 26 Developing Nations 1948 to 1963*, Foreign Agricultural Report No. 27, US Dept. of Agriculture, Washington DC, 1965.

Statistical Abstract of Israel 1967; Venezuela 1949/52 from *Economia Venezolana en los Ultimos Vienticinco Anos*, Banco Central de Venezuela, Caracas, 1966. South Korea pre-war to 1949/51 from UNKRA, *op. cit.*, 'Pre-war' in the second column refers to the average of 1934/8 except for Greece (1935/8), Spain (1931/5), India and Pakistan (1936/8), South Korea (1932/6) and Latin American countries (1935/9).

Table V–2

Growth of Physical Output per Farm Worker 1949/51 to 1964/6

Annual average compound growth rates

Argentina	1·1	Pakistan	−0·3
Brazil	2·4	Peru	2·7
Ceylon	1·8	Philippines	2·4
Chile	1·7	South Korea	5·1
Colombia	1·2	Spain	3·8
Egypt	2·4	Taiwan	5·2
Ghana	n.a.	Thailand	2·1
Greece	4·6	Turkey	3·1
India	1·3	Venezuela	4·4
Israel	5·3	Yugoslavia	4·4
Malaya	2·6		
Mexico	3·3	Average	2·9

Source: Production from Table V–1. Employment from Appendix C.

Argentina, and the low level in Asian countries. But most of the effects of these differences had already made themselves felt before 1950, and differences in natural endowment bore little relation to the *growth* of output from 1950 to 1965. Taiwan had rapid growth with less than half a hectare per farmer and Argentina had no growth with 92 acres per farmer. In Taiwan growth came largely from increased yields and better product mix, and not from increases in area. This does not mean that land endowment is unimportant. It simply emphasizes how impressive Taiwan's performance has been and demonstrates that great progress can be achieved in spite of natural constraints.

From the foregoing evidence, we can reach a few tentative conclusions. The best performance in terms of efficiency was probably obtained in Taiwan, and was well above average in Greece, Israel, Mexico, Korea, Venezuela and Yugoslavia. The worst results were obtained by Argentina, India and Pakistan.

But we cannot make a judgment on agricultural efficiency without considering demand. We must ask whether the countries which did badly did so because demand was stagnant, or whether slow growth also reflects a failure to meet demand. A fifth of farm output consists of raw materials such as rubber and fibres for which demand has been sluggish, but 80 per cent consists of food and it may seem odd to consider demand as a constraint when we know that so many people are hungry. However, when we look at the problem of hunger we must distinguish between effective demand and need.

Demand is simply a measure of people's desires as manifested in the market. The desires are effective only so far as they are effectively backed by income. When we consider need we postulate certain minimum standards which may not be attained or may be overfulfilled.

There is a tendency to judge agricultural performance in the light of needs rather than demand. We would not think of decrying the Indian automobile industry because it fails to meet the 'need' for cars, whereas agriculture is often blamed if food 'needs' are not met. However, economic life is not organized to satisfy 'needs' but to meet effective demand. If a large section of the community is so poor that basic human needs are not being met in the market, then the government should translate this need into effective demand, either by income redistribution or by gifts of food. As long as this is not done, we cannot put the blame on agriculture.

NEEDS FOR FOOD

There is still substantial dispute about food 'needs'. In the 1940s, the Food and Agriculture Organization of the United Nations estimated that two-thirds of world population suffered from inadequate calorie intake. Under criticism from Colin Clark and others,[1] this has now been revised downwards to a more modest figure of 10 to 15 per cent.[2] For developing countries, FAO estimates that a fifth of the population is living below minimum needs.

[1] See C. Clark and M. Haswell, *The Economics of Subsistence Agriculture*, Macmillan, New York, 1968, p. 1. ' "A lifetime of malnutrition and actual hunger is the lot of at least two-thirds of mankind." This extraordinary misstatement, which is in fact based on an arithmetical error, is believed by almost everyone because they have heard it so often: people come to think that any statement which they have heard frequently enough (as Hitler pointed out) must be true. This lack of critical sense however is particularly reprehensible in the prominent men of letters and scientists whose repetition of the statement has done so much to ensure its acceptance.' Clark is Director of the Oxford Institute of Agricultural Economics and his views are similar to those of a former director of the Stanford Food Research Institute; see M. K. Bennett, *The World's Food*, Harper, New York, 1954.

[2] This is the figure in the Third World Food Survey of FAO for 1963. The Director of Statistics of FAO has recently suggested that a third of the world's population suffers from protein deficiency. See P. V. Sukhatme, 'The World's Food Supplies', *Journal of the Royal Statistical Society*, Series A 129 (Part II) 1966, pp. 222–41.

Even the new low estimate of FAO has been challenged by the authoritative report of the US President's Science Advisory Committee.[1] It used FAO calorie and protein standards to measure food requirements in India, Pakistan and Brazil but instead of basing these on hypothetical body sizes (e.g. 143 lb. for a male 25–29) it used actual body sizes which were considerably smaller (e.g. 121 lb. for an Indian male aged 26–29).[2] As a result it came to figures for calorie requirements about 20 per cent lower than FAO for India. And it concluded that Indian and Pakistani consumption of both calories and protein was slightly above the minimum requirements.[3]

This does not mean that there is no malnutrition in these countries. Income is unevenly distributed and the poorest part of the population is living on the verge of starvation. Per capita income in Bihar, the poorest Indian state, is less than half of that in Maharashtra, which is the wealthiest. Income per head in East Pakistan is a third lower than in West Pakistan. So even on the relatively austere criteria of the White House study there are obviously millions of people in the Indian sub-continent whose nutritional levels are so low that they shorten life, damage physical and intellectual development and reduce working capacity. In Africa, where cassava and starchy roots form the basis of the diet, many people suffer from protein deficiency. As a result, there is evidence of kwashiorkor in a number of countries, though except in emergency conditions, as in Biafra, this affects only a part of the population. In a number of countries, there is evidence of dietary deficiency as reflected by pellagra, beri-beri, scurvy and rickets.

Differences in average body size are themselves partially a result of earlier nutritional deficiencies and, in the long run, body size in

[1] *The World Food Problem*, Washington DC, pp. 47, 48 and 53.

[2] This was the figure supplied by the Indian authorities, which the US Commission also thought to be an overstatement. Its own estimate of body sizes was 106 lb. for this age group.

[3] The fact that earlier estimates of food needs have been steadily reduced is also noted by M. C. Burk and M. Ezekiel (himself a former Deputy-Director General of FAO); see 'Food and Nutrition in Developing Economies', in H. M. Southworth and B. F. Johnston, eds., *Agricultural Development and Economic Growth*, Cornell, New York, 1967. They also suggest that the current estimates of output are generally too low and conclude on page 334, 'In the event, when the possible overestimation of requirements is combined with the strong likelihood of underestimation of food supplies available, considerable doubt is cast on current estimates of the extent of under-nutrition and malnutrition.'

the poorer countries will increase as new generations get more food.[1] However, it is not legitimate to take the food consumption of high-income countries as a desirable norm. These countries consume expensive foods as a way of relieving dietary monotony or to provide sensory, aesthetic, or gluttonous satisfactions. The larger body sizes and fat consumption of developed countries are associated with a greater incidence of degenerative diseases such as heart trouble.

It is necessary to keep a reasonable perspective on food needs. Simplistic exaggeration[2] has led to unjusifiable criticism that most developing countries have sacrified agriculture in the interests of uneconomic industrialization, and has distracted attention from the problem of income inequality *within* the developing world. It has confused analysis of the population problem which is often posed in crude Malthusian terms. Exaggerated notions about world famine have served to shelter the surplus food-disposal programmes of developed countries from justified criticism.[3]

We are not suggesting that people in developing countries do not want or deserve better diets. But the present low-quality diets are only one aspect of poverty, and improvement in diets is not everywhere the most pressing need, either for individuals as consumers in these countries, or for government policy. For the poorest groups in the population food 'needs' are urgent, but few governments in developing countries have felt able to afford welfare programmes for the very poor, and, except in the case of emergency relief, food aid has not been directed at helping them, but rather at lowering

[1] Within our group of countries, average weights for males aged 25–29 range from 106 pounds in India to 142 pounds in Chile; see *The World Food Problem*, President's Science Advisory Committee, Washington DC, 1967, pp. 38–9. To some extent the weight differences are genetic.

[2] There are almost daily examples of this simplistic exaggeration, largely because it obviously evokes the natural human sympathies of any normal audience. A typical example is this statement by Lord Snow, a prominent man of letters, a scientist and an ex-Minister of the British Government. 'I have been nearer despair this year 1968, than ever in my life. We may be moving, perhaps in ten years—into large-scale famine. Many millions of people are going to starve. We shall see them doing so upon our television sets.' He went on to advocate, *inter alia*, that the problem be met by massive grants of food. His speech at Fulton, Missouri (where Churchill made his 'iron curtain' speech) was reported by *Time* magazine, November 22, 1968.

[3] See *The Economist*, September 28, 1968, 'Where the influence of the famine mongers has been most pernicious is in the support they have given to the idea of North America being the world's granary'.

Table V–3

Per Capita Calorie and Protein Supplies in 1960

	Calories per capita per day	Protein grams per capita per day
South Asia	1,970	50
Near East	2,470	76
Africa	2,360	61
Latin America	2,510	67
Western Europe	2,910	83
North America	3,110	93

Source: *The World Food Problem*, President's Science Advisory Committee, White House, Washington DC, 1967, p. 317.

food costs for better-off urban consumers. The needs of the poorest group have not therefore been translated into effective demand, and this is not likely to occur unless countries adopt measures for more egalitarian income distribution or changes in landownership.

DEMAND FOR FOOD

If we compare food consumption levels in terms of calories, the range from poorest to richest countries is about 1 to 1·5. The range for proteins is about 1 to 2, but these figures do not give an adequate indication of the difference in demand for food at different income levels.

We can get an idea of differences in demand by using a measure that allows for variations in both the quantity and quality of food. We can do this by comparing the *value* of food consumed. Values at official exchange rates are misleading, because food prices vary a good deal between countries, but we can compare consumption in real terms by converting the quantities into dollars at a common set of prices. We have done this in Appendix A, using data on output and trade for about 100 crop, livestock and fishery items as published by FAO. Table V–4 shows that, at North American prices, food consumption in 1965 varied from $27 per head in India to $156 in France, i.e. a range of about 1 to 6. (The figures refer to food at farm prices and do not include markups for processing, packaging and retailing which are bigger in the more developed countries.) The data are far from perfect, and there are one or two puzzling results (e.g. Greece and Mexico). As a general rule, there

Table V–4

Per Capita Food and Fish Consumption in 1965

$ at US relative prices

Argentina	85	Spain	101
Brazil	67	Taiwan	58
Ceylon	33	Thailand	55
Chile	64	Turkey	60
Colombia	46	Venezuela	70
Egypt	43	Yugoslavia	84
Ghana	34		
Greece	128	Average	59
India	27		
Israel	86		
Malaya	63	France	156
Mexico	36	Germany	126
Pakistan	31	Japan	68
Peru	40	UK	137
Philippines	41	USA	134
South Korea	36	USSR	95

Source: Appendix A. The figures exclude coffee, cocoa, and tea.

is reason to expect under-reporting in the poorer countries, so we may be exaggerating the gap a little.

In the United States, only a tiny fraction of the economy (less than 4 per cent of output) is devoted to agriculture, because demand for food is close to saturation point. Retail expenditure on food has been rising in the past decades, but most of the increase has gone to processing, distribution, restaurant services, etc., and the retail value of food sales is now about three times its farm value. The growth of these types of 'food' expenditure has sometimes given rise to exaggerated notions of likely demand at the 'farm-gate'.

The relationship between changes in per capita demand for food and per capita income growth is known as the elasticity of demand for food. If food demand moved parallel with income the elasticity would be 1, if it did not increase at all the elasticity would be zero. If food demand fell as income rises (as happens with cereals), the elasticity would be negative. Most studies of elasticity are based on consumer budget surveys, and these generally have to be corrected downwards before they can be translated into 'quantitative' elasticities, because they naturally include expenditure on processing, distribution, etc.

The FAO has done a vast amount of work on demand elasticity

for food and its findings are summarized in its 1967 study projecting world food demand for the period 1965–85. This study shows elasticities of demand for dozens of individual food items which also differ between countries because of differences in income levels.[1] The elasticities differ because people reduce their consumption of cereals as they become more prosperous, and switch to more expensive products like meat, milk, eggs and fruit. They also increase their consumption of tea, coffee, cocoa, wine and spirits—but for our purpose we have not treated these as food.

In the FAO study there is no discussion of the aggregate elasticity of demand for food in developing countries, but the overall figure projected for 1965–75 seems to be around 0·4.[2] It is difficult to test this against the historical record, because FAO does not publish indices of aggregate food consumption. However, it publishes indices of food production (including beverages, but excluding fish) for thirty-seven developing countries and we can get a crude idea of aggregate food-consumption trends from the production indices and from trade figures. In the period 1950–65, per capita food production in our twenty-two countries grew on average by 1·1 per cent a year and net food imports of developing countries increased. In 1954 developing countries were net exporters of 4 million tons of grains and in 1965, net importers of 16·5 million tons. Average per capita consumption probably grew by about 1·2 per cent a year. In the same period per capita GDP in these countries grew by 2·9 per cent, and per capita consumption by about 2·5 per cent (an increased share of income being devoted to investment and government). The historical food elasticity was therefore about 0·5,[3] which suggests that food consumption

[1] Basically the FAO operated with four different types of demand function including the log-log inverse function which 'provides for an increase in per capita consumption up to a maximum intake, followed later by a decline, as income rises'. See *Agricultural Commodities—Projections for 1975 and 1985*, FAO, Rome, 1967, vol. II, p. xxiv.

[2] See *Agricultural Commodities—Projections for 1975 and 1985*, FAO, Rome, 1967, which assumes that per capita food consumption will rise by 0·4 per cent a year if per capita GDP rises by 1 per cent a year, or, alternatively, that per capita food consumption will rise by 1·2 per cent a year if per capita GDP rises by 3·0 per cent. However, this is not spelled out very clearly in aggregate form, and no aggregate figure is given for growth in per capita consumption (as distinct from per capita GDP) growth.

[3] The President's Science Advisory Committee suggested a higher figure than FAO, i.e. 0·5 to 0·7, but the evidence for their conclusion is not presented, see *The World Food Problem*, vol. II, p. 648.

Table V–5

Growth of Food Output per Head of Population 1949/51 to 1964/6

Annual average compound growth rates

Country	Rate	Country	Rate
Argentina	−1·5	Pakistan	−0·6
Brazil	2·6	Peru	−0·1
Ceylon	0·0	Philippines	−0·2
Chile	−0·3	South Korea	3·6
Colombia	−0·7	Spain	1·1
Egypt	1·1	Taiwan	2·0
Ghana	n.a.	Thailand	0·8
Greece	3·6	Turkey	1·5
India	0·3	Venezuela	n.a.
Israel	n.a.	Yugoslavia	4·3
Malaya	1·4		
Mexico	2·3	Average	1·1

Source: Same as for Table V–1. Population from Appendix C. The FAO definition of food includes tea, coffee and cocoa.

increased more or less in line with what FAO considered to be normal demand patterns.

This demand was met only with the help of increased imports, which were concentrated on a few countries, particularly India and Pakistan. Agricultural imports are only about 10 per cent of total supply in developing countries as a whole. But given the enormous manpower in agriculture, its low productivity, and the pressure on the balance of payments, one would normally expect most countries to have aimed at an even greater degree of agricultural self-sufficiency. There is every reason to think that further import-substitution in agricultural products in Chile, India and Pakistan would have been more economic than some of the import-substitution which was achieved for industrial goods.

The poor record of India and Pakistan is not typical. Several countries increased food production fast enough to reduce the degree of import dependence. Greece, Israel, South Korea, Venezuela and Yugoslavia were all able to do this on a significant scale. Some countries are indeed reaching the limits of this process. Greece, for instance, has had to sell surplus wheat abroad at a loss, and Israel has had surpluses of milk, eggs and fruit.

For most commodities, agricultural export prospects have been poor, because developed countries have followed extremely protectionist policies, their demand for food, tobacco and beverages is expanding slowly, and they have developed synthetic substitutes for natural fibres and rubber. As a result, world market prices for agricultural products fell by about a fifth from 1950 to 1962, so even where volume increases were attained, a good deal of this was offset by price falls.

Future prospects for food exports to most developed countries are bleak. The USA, Canada, Australia and New Zealand are all big net exporters, and FAO has this to say about prospects in Western Europe:

'For EEC and Northern Europe, net imports (from all outside sources) of cereals and livestock products, as a group, would decline rapidly but for coarse grains and meat, would remain virtually unchanged on the low assumption and increase modestly on the high assumption. There would be a small increase in net import demand for the group of temperate-tropical competing exports on either the low or the high assumption. Import demand for tropical products would rise by 1·4 to 1·7 per cent annually, and net import demand for agricultural raw materials by 0·5 per cent anually.[1]

Only in Japan and the USSR does FAO see markets expanding on a substantial scale.

In spite of the generally poor export markets, some countries had considerable successes. Taiwan built up exports of bananas, mushrooms, pineapples and asparagus. A good deal of these went to the Japanese market to which Taiwan has rather easy access. Mexico increased shrimp exports. Peru developed large markets for fishmeal and fish products. Israel expanded exports of poultry, eggs and citrus. Most of these examples are rather special cases which could not have been generally emulated, but it is also true that some of the export failures were due largely to internal policies. Argentina discouraged meat exporters by unfavourable exchange rates and Brazil prohibited meat exports until 1964 to keep down domestic prices. Brazil could have had bigger exports of cotton, sugar, tobacco and cocoa, if it had offered its producers prices in line with those in world markets, or had had a realistic exchange rate. This would have been a better use of resources than the accumulation of enormous coffee stocks. Malaya could have produced pineapples. Ceylon could have produced coffee, cocoa and cotton as well as tea, rubber and coconuts. But though these countries can be legitimately criticised for not doing more to promote exports, there

[1] See FAO *Agricultural Commodities—Projections for 1975 and 1985*, Rome, 1967, vol. I, p. 57.

is no doubt, in most cases except meat, that if they had all tried much harder they would simply have displaced exports of other developing countries and would have weakened prices further in an already weak market.[1] Thus the success of several countries in increasing sugar exports has been at the expense of Cuba. Increased tea and coffee production in Africa has eaten into the market shares of Brazil, India and Ceylon.

THE IMPACT OF SURPLUS FOOD DISPOSALS

Rising imports of food in developing countries are not simply a reflection of failure of home production to meet demand, but also represent a rational response to a situation in which imported food was available free.

The US policy of income support for domestic agriculture and the extraordinary improvement in US farm efficiency led to embarrassingly large stocks in the early 1950s. By 1953 it was clear that it would not be possible to unload these through normal commercial channels, and there was obviously no point in increasing stocks further. Internal political pressures prevented a cut in US farm output which could have been achieved by a substantial reduction in price support programmes. It was therefore decided to dispose of the surpluses as a form of aid. This aid started on a limited scale in 1953 as part of the Mutual Security Programme, but in 1954 the disposal procedures were elaborated under Public Law 480. Between 1953 and 1966 the US provided other countries with \$14·8 billion of agricultural products under these schemes, usually as a gift. Most of this went to developing countries, and \$10·6 billion went to our twenty-two countries. In 1965, disposals amounted to \$1·7 billion which was equal to 28 per cent of US agricultural exports, or a quarter of the agricultural imports of developing countries. The commodities involved were wheat, flour, cotton, rice, fats and oils, tobacco and dairy products. There have also been food aid programmes by Canada and Australia, but they were small in relation to that of the USA. So far Canada has given away \$350 million of food and Australia somewhat less. However, in the Kennedy Round negotiations in GATT, the USA persuaded other countries to undertake surplus food programmes

[1] This should not be taken as an argument against diversification which will add to the stability of individual country export receipts even if there is no gain in exports for the developing world as a whole.

and the International Grains Arrangement of July 1968 contains provisions for a 13½ million ton food aid programme over a three-year period.

In theory these gifts were intended to be additions to normal supplies, and elaborate precautions were taken to try to ensure this. In the case of disaster or famine relief this was not difficult to achieve, and during the bad harvest years of 1965 and 1966 these shipments saved parts of India from famine and fed 60 million people. However, the continuance of these shipments over fifteen years has obviously had some adverse effects on wheat exports from Argentina and rice exports of Asian countries. They have also probably displaced some sales which the USA might have made on commercial terms. In the early post-war years, when the USA was using its surplus production to build up domestic stockpiles, it effectively *supported* world agricultural markets. At that time its action was helpful, e.g. to Mexico which built up cotton exports rapidly. But Mexico has made little headway with its cotton exports since 1954. Nevertheless, the careful way in which the surplus disposals have been administered has done less damage to the interests of other countries than would have occurred if they had been sold on the free market at whatever price they would fetch.

From the point of view of the aid recipient these extra resources were a valuable contribution to development. Recipient governments sold the products domestically and derived an income which was a painless form of taxation enabling them to increase development expenditures. If they had been able to get an equivalent amount of dollars instead of surplus agricultural products, this would have been more useful to them, but they did not have this option. From the US point of view, this kind of aid was virtually costless. If the stocks had not been given away, they would have had to be destroyed, just as Brazil burned 4·8 million tons of coffee from 1931 to 1944.

Although the surpluses have helped overall economic development, they have weakened incentives for agricultural progress. The availability of supplies which the countries would not normally have bought, helped to keep agricultural prices low and weakened farmers' production incentives. The easy availability of foreign supplies inhibited the development of domestic rural to urban transport and marketing networks. The knowledge that the supplies would be available made recipient governments less eager to promote agricultural development. There was even less incentive for developing countries to try to promote agricultural exports, with these surpluses hanging over the market.

It proved possible to avoid adverse effects on agriculture in some recipient countries. Israel received more US agricultural aid per capita than any other country, and used it to provide a net stimulus to domestic agriculture. Israel cannot economically meet its wheat needs itself and most of the aid shipments displaced imports from other countries rather than damage domestic producers. The US share of Israel's wheat imports doubled whereas the share of Canada, Australia, Argentina and Turkey fell. Imports of surplus coarse grains were even bigger than wheat shipments and these were used as feedstuff in the poultry industry. The government was able to guarantee low and stable cereal prices to poultry farmers and also provided a guaranteed price for eggs. As a result production rocketed and Israel became an egg and poultry exporter instead of an importer (though egg exports initially had to be subsidized). Without the aid, Israel would probably not have thought it worthwhile

Table V–6

Disposals of US Agricultural Surpluses 1953–66

$ million

Argentina	18	Mexico	71
Brazil	706	Pakistan	1,112
Ceylon	190	Peru	88
Chile	72	Philippines	112
Colombia	145	South Korea	753
Egypt	902	Spain	470
Ghana	14	Taiwan	341
Greece	259	Thailand	5
India	3,327	Turkey	441
Israel	346	Venezuela	20
Malaya	10	Yugoslavia	1,153

Source: *US Overseas Loans and Grants*, AID Washington DC, March 1967. Not all of these shipments represented gifts.

to pay for imports of coarse grains on such a large scale to develop the poultry industry. Aid shipments were also used to build up stocks of food products to help stabilize prices.[1]

In India the experience was not so fortunate. India received more

[1] For a description of the Israel experience, see F. Ginor, *Uses of Agricultural Surpluses*, Bank of Israel, Jerusalem, 1963.

surplus food than any other country, about $3·3 billion worth up to 1966. This helped to promote development in general but the availability of surpluses permitted the government to follow policies which retarded agricultural expansion. This is the conclusion of a scholarly Indian study financed by counterpart funds derived from surplus food sales.[1]

'While inflationary pressures have pushed the general price level steadily upwards, the Government with the help of P.L. 480 imports has tried to hold the price of wheat at an artificially low, unchanging level all through. It has meant steady lowering of the price of wheat.'

As a result, P.L. 480 imports became a normal feature of the Indian food economy. In years of high domestic production the Indian government had no incentive to accumulate stocks, but let prices fall.

'The Government had been more anxious to keep a lid on prices of foodgrains, but not to provide a reasonable bottom to them. The wheat prices declining at any time as a consequence of State policy, found the Government very reluctant to support them.'

The pricing and distribution policies have favoured consumers in urban areas and particularly the middle and high income groups.

'The Government has apparently never seriously considered the fact that at least part of the burden of its price policy and the resource for development, is being borne by the farmer, chiefly the wheat famer in India. The lowering of the price of wheat results in adverse terms of trade, which is like a tax on the farmer.'

Since the 1965–6 crisis, Indian policy towards farm prices has changed, and in future it may well be possible to reconcile the continuance of surplus food imports with better incentives to domestic agriculture. Pakistan followed a worse farm policy than India in the 1950s, with compulsory levies on agricultural commodities. Trade was controlled and food was rationed. Since 1960, grain

[1] See N. Rath and V. S. Patvardhan, *Impact of Assistance Under P.L. 480 on Indian Economy*, Asia Publishing House, London, 1967, p. 200. Similar conclusions about the impact of surplus food programmes in Pakistan were reached by C. Beringer, *The Use of Agricultural Surplus Commodities for Economic Development in Pakistan*, Institute of Development Economics, Karachi, 1964.

prices have been freed, and American surplus products have been used to maintain a buffer stock to cushion price fluctuations. The availability of P.L. 480 wheat has permitted the diversion of land from wheat towards export crops. Since Pakistan's policy changed, there has been a sharp upward movement in the trend of its agricultural output. Professor Mason's conclusion on Pakistan's experience is as follows:

'P.L. 480 shipments *may* have had an adverse impact on agricultural output in the 1950s but their availability in the 1960s made possible a number of measures which taken together with other actions bearing on farm incentives set the stage for a very substantial increase in agricultural productivity.'[1]

Having surveyed the production, productivity and market record fairly exhaustively, we can conclude that there were serious failings of agricultural policy in Argentina, India and Pakistan and probably in Chile as well. All of these countries should have given more serious attention to increasing farm output and they should have devoted more resources to this and somewhat less to industry. But to some extent the policy failings of these countries were due to external influences, most notably the farm and commercial policies of the developed world.

THE GREEN REVOLUTION

We must now ask what policies have been most effective in increasing farm output. In fact, there are possibilities in agriculture for promotion of growth by use of labour-intensive technology which do not exist in industry and which hold great promise for the future. The potential of modern agricultural technology is so great, that some observers refer to the possibility of a 'green revolution'. We must now assess whether this is a realistic prospect.

Agriculture is the traditional sector of the economy in which production techniques have developed slowly over the centuries. Because of differences in soil, climate, labour supply, and ownership structure, there is a vast range of alternative techniques to produce a given item. In the past there have been a number of examples of technical diffusion which have greatly increased agricultural productivity. Thus Columbus brought back potatoes from

[1] See E. S. Mason, *Economic Development in India and Pakistan*, Centre for International Affairs, Harvard, 1966, p. 53.

America and greatly increased the production potential of European agriculture. Arthur Young and his scientific contemporaries diffused scientific farming techniques throughout Europe at the end of the eighteenth century, and in the post-war period we have had another wave of these technical transfers. Modern scientfic research has developed seeds and livestock with greatly improved yields. But the new seeds require bigger fertilizer input, increased water supply, as well as new insecticides and weed killers.

The scope for yield increases in developing countries is now enormous. Indian yields per hectare are lower for all crops than they are in the United States, even though Indian agriculture has eighty-five times as much manpower available per hectare as the United States. Some of the yield variation is due to differences in

Table V–7

Yields for Major Food Crops 1964–65

kg. per hectare

	India	USA
Wheat	730	1,770
Maize	990	3,930
Rice	1,610	4,590
Sorghum and Millet	990	2,580
Potatoes	8,300	20,700
Sweet Potatoes and Yams	6,400	9,400

Source: *The World Food Problem.*

use of fertilizer, pesticides and machinery or to soil conditions, but a great deal is attributable to inferior seeds. The gap between traditional seeds and new varieties has grown so large that there are great opportunities for progress.

There is also a great gap in livestock yields, as is obvious from Table V–8. The record is particularly bad in the Far East where meat and milk yields per animal are a small fraction of those in North America or Europe. The hides of these animals are also inferior for leather work. It is true, of course, that Asian cattle provide traction services on a large scale and that a good deal of their food is refuse, but most of the difference in yields is due to inefficient breeding and husbandry, and in India particularly, to religious prejudice.

Table v–8

Meat and Milk Production per Head of Cattle 1962–64

kg. per head of cattle per year

	Beef and Veal	Milk
North America	75	571
Europe	63	1,134
Latin America	28	103
Near East	20	202
Africa	14	87
Far East	5	64

Source: *The World Food Problem*, p. 251.

Research into a new agricultural technology is not something which farmers or commercial enterprises can be expected to perform on their own. The costs are relatively high and the benefits cannot be monopolized by the innovator. But the cost of agricultural research is not high for a government to bear and the benefits in increased output can be large indeed. The classic case is research on hybrid maize which was so successful in raising productivity in the United States. Between the early 1930s and the early 1960s, maize yields trebled in the United States.[1] The total research cost of hybrid maize was $131 million up to 1955, and the net annual return on this innovation has been over $900 million, i.e. about 700 per cent a year.[2] This is clearly a better return than one could hope to get on physical investment, but agricultural research is a long term proposition, and governments must be willing to spend substantial sums over a period of years before major break-throughs can be achieved.

Agricultural research in developing countries tended in the past to be concentrated on export crops such as rubber, sugar or coffee,

[1] See *The World Food Problem*, pp. 196–7: 'Although hybrids gave increased yields, the rise in unit production was attributable to a combination of factors. Hybrids provided the impetus which made other changes in production feasible. Hybrids responded more readily to fertilization, minimized lodging and dropping of ears, and tolerated increased plant populations, thus making profitable the practice of heavy fertilization. Hybrids also made profitable the use of more herbicides and insecticides for pest control. Average applications of nitrogenous fertilizers increased from 2 to 47 pounds per acre during the 30-year period. The combination of desirable practices provided the phenomenal yield increases.'

[2] See T. W. Schultz, *Transforming Traditional Agriculture*, Yale, 1964, p. 159, citing the figures of Griliches.

and to neglect subsistence crops. The exceptions are in countries which have achieved the most progress. In Israel, there has been intensive research on cirtrus fruits, irrigation techniques, desalinization of sea-water, and development of new plant varieties for desert soil conditions, particularly at the Negev Arid Soil Research Station at Beersheba and at the Weitzman Institute of Science at Rehovoth. There has also been a very successful effort to develop an efficient poultry and egg industry using US methods. The rapid growth of rice and sugar output in Taiwan in pre-war years was due to intensive Japanese research, and this tradition has been continued in the post-war period in which rice yields have risen 50 per cent. In 1960 there were 79 Taiwanese research workers per 100,000 engaged in agriculture compared with 1·2 in India.[1] Mexico was also a pioneer in agricultural research. In co-operation with the Rockefeller Foundation, the Mexican government has been conducting research at Chapingo since 1943 to improve seed varieties for corn, beans, wheat and cotton. The return on these efforts began to make itself felt in the 1950s when there were big increases in yields. From 1943 to 1964, Mexican wheat yields rose from 11 to 37 bushels per acre. The total costs have been small in relation to the returns. Between 1941 and 1960 the Rockefeller Foundation spent $9·2 million on agricultural research in Mexico.

These successes contrast sharply with the situation in Argentina where research was run down in the early 1950s. The wheat station at Pergamino had its staff reduced from fourteen to seven, little was done to check foot and mouth disease, or to explore the possible uses of fertilizer. These policies were revised in 1956 when the Instituto Nacional de Tecnologia Agropecuaria was created, but it takes several years for such an institution to produce results.

Agricultural research not only increases yields but adds to the flexibility of agriculture. Taiwan, Israel, and Mexico have been able to diversify their output and exports more readily than other countries because they knew which options were technically feasible. Malaya has been able to diversify from rubber into palm oil because rubber planters had the foresight to finance research into palm oil. But Malayan knowledge of other options such as pineapples has been greatly inferior to that in Taiwan, and is the major reason for lack of further diversification.

It was only in the middle of the 1960s, when two bad Indian

[1] See *Changes in Agriculture in 26 Developing Nations, 1948 to 1963*, US Dept. of Agriculture, 1965, p. 61.

harvests dramatized the deficiencies of farm policy in the developing world, that the value of better seeds began to be generally appreciated. Several Asian countries have now given increased emphasis to research, and donors of aid have also given it greater priority. International co-operation in research is beginning to prove effective. Mexican wheat strains have been successfully used in India, Pakistan, and Turkey. In 1966, India purchased 18,000 tons of Mexican wheat to use as seed, and Turkey 11,000 tons; in 1967 Pakistan purchased 42,000 tons and will soon be making exclusive use of improved varieties. The International Rice Research Institute founded jointly by the Rockefeller and Ford Foundations at Los Banos, in the Philippines, which started operations in 1962, is now producing high-yielding rice strains which are being widely diffused in Asia, though these have not yet been as successful as the new wheat seeds, both for technical reasons and because of consumer preference for traditional types. Work on maize, millet and sorghum is going ahead in India with help from the Rockefeller Foundation,[1] US researchers have now developed a new type of maize (opaque-2) which has about 90 per cent of the protein value of skimmed milk, and other research is also increasing the potential nutritive value of cereals.

Some of the new seeds have been so successful that the climate of opinion about Asian agriculture has now switched from extreme pessimism to rather jaunty optimism. A leading member of the US Department of Agriculture has this to say:

'As of mid-1968, both the food situation and food production prospects in Asia have changed almost beyond belief. The Philippines is self-sufficient in its staple food, rice, for the first time since 1903. Iran with a substantial expansion in wheat acreage, is actually a net exporter of wheat this year. Ceylon's rice harvest climbed 13 per cent above the previous record, as it both expanded the area under cultivation and raised yields.

'Pakistan's wheat crop, harvested in April and May, is estimated to be 30 per cent above the previous record. So is India's. The total Indian food grain crop, officially estimated at 100 million tons, is

[1] See C. Beringer, 'A Green Revolution in the Developing Countries', OECD *Observer*, October, 1968, p. 32: 'In India the area planted with new varieties went up from about 23,000 acres in 1965–66 to nearly 4 million acres one year later. By 1970–71, they are expected to cover 40 million acres, nearly 15 per cent of the total food grain acreage.'

up 32 per cent from last year's drought-depressed levels and, more importantly, up 12 per cent from the previous record.'[1]

The big leap forward of 1968 was greatly helped by technical advance in new seeds, bigger inputs of fertilizers and the major switch in price policy in India and Pakistan. But it should be remembered that the huge harvest increases were strongly influenced by weather. Furthermore, many new seeds require a bigger water supply than old seeds, and had their first big successes in areas such as Punjab or West Pakistan where irrigation has been most extensively developed. Future gains from new seeds, in dry areas or on land where irrigation is meagre, will therefore be more modest than the first results.[2]

There is even more scope for action to improve livestock yields than there is for crops. Technically the livestock sector is more backward than crop production, and future demand for livestock products will rise faster than for cereals. The most rapid improvement in livestock output can probably be achieved with pigs and poultry. Both Mexico and Israel had an enormous increase in output of poultry-meat and eggs, but in Asian countries egg production actually declined between 1953 and 1963.

In some countries technical advance is hindered by religious taboos and traditional prejudices. In most countries these barriers are not too important, e.g. neglect of pig husbandry in Israel. However, the barriers to rational livestock husbandry are a significant influence in some African countries and in India. Indian state governments have reinforced traditional attitudes by strengthening legislation

[1] See L. R. Brown, 'The Agricultural Revolution in Asia', *Foreign Affairs*, July 1968.

[2] K. N. Raj, who is one of India's leading economists, has pointed out the dangers of 'green revolution' optimism and questioned the feasibility of the 5 per cent growth rate for agriculture in the Fourth Indian Five Year Plan; see 'Some Questions Concerning Growth, Transformation and Planning of Agriculture in the Developing Countries', *Journal of Development Studies*, UN, New York, 1968–69, and 'Plan or No Plan?', *Economic and Political Weekly*, Bombay, July 1968. Raj argues that some areas of India (Punjab, Gujerat and Madras) have had successes in agriculture comparable with Mexico because they have also benefited very substantially from previous investment in irrigation. He questions whether progress in these areas and in Mexico is really an example of quick transformation of traditional agriculture. He feels that the process of transforming traditional agriculture is more complicated than most green revolutionaries would admit, and points out that the acknowledged success of Taiwan in this respect took several decades of research and extension work.

against cow slaughter. In fact, Indian practice is not entirely in accord with the legislation that has been passed. Cattle census records reveal a big variation in the ratio of cows to bulls in different parts of the country, which is clear evidence of surreptitious slaughter. Ten per cent of the population are Muslims who eat beef when they can get it, and many Hindus eat meat. But instead of trying to break the old taboos through propaganda and education, the government has done very little, except for isolated efforts to castrate scrub bulls, and some advocacy of intra-uterine contraceptive devices for cows!

Apart from better livestock husbandry, Asian agriculture could gain a good deal from better pest control and storage. Indian losses from monkeys, rodents, insects and poor storage are about 15 per cent of output. Governments could help here by education, propaganda advocating monkey and rat destruction, by provision of more public warehouse facilities, more veterinarians and epizootic controls.

In almost all of the countries where agriculture has made rapid progress, foreign technical assistance has made a considerable contribution. Thus the rapid pre-war growth of agriculture in Taiwan owed a great deal to Japanese research, and post-war development was greatly stimulated by the establishment of the Joint Commission on Rural Reconstruction. This enabled the US Aid authorities to work closely with the Taiwan government, and $135 million were spent on 6,000 rural development projects. In Mexico, the research effort depended heavily on the Rockefeller Foundation. In Israel, US technical assistance and aid-financed supplies of feeding stuffs were responsible for the success of the poultry industry, and in Greece and South Korea, US aid was also very important. Both Israel and Taiwan now provide technical assistance to other countries in agriculture.

PERSUADING FARMERS TO USE NEW TECHNIQUES

Research is only the beginning of a development policy in agriculture. Once the new knowledge is available, farmers must be persuaded to adopt it. The diffusion of new technology is more difficult than in industry, because there are many more production units and they are more widely scattered geographically. In most cases farmers are using techniques which have been tested over generations and with which they are thoroughly familiar. The experiment with new strains or methods will involve unknown risks, and even if they can see that something works well in normal conditions, they will still need to be assured that the results will not be disastrous in a bad year. In many cases, agricultural innovation involves far-ranging change in production techniques. If fertilizer is applied to traditional strains of wheat and rice they often grow so high that the stalk collapses. If new seeds and fertilizer are both applied, more water will often be necessary. Therefore most farmers will prefer to let their neighbours bear the risk of making the first experiments. Quite apart from this, the cost of new seeds, water, fertilizers, pesticides, etc., may initially be high because of the limited scale of production. If production is to be raised and costs lowered, the government may have to subsidize a whole range of new inputs for a period, until they become commercially attractive on their own account. The argument for such subsidies is exactly the same as that for protecting 'infant industries'. It has taken most governments a long time to apply this kind of logic to agriculture, though they have accepted it very readily for industry. In fact, in India and Argentina, government policies to protect industry raised the price of agricultural inputs, and thus hindered technical change. In Egypt, Greece, Israel, Taiwan and Yugoslavia there have been very big increases in the use of fertilizers, whereas in Argentina there has been no progress at all.

The benefits of new inputs will depend on the capacity of farmers to absorb new knowledge and adjust their working techniques accordingly. The process will often be slow, because running a farm involves a complex variety of managerial skills which can only be adapted gradually to new production techniques. The speed of adaptation will depend on the level of education. If they are literate as in Israel and Taiwan, farmers will be able to use published material, such as government pamphlets and farm journals. Otherwise, new techniques will be difficult to put across, particularly if access to radio and TV is limited. Until farmers are consuming new inputs on a large scale, it will not pay commercial firms to educate farmers, as is done by fertilizer and seed salesmen in developed countries. The government will therefore need to provide extension services and demonstration projects, to encourage farmers associations and co-operatives. These played a large role in the success of agriculture in Japan and Denmark, but in most developing countries, agricultural extension is still weak. If all farmers are to have some contact with the extension work, it will usually be necessary to have one extension worker for every 300 farm families. This would give a potential coverage of less than one working day of extension per farm family, but as extension work is usually done in groups, this ratio would be adequate. Only in Israel and Greece are extension services provided on anything like this scale. In the past decade, the effort to provide agricultural extension services has been pushed much further in Asia than in Latin America. In India there is a very large programme to provide village development officers. Unfortunately, many of them are not properly qualified for agricultural extension work, but have concentrated on social projects. In East Pakistan, where it was found that extension workers were having little success, the Academy for Rural Development at Comilla started in 1959 to provide part-time training for village leaders and model farmers, and this technique has proved very successful, just as it did earlier in both Denmark and Japan.

INVESTMENT

In most developing countries, it is not appropriate to promote agricultural development by large-scale mechanization.[1] In view of the possibilities of using labour more intensively, such expenditures are generally wasteful in the lower income countries, though not of course in Argentina or Israel. Large scale mechanization would raise productivity and release labour not employable elsewhere. There are several examples of the wastes involved in highly capitalized farming in poor countries, the most noticeable being the fiasco of the British government's groundnut scheme in Tanganyika, the French project in the Casamance Valley in Senegal, and the state farms in Ghana. However, there may be quite serious seasonal bottlenecks even in countries with a normally abundant labour supply and there will probably be a growing need for new types of farm implements to deal with new seed varieties which require more seed-bed preparation and more labour to harvest the higher yields.

One of the important reasons for fast agricultural growth in Israel, Mexico, Taiwan, Venezuela and Greece has been heavy investment in irrigation. Irrigation increases yields, permits new seeds to be used and adds greatly to the reliability of harvests. In Israel the water supply to agriculture was raised threefold between

[1] Availability of mechanical horsepower per hectare of arable land is 0·05 in Asia, 0·03 in Africa, 0·18 in Latin America, 1·01 in the USA and 0·8 in Europe; see *The World Food Problem*, p. 397.

1950 and 1965 and has permitted a large extension of the cultivated area as well as raising the fertility of land already cultivated. In the arid climate of Israel, irrigation can raise the yield of land from four to seven times. Israel's increased water supply has involved draining the Hula swamps, putting a pipeline into the Negev, diverting the Yarkon and Jordan waters, digging wells, and more recently, de-salting sea water. The investment in irrigation has been very high and has been justified by the political need to extend the area of settlement throughout the country. In terms of its agricultural benefits alone, it would not have been economic to put such large resources into irrigation. The Israeli government has spent more on agricultural investment than it has on industry. In Venezuela and Mexico there has also been heavy spending on irrigation. On the arid areas of the Mexican Pacific Coast, where water from the mountains is relatively easy to trap, irrigation has had a high pay-off, but there have been some other areas of the country where the returns have been small, as in the massive Papaloapan project. The efficiency of irrigation projects has come in for criticism in several countries. This is true of water development projects in Brazil,[1] Turkey,[2] Ceylon,[3] Pakistan and Taiwan. Thus the biggest agricultural aid project in Taiwan was the Shihmen Dam and Reservoir which cost $70 million to construct. Jacoby suggests that the return on this investment has only been about 1·5 per cent a year in a country where long-term riskless loans yielded 12 per cent or more. 'It stands as an engineering monument of which the Chinese people may be proud. But it was purchased at far too high a cost in terms of tens of millions of dollars of alternative developmental opportunities foregone.'[4] In Pakistan the First Plan allocated four times as much to irrigation as to fertilizers, better seeds, plant protection and improved farm techniques. As Pakistan's chief economic planner said in retrospect:

[1] See A. O. Hirschman, *Journeys Toward Progress*, Twentieth Century Fund, New York, 1963.

[2] See W. Friedmann, editor, *Public International Development Financing in Turkey*, Columbia University School of Law, New York, 1962 (mimeographed), p. 150; 'The reality is that the Seyhan Project is a half-finished monument, a very heavy burden on the national economy.' The total costs of the project including work not completed would be 'three times Turkey's national budget'.

[3] In Ceylon, $125 million was spent on the Galoya project which has so far shown very poor returns. The post-war emphasis on large scale tank and canal irrigation of the traditional type has recently been criticized by visiting Israeli experts.

[4] See N. H. Jacoby, *US Aid to Taiwan*, Praeger, New York, 1966, p. 199.

'The only explanation can be that the planners have treated irrigation projects as part of the effort to build up the infra-structure of the economy, taken their need for granted, and never really bothered to question their economic rationale.'[1]

Since then Pakistan has given much more emphasis to small-scale irrigation. Subsidies to provide individual farms with tube-wells have had good results in terms of increased yields.

In some countries, the creation of new road networks has had a major effect in opening up new land for cultivation. This was true in Brazil. The roads built to link Brasilia with the rest of the country permitted large new areas to be settled in the interior. Venezuela has also spent heavily on roads to open up new areas to settlement. The large strategic road building in Turkey under NATO programmes permitted farmers to increase their marketed output. Mexico has spent a good deal on roads deliberately designed to promote marketing facilities of farm products.

As a result of investment in irrigation and roads, several countries were able to make a substantial increase in their cultivated area.

IMPACT OF PRICE AND TAX POLICY ON OUTPUT

In developed countries, farmers are now a small fraction of the labour force and receive massive welfare payments in the form of price and income support. In the USA a quarter of farm income is subsidy, and, in Western Europe, the ratio is higher. But in the early stages of development, when most people are farm-workers, agriculture must be squeezed to provide resources for development elsewhere in the economy. Meiji Japan, where land taxes absorbed a third of agricultural income, is a striking example of what can be done. But if the sacrifices demanded are too great or are inefficiently levied, production will suffer, as it did in the USSR under Stalin.

Most developing countries have squeezed agricultural income by the price scissors, rather than by direct taxation, i.e. they have kept down food prices by controls, by surplus food imports, export controls or unfavourable exchange rates for farm exports. At the same time protection for industry has raised the price of manufactured goods either for consumption or production purposes. The advantage of this kind of taxation is that it is surreptitious. It requires less political courage than direct taxation. In many countries, the

[1] See M. ul Haq, *The Strategy of Economic Planning*, Oxford University Press, Karachi, 1966, p. 35.

farm sector is privileged by exemption from income tax and land taxes are negligible, but the effective tax burden on agriculture may be high if the price scissors are sharp.

Some countries have been in the fortunate position that they did not need to squeeze farm income. Israel, Taiwan, Greece and Korea were large recipients of external finance, and Venezuela had a very large income from oil, so none of them needed to squeeze farms in the way that was necessary in India and Pakistan, where aid was much smaller and where farmers are a bigger part of the economy.

Some countries helped protect farmers against income fluctuations by significant programmes of price support and public storage. This was the case in Mexico, and could well have been practised by many other countries if they had used surplus food disposals more efficiently.

In Argentina, India and Pakistan, where agricultural performance was relatively poor, it is quite clear that the price scissors policy was too extreme. It dulled incentives and lowered incomes so that farmers were not motivated or able to increase investment or modernize their inputs. In all these countries, a good deal of the farmer's sacrifice was not devoted to development but simply increased consumption standards or urban dwellers who got cheaper food.

Government manipulation of the price system was carried to the most extreme lengths in Argentina, where the parity price for agricultural products (i.e. the ratio of prices received by farmers to those they paid for farm inputs and their own consumption) fell from 100 in 1929 to 51 in 1953–55. It rose again to 61 in 1965, but the 1965 terms of trade for agriculture were about 20 points worse than the price experience of US farmers in relation to 1929. The price of industrial goods was raised by tariffs and import controls. Farmers had to pay more for consumption goods, fertilizers and tractors, whilst their receipts for farm products were reduced by the multiple exchange rate system, and by price controls on food intended to keep down the cost of living. State trading agencies purchased crops at lower prices than they sold them abroad. The price squeeze on Argentine farmers is a major reason why output stagnated, and why there was no progress in use of fertilizers or tractors. In 1964, fertilizers (ammonium sulphate) cost twice as much in Argentina as in the USA, and farm prices were lower. Tractor prices were about one and three-quarter times the US level.

In Pakistan, wartime controls on food prices were maintained until the late 1950s, farmers were obliged to make compulsory deliveries to the government, and there were heavy export taxes on jute and cotton. This policy had a catastrophic effect on farm output and was sharply reversed in 1960. Pakistan farmers now get subsidies for fertilizers and tubewell irrigation, they have free markets for farm products, food surpluses have been used to cushion price fluctuations, and production is rising fast.

In India farm price policy was less extreme than in the other two countries, but incentives were hurt by policies designed to keep retail prices down, and inputs were made expensive by protection for the domestic fertilizer industry. In 1965 fertilizer prices in India were 50 per cent higher than in the USA. The government made no attempt to even out food price fluctuations by maintaining a buffer stock which it could have built up in some of the years of high production. Instead it let prices collapse when harvests were good and tried to allocate supplies at controlled prices in bad years by a loose system of zonal rationing. In response to the harvest failure and food crisis of 1965–66, Indian food prices rose considerably, and government policy changed. It used the bumper harvest of 1967 to increase government stocks and this is now helping to keep prices up.

In countries where agriculture has expanded fast, price policy has been different. Fairly high support prices have been maintained in Taiwan, Israel and Greece, and in Mexico they were maintained at a reasonable level. In all these countries and in Egypt as well, government price operations have also tended to reduce fluctuations in farm income. Several of these countries have been able to supply farmers with substantial credit. Farmers have been much more responsive to price incentives than many governments anticipated. Recent research suggests that this is so even in an extremely conservative country like India.[1]

If governments wish to raise revenue from the agricultural sector in order to finance development, they should make greater use of direct taxation and less use of price manipulation. Direct taxes on agriculture are generally less significant than they were in pre-war years. In India, land taxes provided a fifth of government revenue before the war, but now yield only 5 per cent. In other countries they are even lower. Only in South Korea have they been high in the

[1] See D. Narain, *Impact of Price Movements on Areas Under Selected Crops in India, 1900–1939*, Cambridge, 1965.

post-war period.[1] Land taxes can have a positive effect on production incentives by forcing farmers to increase their marketed surplus, just as they did in Meiji Japan where they provided three-quarters of government revenue. If agricultural taxation is based on the potential output of the land, it will provide an incentive to raise productivity. Farmers with higher than average yields will have a bigger margin of profit, and those with lower yields will be penalized. Furthermore, the land tax can be made progressive according to the size of the holding, and can provide a fiscal incentive to break up large, inefficient estates.

There are several reasons for the reluctance to tax agriculture more heavily in a direct form. The first is the political opposition of farmers, particularly as they would expect it to be additional rather than an alternative to their indirect tax burden. In some countries, land taxation is regarded as a heritage of colonial rule and is politically unpopular for this reason. There are also technical difficulties in levying land taxes. They require an up-to-date land register with details of the area cultivated, land ownership, quality of the soil, etc. Finally, in countries with rapid inflation, any tax which is collected with a lag is of much less value to government than those collected when they fall due.

LAND REFORM AND OTHER INSTITUTIONAL PROBLEMS

Many writers assert that agrarian reform is a 'pre-condition' for increased production in developing countries.[2] We doubt whether this is generally true, for several countries made significant progress with unsatisfactory agrarian structures. One of these is Greece, which has had two major agrarian reforms, but where the average holding is now divided into fifteen small strips. Another is Mexico, which we shall discuss later. The discussion of agrarian reform

[1] See H. P. Wald, *Taxation of Agricultural Land in Underdeveloped Economies*, Harvard, 1959, p. 62.

[2] See G. Myrdal, *Asian Drama*, Pantheon, New York, 1968, pp. 1369 and 1374, who holds this position for South Asia: 'the South Asian case may thus be one in which the promotion of social and economic equality is a pre-condition for obtaining substantial long-term increases in production'. He is also sceptical about price incentives: 'where only a minor fraction of the farming units at present make significant contributions to marketed food supplies it is often pointed out that a normal market situation does not exist. Higher prices would not call forth greater production as economists reared in Western thinking are inclined to suppose.'

includes several issues which are related but different. The physical agrarian structure may be inefficient and impede production for technical reasons, as in the Greek case. On the other hand, the system of ownership may damage incentives because the benefits of increased productivity accrue to landlords and money-lenders, rather than the cultivator. Finally, inequality of income is socially unjust and may be justifiable simply on moral grounds.

As land tenure varies so much from country to country, it is difficult to derive generally valid conclusions about the desirability of reform. It has obviously been helpful to productivity growth in the past, e.g. the Meiji reforms which ended Japanese feudalism and established a market economy for agriculture with a very big land tax, and the enclosure movement in British agriculture which dispossessed the peasantry of their rights over common land. But other land reforms have hindered productivity, e.g. Soviet collectivization. And they have nearly all had a fairly high initial cost because of disturbed production schedules or civil war. The changeover from the Tokugawa system probably reduced Japanese farm output for a decade. The Mexican reforms prevented any agricultural progress between 1910 and 1940. The Soviet losses from collectivization were very large and agrarian reform in Bolivia and Cuba has also been very costly. Governments must obviously weigh these possible costs carefully against the likely benefits.

Often the purpose of land reform in the past was to break feudal obstacles and introduce a system responsive to modern market forces. When the choice is of this kind, it may be worth making a revolutionary break even if the transition involves a temporary fall in output. However, most contemporary countries have more dynamic economies than was true in Japan in the 1860s, or the UK in the eighteenth century. Most systems of landownership are responsive to modern market incentives, even when there is quite a sizeable element of feudalism left. Therefore land reform is not now likely to be a *primum mobile* of economic development.

There may be strong arguments for land reform on grounds of social justice, and these may be so compelling that quasi-confiscatory measures may be necessary. In applying criteria of social justice, it is desirable to keep a perspective which encompasses the whole economy. In Latin America the biggest disparities in income and the biggest degree of exploitation are often found in the agricultural sector and land reform may have high priority. In Asia, by contrast, there are several countries where landowners are quite poor by the standards of civil servants and the middle class in urban areas. There may be some case for penalising them if they use their income in a less useful way than the industrial rich, e.g. for marriage feasts rather than investment. But this problem might equally well be tackled by creating rural savings banks and propaganda in favour of cheaper marriage feasts. However, there may be a case for further land reform of a non-confiscatory character in India, where there is a landless rural proletariat whose living standards are subhuman. We shall return to this later.

If reform is undertaken it is necessary to ensure that the newly created structures will be reasonably flexible and responsive to future changes in technology or in the size of the agricultural labour force. Post-war Italian land reform and settlement schemes have involved waste because farm houses were built on plots which soon became too small for economic exploitation. Post-war Japanese land reform has also made it difficult to enlarge the size of farms, which is now desirable. Any system which freezes rents or fixes maximum sizes of individual holdings is likely to affect resource allocation adversely in the long run. For this reason, land reform should never be regarded as a final utopian panacea.

Most governments which are strong enough to enforce land reform are also capable of taxing agriculture more heavily and imposing a degree of progressivity which will encourage sale of large land holdings. This may well be just as effective as land reform legislation, and it will not require expenditure on compensation, survey and legal costs.

Land ownership is most highly concentrated in Latin America:

'In 1950, agricultural enterprises of more than 1,000 hectares comprised only 1·5 per cent of the total number of farms, but held 65 per cent of the land area. At the opposite extreme, farms of no more than 20 hectares made up 73 per cent of the total number, but occupied only 3·7 per cent of the land. In Venezuela, until 1959, 1·69 per cent of the agricultural properties held 74 per cent of the farm land. In Brazil 1·6 per cent of the landowners control one-third of the agricultural area. In Chile, 1·5 per cent of the agricultural properties control 75 per cent of the farm area.'[1]

The heavy concentration of landownership is derived historically from that in Spain and Portugal, where it still persists, but in several

[1] See V. L. Urquidi, *The Challenge of Development in Latin America*, Praeger, New York, 1964.

countries the large properties are run on a capitalist basis with wage labour, and respond to production incentives in the same way as large farmers in the United States. This is true of large farms in Mexico and Argentina and of those in Southern Brazil. The lack of progress in Argentine agriculture is due more to low prices than to the conservatism of landowners. Argentine agriculture expanded quickly up to the 1930s, and had the same ownership structure then as now.[1] Chile, however, is a case where the system is semi-feudal. Half the peasants are tied to large estates and have no property rights or leaseholds. They provide labour services in return for a very low cash wage and free housing. Their other income is derived from small plots which they farm on a sharecropping basis, with half of the crop going to the proprietor. The rest of the peasantry has very small holdings or are casual labourers. The system provides little incentive for increased output or investment, and incentives have been further squeezed by price controls on practically all farm products sold on the domestic market, low exchange rates for export products and preferential exchange rates for imports of food and raw materials.

The Economic Commission for Latin America and the Alliance for Progress have urged that changes be made in the agrarian structure of Latin America with a switch to peasant proprietorship, or at least to a tenancy system in which the peasant can keep the benefits of agricultural improvement for himself. But the political power of landlords is usually great enough to resist effective programmes of land redistribution, and the three really big changes in ownership structure, in Cuba, Bolivia and Mexico, have been achieved by revolution.[2] In Chile, the ownership structure is now being changed

[1] Some Argentine economists would not agree, e.g. Aldo Ferrer, *The Argentine Economy*, Berkeley, 1967, pp. 160–1, who argues that the system worked up to 1930 only because of the expansion into new land. He holds that landlords are interested in their property as a source of social status rather than for profit. It is also true that there has been some improvement in prices for farmers since the mid-1950s, and that this has had little effect on output. However, the Prebisch report of 1955 which outlined solutions to most Argentine economic problems n the post-Peron era did not even mention land reform; see 'The Prebisch Report', *The Review of the River Plate*, October 31 and November 11, 1955.

[2] Since 1960, under US pressure in the Alliance for Progress, fourteen Latin American countries have passed land-reform laws, but in most cases they have been permissive, rather than compulsory, and are intended to have a piecemeal impact. So far, land distribution has proceeded furthest in Venezuela where publicly-owned virgin lands were available. See *Progress in Land Reform*, UN, New York, 1966.

by legislation, but Chilean discussion of land reform has been so protracted, and fears of inadequate compensation so strong, that this has acted as a further disincentive to increased productivity.[1]

Mexico is the only one of our Latin American countries which has had a major land reform. Before the revolution of 1910, the concentration of land ownership inherited from Spanish colonialism had been increased by the policies of the Diaz régime, which distributed almost 80 million hectares of communal land to survey companies and big investors. In 1910, 834 *haciendas* possessed 90 per cent of the land. 32 million hectares (12 per cent of landed property) belonged to foreigners. The biggest foreign ranch was the Hearst estate in Chihuahua with 3 million hectares. During the revolution some land was seized in local peasant revolts such as those led by Emiliano Zapata and a good deal of church land and foreign land was expropriated. Peasants ceased to be peons held in debt bondage, and were free to move from one employer to another. But the process of handing land to the peasants was remarkably slow until Cardenas came to power in 1934. Between 1915 and 1934 only 7·7 million hectares were distributed to peasants. Cardenas distributed 18 million hectares in six years, the three succeeding Presidents 12·6 million and Lopez Mateos 16 million.[2] The total redistribution is still less than the sales and gifts of Porfirio Diaz. Most of the land was given free to the peasants, but they did not receive it in individual ownership. It was used to create *ejidos* in collective ownership by villages. This arrangement was intended to be a return to the old Aztec system of land ownership. In some *ejidos* cultivation is carried out collectively, and in others by individual peasants. In neither case, however, can peasants sell, mortgage, rent or transfer their land, and the distribution of land between peasants can be changed periodically. This system has strong disadvantages from the standpoint of production incentives and provision of agricultural credit, and it also subjects the peasants to pressure from local political bosses. In many ways it is as inefficient as the 1860 land reforms in Russia which were also intended to be a reversion to an old system of collective ownership.

1 Hesitation over land reform has also acted as a disincentive in Ceylon. Nationalization of foreign tea plantations was proclaimed as government 'policy', but was not carried out. The uncertainty inhibited replanting which could have released land for rice growing, and it also stimulated an outflow of private capital. See N. Kaldor, *Essays on Economic Policy*, vol. II, Duckworth, London, 1964, p. 297.

2 See *La Economia Mexicana en Cifras*, Nacional Financiera, Mexico, 1966.

Mexico still has some very large landowners. Flores cites a figure of 9,600 proprietors who owned 80 million hectares in 1960.[1] This is almost twice as much land as the *ejidos* hold. In theory these big estates should have been eliminated except where they occupy very poor land, but in practice, politically influential landlords have retained large properties. The other main category of landholding is the so-called small properties (*pequenas propiedades*) which were not affected by the land reforms. These were defined rather generously as units of 150 hectares of irrigated cotton land up to 5,000 hectares for cultivation of guayale. Half of the landholdings in Mexico consist of such units. These farms and the *haciendas* are now capitalist enterprises hiring wage labour. In fact, the big post-war expansion in Mexican agricultural output has been concentrated on these properties, which have been the main beneficiaries of government irrigation programmes. Productivity is much higher on capitalist farms than on *ejidos*, so it can hardly be claimed that land reform has been a major cause of Mexico's agricultural growth. Land reform has been more important as a political symbol. Some Mexicans attribute to it a more or less mystical importance. A leading Mexican agricultural economist describes its effects as follows:

'The break-up of the *hacienda* was the catalyst which released and set in motion the multitude of complex forces to which Mexico owes its sustained rates of agricultural and industrial growth. It gave the rural population an opportunity for both horizontal and vertical mobility; it destroyed the "caste" system, it profoundly affected the political environment and brought the country out of the colonial impasse.'[2]

[1] See E. Flores, *Tratado de Economia Agricola*, Fondo de Cultura Economica, Mexico, 1964, p. 320.

[2] See E. Flores, 'Land Reform and the Alliance for Progress', in L. Randall, ed., *Economic Development*, Heath, Boston, 1964, p. 48. The romanticism of Flores and other Mexican writers about the *ejido* is similar to that of the Narodniks in Tsarist Russia in relation to the *mir* (village communes) which were strengthened by the 1861 land reforms. It is worth noting that Lenin attacked the Narodnik position and pointed out that the abolition of the *mir* and installation of private property in land would be a spur to increased productivity; see V. I. Lenin, 'Development of Capitalism in Russia' (1899), and 'The Agrarian Question in Russia at the End of the Nineteenth Century' (1908), in *Selected Works*, vol. I, London, 1936.

Its real contribution has been to create a foundation of political stability which has enabled the government to pursue strong and consistent development policies of a kind not possible elsewhere in Latin America, but land reform itself has not contributed much to increased productivity, and income distribution in Mexico is more unequal than in several other Latin American countries. The basic reasons for the success of Mexican agriculture have been large-scale investment in irrigation and farm-to-market roads, a long-term commitment to research and extension work, ample provision of funds for farm credit and pursuit of reasonable price policies for farmers. Given these ingredients, agriculture would perform reasonably well in most economies whatever the tenure system.

Post-war land reform seems to have had beneficial effects on production efficiency in Egypt, South Korea, Taiwan and Yugoslavia.

In Egypt, land reform has been only one aspect of the process of gradual abolition of large-scale private property. There were two agrarian reform laws in 1952 and 1961 which have reduced the maximum holding to 100 feddans (about 24 hectares). The maximum holding by any one family is limited to 300 feddans to prevent evasion by splitting up large family properties. Compensation was well below the market value of the properties. In the 1950s about 10 per cent of the land was distributed to small holders. Rent control has been established at about two-thirds of previous levels for all tenants, and peasants have much greater security of tenure. Ultimately it is planned to reduce the maximum holding to 25 feddans which has provoked landlords into anticipatory sales. The share of absentee owners in farm income has been reduced by about half, and tenants have increased their share by a third.

In order to avoid a fall in productivity on large estates which were broken up, co-operatives have been created which make farmers conform to a planned system of crop rotation, and land is ploughed collectively by tractors belonging to the co-operative. Fertilizers and insecticides are provided by the co-operatives.

'This ingenious combination of collective farming and individual ownership seems, according to survey studies, to have brought an increase in production. The system also seems to be appreciated by the farmers. Attempts have been made to introduce *voluntary* systems of co-operative farming, coupled with individual ownership, in villages outside the land reform areas. These have proved a success and it is possible that the system may spread to all agriculture in Egypt.'[1]

The Egyptian land reform was also accompanied by a major expansion of agricultural credit. Before the reforms this was not available to small proprietors or tenants, but they were the main beneficiaries of the fourfold increase in credit which took place between 1952 and 1965, so that the role of money-lenders in rural society has been greatly reduced.[2]

The growth of Egyptian farm output has not been spectacular since 1950, but it has been more than three times as rapid as in the preceding forty years in spite of the disturbance which might have been expected from the large changes in ownership and the significant improvement in income distribution.

In South Korea and Taiwan, very significant land reforms have been accomplished which undoubtedly contributed to the increase in output. In Taiwan the reform affected about 60 per cent of farm families and about 70 per cent of the previously leased land became owner-occupied. The reform was carried out in three successive stages. In 1949 a ceiling was put on the proportion of the crop payable as rent, and this encouraged some landlords to sell. The government then sold public lands which had belonged to Japanese in the colonial period. Finally, under the Land-to-the-Tiller Act of 1953 it placed ceilings on the land holding of landlords and resold the land to tenants. The government paid reasonable compensation, 70 per cent in bonds indexed to the price of rice and sweet potatoes, and 30 per cent in shares of industrial companies confiscated from the Japanese. The Taiwan programme was unusually successful for three reasons: (*a*) it was carried out by a government completely indifferent to local pressure groups, backed with an army of half a million men, conscious of past mistakes and knowing that another failure would probably mean death; (*b*) part of the property transfer involved confiscation of land owned by foreigners just defeated in war; (*c*) compensation could be reasonable because government revenues were boosted by foreign aid. These are not normal circumstances and it would obviously be naïve to assume that the Taiwan

[1] See B. Hansen and G. A. Marzouk, *Development and Economic Policy in the UAR (Egypt)*, North-Holland, Amsterdam, 1965, p. 92.

[2] See E. Eshag and M. A. Kamal, 'A Note on the Reform of the Rural Credit System in UAR (Egypt)', *Bulletin of the Oxford University Institute of Economics and Statistics*, May 1967.

example would be easy for other governments to follow. Even so, the reform left a good deal of land in small fragmented holdings.

In both South Korea and Taiwan, the reforms limited the holding of land suitable for rice paddies to three hectares and redistributed larger holdings to peasants on very favourable terms. Tenants were given security of tenure and rents for all tenants were fixed at about a third of the value of the crop instead of roughly half as had previously been the case. The land was thus distributed fairly evenly and few peasants were left without land. In both countries this system provided peasants with substantial new incentives to increase output, which were greatly reinforced by extension and research programmes and the provision of irrigation water, fertilizer, credit and improved seeds.

In Yugoslavia, agricultural progress owes a good deal to favourable price policies and to the reversal of collectivization. Since land was redistributed in independent peasant holdings, output and productivity have grown steadily.

In Venezuela, land reform has largely taken the form of resettlement on public land.

In Greece and Ghana where production grew faster than average, land ownership was already concentrated on small owner-cultivators. In Israel, all land belongs to the Jewish agency and most farms are individually cultivated but have a large element of co-operation for supplies, irrigation and marketing. The *Kibbutzim* are communal settlements which have had an important moral and political significance but which are not any more efficient than the rest of the farm sector. Israeli farmers are mostly new settlers who often had no previous experience of farming and have been much more receptive to new techniques than farmers in other countries. They are also trained and helped by the land settlement department of the Jewish agency, so their situation is really quite different from that of farmers in other countries.

India and Pakistan are countries where land reform has been a political symbol of the break with colonialism. The major feature of the reforms was the elimination of the top layer of landlords created by British rule, i.e. the *zamindars* (in Bengal and Uttar Pradesh), and their counterpart in the ex-princely states, the *jagirdars* (in Rajasthan and Hyderabad). These were intermediaries rather than proprietors in the normal sense, as they had heavier land tax obligations to the government than other landowners and their wealthier tenants had security of tenure and fixed rents. A good deal of their land was redistributed to 'cultivators' who do not in fact farm the land themselves but sublet it. The *zamindars* had been closely associated with the colonial power and were particularly easy to remove in East Pakistan where most of them were Hindus. In India they put up more resistance and agrarian reform was handled by each of the states separately in the 1950s. In West Pakistan the reform did not take place until 1959. In many of the Indian states rents have been fixed, tenants have been given some security of tenure, and minimum wages have been set for agricultural workers. However, a good deal of land remains in unconsolidated strips and there has been very little redistribution to smaller peasants. The legislation establishing ceilings on land holdings was usually unsatisfactory or evaded.[1] Smaller tenants were often evicted from their traditional holdings, on order to establish the claims of the bigger tenants that they were cultivators. In most cases the *panchayats* (village councils) are dominated by the old landowners and the intended effect of land reforms was frequently evaded by splitting up the titles to large plots amongst the family of the old landowners. The top group of landlords includes only 2·4 per cent of the holdings but holds 28 per cent of the land. This is not inequality on the Latin American scale but it hardly reflects a 'socialist' policy.[2] About a fifth of the rural population (including 40 million of the untouchables) still own no land and many regulations on rent control and minimum wages are a dead letter. There is a movement led by Vinoba Bhave which encouraged landlords to make voluntary gifts of land (bhoodan) for redistribution, but its impact has been rather small and many of the gifts were of poor land.

A major problem of the Indian peasantry is that many of them are heavily in debt to local money-lenders who are their only source of credit and are sometimes their landlords. Debt is often passed on for several generations (though the wartime inflation temporarily

[1] See A. M. Khusro, 'Land Reforms since Independence', in V. B. Singh, ed. *Economic History of India: 1857–1956*, Allied Publishers, Bombay, 1965, p. 199: 'Legislative measures about ceilings imposition, some of which were never passed and some remained on the statute books, seem to be a dark spot in the history of Indian land reforms. The net benefits of ceilings legislation seemed in the end to be negligible.'

[2] Figures on distribution of rural property in India are given by I. M. D. Little in P. N. Rosenstein-Rodan, ed., *Pricing and Fiscal Policies*, MIT, Cambridge, Mass., 1964, p. 67. In West Pakistan, the top 2·1 per cent of holdings cover 23·4 per cent of the land, see *Census of Agriculture*, Pakistan, 1960.

eased the problem). So far, little has been done to provide alternative forms of credit, so the poor peasant has little hope of improving his lot. The land reform programme has therefore been rather modest in social terms and has not had any favourable effect on productivity.

The chief gainers from the expansion of Indian agriculture have been the more prosperous peasants, and landlords who have taken up active cultivation. If land reform had been more vigorous and the ceilings on individual holdings had actually been applied, there would have been some land to distribute to the poorest section of the population, who might then have been able to pull themselves up by their bootstraps. Unfortunately, the occasion was missed, and other methods of income redistribution are difficult to envisage, so that most of these people will have to live out their lives as miserably and bleakly as in the past.[1]

If we are to derive lessons for agricultural policy from past experience, they would be along the following lines. Governments should give every encouragement to agricultural research and the diffusion of new technology to farmers. They should be careful to maintain a price system that will foster production incentives, and even subsidize new inputs of fertilizer and seeds whilst the new farm technology is in its infant stage. They should tax farmers by means which will have the least harmful effect on production incentives. If they have access to surplus food aid, it should be used as far as possible to build government stockpiles for stabilization purposes and to help farmers move into new fields such as livestock production. However, one cannot expect most countries to do as well as Israel, Taiwan, Mexico or Venezuela in raising output. In the first place, the export performances of Israel and Taiwan were special cases which cannot be repeated on a large scale because of protectionism

[1] The picture is further complicated by social and caste barriers. The impact of these on productivity in Indian agriculture are brilliantly set out in Kusum Nair's survey of life in Indian villages. See her *Blossoms in the Dust*, London, 1961. Interestingly enough, the two cases where she found the most progressive attitude to change and greatest success in raising income were in areas settled by refugees from Pakistan. In the Punjab she found displaced ex-landowners who were forced to cultivate their new land to survive, tradesmen who were forced to give up the trades prescribed for their caste who became rural entrepreneurs, and a general weakening of tabus and caste barriers. In a Muslim area of Assam, she found that refugees were willing to cultivate vegetables as well as jute, whereas the local farmers would not suffer the indignity of carrying vegetables to market on their heads: 'That we cannot do. It is below our dignity.'

and the inherent sluggishness of demand in developed countries. Secondly, these four countries were rich enough to give farmers reasonable prices and to afford irrigation investment on a scale which would be uneconomic in countries at a lower income level or with smaller access to external finance. Thirdly, there are limits to which the results of foreign research can be applied quickly, and it will take at least a decade for most countries to mount an indigenous research effort as effective as Israel, Taiwan or Mexico.

There are no grounds for believing that neglect of agriculture has produced a Malthusian crisis of world hunger. Most developing countries have pursued a reasonably balanced policy towards agriculture, and in two of the countries where it was neglected, i.e. India and Pakistan, there has been a substantial revision of policy that augurs well for the future. The problem of nutritional deficiency in developing countries is not an agricultural problem, but one of income distribution and social policy. If governments are willing to promote greater social justice there is no reason to believe that agriculture will fail to supply the food.

In the past twenty years, agricultural output in our twenty-two countries increased at about 3·7 per cent a year. If some degree of import substitution is to be attained in future, a 4 per cent growth rate will probably be adequate to meet needs in the 1970s, i.e. if birth control keeps down population growth to the same rate as in the 1960s. This kind of growth rate should be attainable by most countries, however poor their natural resources.

Agriculture, which is generally organized on a family basis, has to support most of the labour which cannot find employment elsewhere. As demand for agricultural products is increasing slowly, agricultural income per head depends a great deal on job opportunities in other parts of the economy. If the non-agrarian sector is small or growing slowly, and population is growing fast, farm income and productivity will stagnate. If population grows slowly and the rest of the economy is growing fast, workers will be pulled out of agriculture on a substantial scale, and ways will readily be found to increase the productivity of the remaining farmworkers. Thus the prosperity of farmers depends very much on the success of economic policy as a whole and not just on policies toward agriculture.

Chapter VI

Has Industrialization Been Too Costly?

In all the countries under study, industrial output grew rapidly from 1950 to 1965. Both the weighted and the unweighted averages rose by more than 8 per cent a year, and in every case industry was the most rapidly expanding sector of the economy. It would not be true to say that industry was always the 'leading sector'. In Ceylon, Ghana, and Thailand, industrial output is still much smaller than that of agriculture and contributed less to the growth of total output. But, everywhere else, industry contributed more than farming. The biggest gains were registered by Israel, Spain, Taiwan and Yugoslavia where industry grew by more than 10 per cent a year.

One reason why industry was able to expand so quickly was the abundant supply of labour. The employment figures for individual countries in Table VI–2 should be treated with reserve, but the average figure for all the countries is probably near the mark. This shows an increase in industrial employment of 4·2 per cent a year, compared with 0·8 per cent for agriculture. It is often argued that developing countries should have tried to provide even more employment in industry, and this is a legitimate criticism. However, we must keep some sense of perspective in this matter. Industrial productivity grew by 3·8 per cent a year compared with 2·7 per cent for agriculture, so the scope for a more labour-intensive approach, with slower-productivity growth, was presumably not very great. As industrialization is in part a displacement of handicraft trades some rise in productivity is almost inevitable.

Industry received a much bigger share of investment than agriculture. Unfortunately, it is not possible to estimate just how fast industrial capital has grown, but if we allow for bigger inputs of both labour and capital, it would not seem that industrial efficiency has risen any faster than that in farming.

Table VI–1

Growth of Industrial Output 1913–65

Annual average compound growth rates

	1913–50	1950–65		1913–50	1950–65
Argentina	4·3*	4·0	Pakistan	n.a.	8·2
Brazil*	6·7	7·5	Peru*	n.a.	7·8§
Ceylon*	n.a.	4·8†	Philippines	n.a.	8·8
Chile	2·4	5·7	South Korea*	n.a.	9·2
Colombia*	8·5‡	7·2§	Spain	n.a.	10·2
Egypt*	n.a.	5·8‖	Taiwan	n.a.	13·7
Ghana	n.a.	n.a.	Thailand	n.a.	n.a.
Greece	5·1*	8·6	Turkey*	n.a.	9·9
India	2·7	6·7	Venezuela	n.a.	9·1
Israel	n.a.	10·8	Yugoslavia	n.a.	11·2
Malaya	n.a.	n.a.			
Mexico	3·8	6·7	Average	4·8	8·2

* manufacturing; † 1952/6–65; ‡ 1929–50; § 1950–63; ‖ 1950–62.

Source: *The Process of Industrialisation in Latin America* (Statistical Annex), ECLA, Santiago, 1966 (mimeographed). F. Hilgerdt, *Industrialisation and Foreign Trade*, League of Nations, Geneva, 1945. UN *Monthly Bulletin of Statistics* and UN *Statistical Yearbooks*. Pakistan, *National Accounts of Less Developed Countries*, OECD Development Centre, Paris, 1967, index for large and small scale manufacturing combined with mining. Egypt from B. Hansen and G. A. Marzouk, *Development and Economic Policy in the UAR (Egypt)*, North-Holland, Amsterdam, 1965, p. 115. Ceylon and South Korea from *The Growth of World Industry 1953–65*, UN, New York, 1967. Brazil, 1963–65 estimates supplied by Vargas Foundation, Israel figure supplied by the Bank of Israel. Mexico 1910–50 from *La Economia Mexicana en Cifras*, Nacional Financiera, Mexico, 1966.

A good deal of the benefit of increased industrial output has gone to capitalists in the form of profits. This has strengthened the savings capacity of the economies, and has helped to make the industrialization process self-reinforcing, for a good deal of the profits are reinvested.

THE NATURE OF DEMAND

Domestic demand provided the major market for industry and expanded much faster than total income. The poverty of developing countries is much more marked in industrial products than in farm commodities. Indian consumption of food per head is a fifth of that

Table VI–2

Growth of Employment by Sector 1950–65

Annual average compound growth rate

	Industry	Agriculture	Services
Argentina	2·4	−1·0	2·0
Brazil	4·5	1·6	4·2
Ceylon	3·0	0·7	3·0
Chile	0·8	0·3	2·0
Colombia	2·6	1·2	3·6
Egypt	1·5	0·7	3·2
Ghana	n.a.	n.a.	n.a.
Greece	1·1	0·1	3·3
India	5·2	1·3	4·0
Israel	6·3	3·8	5·3
Malaya	2·2	0·0	4·7
Mexico	4·9	2·2	4·0
Pakistan	4·5	2·2	2·3
Peru	1·2	0·1	3·2
Philippines	6·0	0·7	4·5
South Korea	12·1	−0·1	4·2
Spain	2·6	−1·6	2·8
Taiwan	7·3	0·2	1·8
Thailand	8·2	2·3	5·1
Turkey	2·9	1·3	3·5
Venezuela	4·6	0·9	5·4
Yugoslavia	4·3	−0·5	1·9
Average	4·2	0·8	3·5

Source: Appendix C.

in the USA, but India uses only one fortieth the manufactured products per head that the USA does. 'Balanced' growth therefore requires much faster expansion in industry than in agriculture. If agriculture expands too fast a country may face embarrassing and unsaleable surpluses. This does not often happen with industrial products.

Not only is demand increasing fast, but domestic producers have increased their share of the home market. These countries are all net importers of manufactures. They imported $15 billion worth in 1965, but imports have been restricted in various ways, and were reduced from about a quarter of consumption in 1950 to a fifth in 1965. The substitution of domestic products for imports has been most complete for consumer items. Imports are now concentrated on capital goods and intermediate products, although there has also been import replacement in these lines. Import substitution has been carried furthest in Argentina, Brazil, Chile, Egypt and India, where a significant part of output is produced at prices a good deal higher than imports would cost.

Foreign demand for manufactures has been buoyant. Exports rose by 9 per cent a year in value from 1953 to 1967 compared with 2·4 per cent for foodstuffs. But many countries have not fully exploited their opportunities and export sales have generally risen more slowly in volume than home sales. For our group of countries as a whole, manufactured exports in 1965 were only about 8 per cent of production. Developing countries supply less than 5 per cent of world exports of manufactures, and there is little doubt that they could increase this substantially.

STATE ENTERPRISE

Many governments have fostered industrial development by creating state enterprises. In Egypt and Yugoslavia the government undertakes four-fifths of total investment, and in India about 60 per cent. In Brazil, Israel, Malaya, Mexico, Pakistan and Turkey, government investment is also very large, and there are only a few countries where government investment is unimportant. TableVI–3 shows the share of government in all investment. The government share of industrial investment is probably somewhat lower than the overall ratio.

The motivations for direct government participation have been mixed. Only Egypt and Yugoslavia have pursued an active socialist policy involving the nationalization of foreign and domestic enterprise and concentrating all new investment in the government sector. India has also proclaimed socialist intentions and has nationalized airlines and insurance, but it has not nationalized any private firms in industry. It has reserved new developments in certain fields for the government, i.e. in steel, machine tools, heavy engineering, chemicals and coal mines, but even this policy has now been eased to encourage the private sector to expand steel production, and foreigners to invest in chemicals. Ghana and Ceylon also had socialist governments for part of the period under review and the extent of their socialism was somewhat similar to that in India. In both cases, the most recent trend is to look more favourably on the role of the private sector.

Table VI–3

Percentage Share of Government in Total Gross Fixed Investment 1965

Country	%	Country	%
Argentina	27·7	Mexico	41·8
Brazil	48·3	Pakistan	50·3
Ceylon	38·1	Peru	18·1
Chile	n.a.	Philippines	11·9
Colombia	18·3	South Korea	22·0
Egypt	80·7*	Spain	26·3
Ghana	n.a.	Taiwan	34·6
Greece	25·3	Thailand	32·4
India	61·0	Turkey	50·0
Israel	40·5	Venezuela	(26·4)‡
Malaya	44·0†	Yugoslavia	87·7

* 1961; † 1964–5; ‡ excludes public corporations.

Source: Latin American figures supplied by ECLA, Santiago. Ceylon, Egypt, Greece, Malaya, South Korea, Taiwan and Yugoslavia from *Yearbook of National Accounts Statistics 1966*, UN, New York, 1967. India from *Fourth Five Year Plan, A Draft Outline*, Delhi, 1966, p. 42; the estimate refers to the level envisaged for the third plan. Israel from *Annual Report 1966*, Bank of Israel, Jerusalem, 1967. Pakistan from *Mid-Plan Review of the Third Five Year Plan 1965–70*, Karachi, April 1967. South Korea, *Economic Survey 1967*, Economic Planning Board, Seoul, December 1967. Spain, *Contabilidad Nacional de Espana Ano 1965*, Instituto de Estadistica, Madrid 1967. Thailand, *National Accounts of Thailand 1966*, National Economic Development Board, Bangkok 1967. Turkey, *National Income, Total Expenditure and Investment of Turkey 1948, 1958–65*, State Institute of Statistics, Ankara, 1966.

In Mexico, government responsibility is large because of the strong desire for national independence. The government acquired large enterprises by nationalization of foreign-owned railways, oil and electric power, and it has reserved the exploitation of natural resources for itself. However, the Mexican government's ownership stake in the form of joint enterprises with local or foreign entrepreneurs is probably more important than industries which it owns directly.

In other countries there is no strong ideological commitment to state enterprise, but for pragmatic reasons the public sector has come to be relatively large. Governments felt that individual investments were too large for private firms, or that industries had to be nursed through an unprofitable initial period. Foreign aid increased the size of the public sector either directly through financing state enterprise, or simply by increasing the funds available to government. Amongst countries with a basically free enterprise orientation, Brazil, Pakistan and Turkey have the biggest state sectors. In Brazil (at least prior to the Kubitschek period, when the motivation, as in Mexico, became one of national pride) state enterprises were usually started reluctantly after foreign or domestic entrepreneurs had refused to enter because of difficulty in financing or an uncertain profit outlook. Before building the steel mill at Volta Redonda Brazil tried to induce the US Steel Corporation to undertake the project. To some extent, the growth of Brazilian government responsibility was simply due to the inability of the private sector to make profits because of anti-inflationary price controls. This was particularly true of public utilities.

Some governments with a rather strong preference for private enterprise have started up state plants and then sold them. This happened in Argentina, Chile and Pakistan. The Philippine government also tried hard to sell its enterprises, but had difficulty in finding buyers. Taiwan distributed shares in government enterprises taken from the Japanese as part compensation in its land reforms.

There does not seem to be any inherent dilemma[1] in running a mixed economy with both a large public and private sector, if the relation of the two parts is complementary. In Brazil and Mexico, there has been a close symbiosis between private and public activity in terms of finance, technical co-operation, transfer of managerial personnel, and joint planning of investments. In India, on the other hand, the sharp segregation of the two sectors has been harmful. The government prevented private industrialists (both home and foreign) from expanding in fields in which its own technical and managerial resources were stretched to the limit. This mixed system has therefore been more harmful to efficiency than the fully fledged state enterprise of Egypt or Yugoslavia.

Efficiency within state enterprise varies a great deal. In Brazil and Mexico firms have been free to respond to market forces in more or less the same ways as private enterprise, and as the management has been well paid it has generally been competent. In Argentina and Turkey, state enterprise was subject to bureaucratic constraints particularly on pricing policy, and had to employ excessive numbers of workers. In Ghana, government plants had a

[1] Raymond Vernon sees such a problem in Mexico, see his *Dilemma of Mexico's Development*, Harvard, 1963, but we did not find his case very convincing, nor does Mexico seem to have run into the problems which he forecast.

very poor record because of the great shortage of local skills. Instead of seeking partnership agreements with foreign firms, the government gave them turnkey contracts to build plants, or management contracts to run them. As the foreign firms had no financial interest in the success of these ventures, several of them have been disastrous failures.

The record of state enterprise has been most closely scrutinized in India. In the state steel plants the top managerial positions went to civil servants without industrial experience. Middle management was not able to take 'decisions about promotions and dismissals, spare parts and replacements, and a number of other matters, some extraordinarily trivial, were often delayed. The plants' financial advisors have been especially difficult obstacles to day-to-day decision making and, in some instances, have even vetoed decisions by their nominal supervisors, the general managers. Adding to the difficulties created by this system was the seeming inability of the plants' administrative offices to make any of the decisions referred to them. The general manager and his subordinates frequently had a distinguished record with a state or central ministry. Often the general manager was nearing retirement or was brought out of retirement to manage the plant. Thus, Rourkela has had seven general managers in about as many years; Bhilai and Durgapur have each had four. Some plant officials have regarded their tenure at the plant as way stations in their careers not to be tarnished by a wrong decision.'[1]

In spite of the weakness of management in the state sector and serious delays in the planned schedule of operations, India expanded its steel industry very quickly from 1956 onwards, and the length of time involved in getting new plants working at normal capacity was no longer than has been the case in some other countries. In Brazil, it took six years to get Volta Redonda into operation and there were long delays and escalating costs in starting the Cosipa plant. The major drawback of the Indian policy of relying entirely on the state sector for new developments is that it wasted opportunities which existed in the private sector. It would have been cheaper to expand existing capacity than to create as many as three completely new plants. It took about four decades before the Tata Company was able to Indianize its top management completely, and it was obviously unwise not to use these talents more fully. If it had not been for official controls, the private sector would have expanded

[1] W. A. Johnson, *The Steel Industry of India*, Harvard, 1966.

capacity to some extent from the early 1950s onwards, but it was only in the 1960s, when it was apparent that the official plan targets would not be met, that the private sector was allowed to expand. The same is also true of the fertilizer industry. Government progress with fertilizers was slow, at a time when foreign investors were being discouraged from investment in this industry.

PRIVATE SECTOR

Most governments have done a lot to help private industry, even though the stimuli were sometimes inadvertent. There was no scarcity of entrepreneurship when adequate profit opportunities were created. In Pakistan, industry had to start more or less from scratch and although Muslims in pre-partition India had very rarely been industrialists, the supply of successful Pakistani entrepreneurs proved surprisingly large.[1]

There are four main ways in which governments helped the private sector.

(*a*) Protection of the home market against imports enabled local industry to charge high prices. The economic impact of this was the same as a massive subsidy, which was borne by consumers and not by government;

(*b*) Direct financial help mainly in the form of subsidized credit from development banks;

(*c*) 'Decolonialization' of foreign private investment helped the entry of local entrepreneurs into many lines of business, but the check to new foreign investment created some technical problems;

(*d*) Governments have given some technical support to private industry, but, in most countries, industrial research and training have been neglected.

We can now analyse each of these lines of policy towards the private sector in more detail.

a. *Protection*

Several instruments have been used to restrict imports or to raise their price. These include quantitative restrictions, customs tariffs and multiple exchange rates. The crudest instrument is quantitative restrictions, both in terms of its impact on industrial efficiency and government revenue.

Import controls can be a useful temporary instrument in times of

[1] See G. F. Papanek, *Pakistan's Development: Social Goals and Private Incentives*, Harvard, 1967, for the evidence.

balance of payments crisis, but as a permanent means of protecting domestic industry they have distinct dangers. If imports are prohibited there is no competition for the domestic producer, who can charge a price which gives him exorbitant profits. If imports are licensed, the people who get them have a special privilege and profit opportunity without paying for it. They tend to be the old-established producers. The procedure keeps out new firms and restrains dynamic ones. This difficulty can be removed by selling import licences, but this is not usually done. Brazil is the only country to have auctioned licences on a large scale (from 1953 to 1957, after having allocated them without charge from 1947 to 1953). The two countries which have relied most consistently on import controls are India and Mexico. Mexico succeeded in applying a flexible policy largely because of the power of the government relative to business interests. It imposed price controls on the domestic market, and occasionally forced prices down by threats to reduce trade barriers.[1] An import licence decision usually takes a month, whereas in India it may take more than a year. Furthermore, Mexico has a convertible currency and a realistic exchange rate, so the system works reasonably well.

In India, some alleged import-substitutes have had a higher *foreign exchange* cost than the imports they replaced. A detailed study of the cost of producing Cummins Diesel engines illustrates the point. In the first year of production the cost of engines produced in India was $7,300 as compared with an import price (ex duty) of $4,549. But the import content of the Indian product (allowing for the cost of foreign technicians working in India) was higher than the cost of importing the final product. Furthermore, there did not seem any prospect of net foreign exchange savings for several years.[2] It is not clear how often this has happened but it is not an isolated case. Fortunately, India eased a good many of her import restrictions after devaluing in 1966, just as Pakistan did earlier. Nevertheless, they are still applied on a fairly large scale.

In theory, tariffs are a better instrument of protection than

[1] For a description of Mexican policy in this field, see R. Izquierdo, 'Protectionism in Mexico', in R. Vernon, ed., *Public Policy and Private Enterprise in Mexico*, Harvard, 1964. As evidence of the move towards more selective policies, Izquierdo quotes a presidential report of 1961: 'It was decided to reduce tariffs and abolish import controls in the case of certain industrial products and basic raw materials whose local prices were manifestly and unjustifiably higher than the international prices.'

[2] See J. Baranson, *Manufacturing Problems in India*, Syracuse, 1967, p. 83.

licensing because they fix an explicit upper limit on the price the domestic producer can charge. They also give him a greater certainty about the duration and extent of protection than he has with quantitative restrictions and they provide the government with revenue. For these reasons Brazil started to use tariffs as the main instrument of protection in 1957, and abandoned quantitative restrictions.

Tariffs normally require legislation, whereas quantitative restrictions can be imposed by administrative action where there are fewer checks on mistakes or corruption and where there may be less consideration of consumer interests. But tariff-fixing procedure varies a good deal from country to country. In India and Pakistan there are tariff boards, which have public hearings and publish evidence for their decisions. They are taken in articulate fashion, even though they may be wrong or be nullified by the influence of quantitative restrictions. In Brazil, the Commission on Tariff Policy (CPA) represents industry, trade unions, importers and government, but not consumers. Its hearings are private, and although some of its material is available to interested parties in mimeographed form, the evidence is often not available, or indeed, ever written down. In Argentina, the tariff fixing procedure is almost entirely hidden from public surveillance. This is also the situation in Mexico.[1]

In practice, therefore, tariffs have almost invariably been an *ad hoc* response to pressures from the private sector. For big industrialization schemes financed by government, there is usually some strategic consideration of comparative advantage, but this is not the case for the private sector. Thus in Brazil, the guideline for protection to private industry is the Law of Similars, which gives tariff protection to a private industry if it can prove its physical capacity to produce a product similar to that being imported. Often protection was given without any close consideration of the costs of the local product, and there seems to be no case where a tariff commission has been given general guidance as to the size of the cost differential it should permit.

Measurement of tariff incidence is usually carried out by calculating the difference which the tariff makes to the domestic price of the final product which is produced as an import substitute. Recently, Professors H. G. Johnson and B. Balassa have emphasized the need to calculate the incidence of protection in relation to the

[1] See R. Izquierdo, in R. Vernon, *op. cit.*, p. 253.

'value added' by domestic industry.[1] If half of a manufacturer's final product represents the costs of materials he has purchased from other sectors of the economy, the 'value added' will be only half of the value of the final product. In this case a 30 per cent tariff on the final product would represent 60 per cent protection on value added, if there are no tariffs on the materials used as inputs in the industry. If there were a 30 per cent tariff on all the inputs, the tariff on value added would be the same as on the final product, but if the tariff is higher on the inputs than on the final products, the protection on the value added will be lower than on the final product, and may even be negative.[2] In order to calculate 'effective' tariff incidence, a detailed knowledge of the cost structure of industry is required, which

Table VI–4

Comparison of Tariff on Final Product and on Value Added in Brazil in 1966

	Percentage tariff on final product (nominal tariff)	Percentage tariff on value added (effective tariff)
Diesel engines	30	−35
Bulldozers	10	−28
Refrigerators	220	360
Television sets	200	299
Radios	200	298
Automobile tyres	100	82
Automobile batteries	120	168
Electric fans	220	373
Cotton shirts	220	276
Woollen yarn	220	679
Cotton dresses	220	226

Source: J. Bergsman, *The Structure of Protection in Brazil*, EPEA, Rio de Janeiro, November 1967 (mimeographed).

[1] See B. Balassa, 'Tariff Protection in Industrial Countries: An Evaluation', *Journal of Political Economy*, December, 1965, and H. G. Johnson, *US Economic Policies Towards the Less Developed Countries*, Brookings, Washington DC, 1966. The concept of effective protection was brought into economic literature in 1955 by C. L. Barber, 'Canadian Tariff Policy', *Canadian Journal of Economics and Political Science*, November 1955.

[2] The costs of an industry may also be raised by an obligation to use a fixed proportion of a high cost domestic product which may not be protected by a tariff, e.g. the obligation on the Brazilian steel industry to take a quarter of its coal requirements from high-cost local producers.

governments have never had available in the past when fixing tariffs. However, information is available to make it clear that there can be very wide differences between the effective and nominal tariff incidence. This is illustrated in Table VI–4, for Brazil. These very wide differences in the effective incidence of protection were not envisaged by those who created the tariffs on the final products, and it can be seen that in some fields tariff protection has been carried to absurd lengths. The highest nominal tariff is 220 per cent, but the highest effective rate is 680 per cent. In Brazil some industries were able to get protection of 300 per cent or more, whereas others were injured by negative protection, i.e. tariffs on their inputs much higher than on the final product. The most highly protected sector in Brazil has been the textile industry, which has been so sheltered that its competitiveness has declined greatly from the early post-war years when it was a significant exporter. It is clear therefore that tariffs can have a highly distorting effect on resource allocation.

Table VI–5 shows an unweighted average of Latin American tariffs on 125 industrial products. The protection ranges from 34 to

Table VI–5

Average Nominal Per cent Tariff and Other Charges on Imports of 125 Representative Items

Argentina	131	Mexico	61
Brazil	168	Peru	34
Chile	138	Average of above	107
Colombia	112	European Common Market	13

Source: S. Macario, 'Protectionism and Industrialization in Latin America', *Economic Bulletin for Latin America*, Santiago, March 1964, p. 75.

168 per cent and the average is 107 per cent as compared with 13 per cent in the European Common Market countries, and was further bolstered by quantitative restrictions and multiple exchange rates. Although protectionism has a longer history in Latin America than in Asia, it would seem that tariff rates in India and Pakistan are now near to Latin American levels.[1] This is also true of Egypt, where the

[1] Calculations of 'effective' tariff incidence for Pakistan show protection which varies from −27 per cent for grain milling to 311 per cent for canning and preserving. See R. Soligo and J. J. Stern, 'Tariff Protection Import Substitution and Investment Efficiency', *Pakistan Development Review*, Summer, 1965.

effective incidence of tariffs has increased greatly since the 1950s.[1] The evidence suggests that tariffs in developing countries may well be ten times as high as in the Common Market or USA!

Many countries need a complete overhaul of their tariff so that it can be used as a more efficient method of protection. Given the difficulty of getting up-to-date information on cost structures, it would seem desirable to have a fairly uniform rate of protection, no higher than 50 per cent, because an industry which cannot survive without more than this is unlikely ever to be competitive. If higher margins are exceptionally and temporarily required, they should be met by government subsidy. Both Pakistan and Brazil made unilateral reductions in tariffs in the mid-1960s, after realizing the harm that they did to their industrial efficiency. In Brazil the 1967 cut was very large indeed. Bergsman estimates that the cuts reduced protection on his sample of 200 products from 107 to 38 per cent. As a result there was no enormous increase in imports but an immediate increase in competition and a lowering in prices in certain industries, particularly automobiles. Spain and Yugoslavia had a similar experience earlier when they reduced tariffs in the course of their stabilization programmes.

b. *Financial Aid*

Governments have stimulated private industrial development by providing financial help. This has sometimes been done by subsidies and tax privileges or preferential margins to local manufacturers bidding for government contracts. Privileges of this kind were important in Mexico and Taiwan, but in most countries the major direct government financial contribution to the private sector has been through Development Banks. These special government banks provide medium- and long-term credit to promising lines of industry, help support local entrepreneurs, and often give technical help or advice on marketing. Given the weakness of capital markets, they perform a particularly useful function. Often they provide government funds at subsidized interest rates, and many of them help to mobilize private capital through bond issues. Some of them have set up joint ventures with domestic and foreign private enterprise. These institutions are particularly important in Latin America,

1 See B. Hansen and G. A. Marzouk, *Development and Economic Policy in the UAR (Egypt)*, North-Holland, Amsterdam, 1965, p. 152, which gives a crude impression of the change by relating import duties to non-essential imports. The ratio rose from 70 per cent in 1952 to 114 per cent in 1961.

Table VI–6

Leading Industrial Development Banks

	Title	Date operations started	Net worth in 1963–66 $ million
Argentina	Banco Industrial de la Republica Argentina	1944	394
Brazil	Banco Nacional de Desenvolvimento Economico	1952	304
Ceylon	Agricultural and Industrial Credit Corporation	1943	7
Chile	Corporacion de Fomento de la Produccion	1940	611
Colombia	Caja de Credito Agrario, Industrial y Minero	1932	244
Egypt	Industrial Bank (UAR)	1949	34
Ghana	National Investment Bank	1963	11
Greece	Hellenic Industrial Development Bank	1964	229
India	Industrial Finance Corporation of India	1948	201
Israel	Industrial Development Bank	1957	206
Malaya	Malaysian Industrial Development Finance Ltd.	1960	15
Mexico	Nacional Financiera	1934	1,262
Nigeria	Western Nigeria Development Corporation	1963	42
Pakistan	Industrial Development Bank of Pakistan	1961	177
Peru	Banco Industrial del Peru	1936	71
Philippines	Development Bank of the Philippines	1947	310
South Korea	Korean Reconstruction Bank	1954	141
Spain	Banco de Credito Industrial	1920	317
Taiwan	China Development Corporation	1959	22
Thailand	Industrial Finance Corporation of Thailand	1959	4
Turkey	State Investment Bank	1964	342
Venezuela	Corporacion Venezolana de Fomento	1946	470
Yugoslavia	Yugoslavenska Investiciona Banka	1956	2,761

Source: N. D. Nyhart and E. F. Janssens, *A Global Directory of Development Finance Institutions in Developing Countries*, OECD Development Centre, Paris, 1967.

where they have been operating since the 1930s and have experienced and capable staffs. The biggest ones are the Nacional Financiera in Mexico, the CORFO in Chile and the Venezuelan Corporacion de Fomento. In Argentina and Chile their activity has declined in recent years. In Mexico, Nacional Financiera had financial interests of some sort in 533 business enterprises in 1961.[1] Its assets are about $1·3 billion. Banks of this type have also been important in Israel, Spain and Turkey. In Asian countries, where industry is less developed and where greater emphasis has been placed on the state sector, these banks have generally played a minor role, though Pakistan and the Philippines are exceptions. Table VI–6 lists the biggest institution in each country, but some countries have several important development banks. In Mexico there are many government *financieras*, and the central bank itself operates as a development agency. In Brazil there are powerful financial agencies for regional development, such as SUDENE for the north-east. In Venezuela there is an important agency to finance development in Guyana province, where immense investments have been made to provide an infrastructure for industry. Apart from these special banks, governments often own a large part of the commercial banking sector (over a third in Brazil and Argentina) and these have also provided finance on favourable terms for industrialization. In Mexico the government has issued instructions to *financieras*, banks and insurance companies, specifying where they should invest a certain portion of their funds, and several other countries have also issued directives of this kind.

The general price policy of governments has tended to favour industry. Food prices have been kept down to hold wages in check. Publicly owned utilities such as electricity have often sold their services at cheap rates. In India, the government has provided the private sector with steel at artificially low prices.

c. *Decolonializing Foreign Investment*

Foreign private investment can be of great help in providing finance, transferring technology, and filling gaps in management. But many countries have been chary of encouraging it because of the undesirable features it used to have in the colonial period.[2] By keeping out foreign investors they created technical bottlenecks, but thought it

[1] See R. Vernon, ed., *Public Policy and Private Enterprise in Mexico*, Harvard, 1964, p. 194.

[2] These are described in detail in Chapter VIII.

was worth doing in order to help local entrepreneurs, and wean foreigners away from colonial habits. Exchange control has forced foreign banks to concentrate their lending on domestic projects, and the pre-war dominance of these institutions, particularly in ex-colonies, has been reduced by government legislation to promote local banking. These policies were popular with local industry. Government policy in restricting foreign investors received little criticism from Indian industry, whereas the Brazilian policy of welcoming them after 1955 met vociferous criticism from local business interests.

In most countries which were colonies, the phase of decolonialization was necessary. But once the exploitative elements have been removed, some foreign investment becomes vital for technical progress. Therefore most countries have shown a characteristic cycle in their attitude to foreign capital, first hostile then welcoming.

In this respect, the earlier switch in attitudes towards foreign capital in Latin America than in Asia did not represent greater enlightenment, but simply a different historical phasing of the same problem. Mexico was one of the countries most violently opposed to foreign capital in pre-war years, but settled its debts amicably in wartime and has cultivated foreign capital since 1945. In Brazil and Argentina, policies favouring foreign capital date from 1955. As a result these three countries have received more foreign private investment in industry than the whole of Asia.

As foreigners only invest in lines which are likely to be highly profitable, the main point in attracting direct investment is not its financial contribution but the technical help and training which it provides. The process needs to be vetted, and governments have to ensure that foreign companies train local personnel. Such supervision has probably been most successfully developed in Mexico, where Nacional Financiera and the Bank of Mexico actively seek out foreign partners for joint ventures in novel fields, ensure a fairly rapid Mexicanization of top level posts, and prevent foreign entry into fields where local firms have adequate capacity.

d. *Training and Technical help to Industry*

The rapid growth in demand for technical, managerial and supervisory skills imposed constraints on industrial development in some countries. In Israel and Taiwan skills were available in abundance because of large-scale immigration of experienced and trained people. Some other countries like Venezuela and Brazil[1] also attracted well-trained immigrants. But India, Pakistan and Ghana had to pay foreigners high salaries to fill the skill gap or suffered from inefficiency. To some extent these countries suffer from neo-colonial emphasis on formal educational requirements, have little upgrading or mobility, and do not have adequate pay differentials for skills. In the long run, improvements in formal education can ease the problem, but government policy can also do a great deal to help promote practical training. Brazil is a country with a very poor educational system, which was forced at an early stage of its industrialization to improve practical training facilities. The problem was tackled by the creation of an apprenticeship programme in São Paulo in 1941 which has since grown to cover the whole country. This industrial apprenticeship service (SENAI) was financed by a compulsory 1 per cent levy on the payrolls of industrial firms which was collected by the tax authorities. Rebates were made to firms which provided training in their own plants, and the scheme provided firms with training personnel when required. At the beginning of the system much of the training was done in special schools, but the trainees were on the payroll of the firms and their training was geared specifically to the jobs they had. The schools are well-enough financed to buy the latest machinery, and in São Paulo the value of machinery per pupil is about $3,000. The system is now more heavily geared to in-plant training. Some of the more technically advanced industries in Brazil spend up to 2 per cent of their payroll on training programmes. In São Paulo, about two-thirds of juveniles in industry are involved in SENAI training programmes or schools. The proportion in other states of Brazil is lower than this and the programme is weak in the underdeveloped north-east. The Brazilian system of industrial training has already served as a model for Peru and Colombia and could well be emulated elsewhere. Egypt is another country which has built up its apprenticeship system rapidly from three centres with eighty apprentices in 1957 to thirty-five centres with 5,000 apprentices in 1965. She had considerable technical assistance from Germany in building up this system.

In India and Pakistan, training schemes are more badly needed than

[1] See N. H. Leff, *The Brazilian Capital Goods Industry 1929–1964*, Harvard, 1968, p. 52: 'During the years 1924–62, some two million people emigrated from Europe, Japan and Mediterranean countries to Brazil. Most of the immigrants were better educated, more skilled and had more industrial experience than the average Brazilian worker.'

in most other countries because of the low level of basic education. But both countries have followed the old British pattern of industrial apprenticeship, where there is only a formal legal obligation to provide training to juveniles. In Pakistan, the proportion of apprentices who get properly supervised training is under 1 per cent of the industrial labour force, and is largely confined to railway workshops. Left to themselves, individual entrepreneurs will seldom spend enough on training, because they cannot be sure that the people they train will continue to work for them, but if all employers are subject to a training levy with rebates for training performed in the plant, their attitudes change.

In many countries, the existing stock of skills is misused or incentives to acquire scarce skills are weak because the salary structure is not geared to the needs of the economy. It may still represent priorities established under colonial rule, or reflect distortions due to inflation. It is usually particularly inadequate in attracting people to acquire middle-level skills. In some jobs, there is an unnecessarily restrictive emphasis on formal qualifications, when intelligence and short vocational courses will equip people adequately.

In Mexico there has been outstanding success in creating an efficient technocratic cadre of people to run government economic agencies, as well as industrial plants in the private sector. In spite of the proximity to the United States, there is very little emigration of skilled people. The reason for this is that the government was willing to pay high salaries to technically trained people such as economists or engineers, either directly, or through the subterfuge of multiple jobs, some of which are sinecures. Income tax is also very low, so that in most professions where the supply of skills is scarce, money incomes are as high as in the USA, and real incomes are higher because of the lower cost of living. The government has also been generous with grants for special graduate training. Between 1940 and 1960, the Bank of Mexico provided 600 fellowships for economists and engineers to do graduate work in the United States.

There is very little industrial research in developing countries and most of the technology used in industry is taken directly from that of the developed world. In many cases the countries are too small for industrial research to have any significant pay-off, and attempts to devise labour intensive technologies, even in big countries like communist China, have had little success. In spite of this there is considerable scope for useful industrial research. One obvious field is mineral prospecting and survey, but there is also need for research into new processing techniques for local raw materials and design of products suitable for low income consumers. In this respect, Mexico and Brazil have done more than other countries. The Institute for Technological Research at the São Paulo Polytechnical School has played an important role in Brazil since the 1920s. In Mexico the Institute of Industrial Research at Monterrey, and the Instituto Mexicano de Investigaciones Tecnologicas in Mexico City have developed techniques for using sugar waste in paper making, produced improvements in Mexican glassware, devised methods for using Mexican cereals in US baby foods, and a wide variety of other processes and patents. In countries where firms in the private sector are too small to support research on an economic basis, publicly supported institutes can play a valuable role. In most countries there is no real effort to ensure that research is oriented to the needs of economic development. In Greece, for instance, half the research expenditure of the country goes to the Demokritos Atomic Centre which was set up with help from AID and the International Atomic Energy Agency. The Centre is too small to make a significant contribution to knowledge in its field, and the resources involved could more profitably have been used elsewhere. In many other countries, the research pattern is equally irrational in terms of its contribution to economic growth.

Governments can also help industrial development by carrying out feasibility studies and pre-investment surveys. Mexico has done this in the Bank of Mexico and Nacional Financiera. These agencies have large staffs of economists and engineers, and have carried out feasibility and pre-investment studies for a wide variety of industrial projects. For the steel industry, for instance, they carried out a detailed investigation of likely production costs for a new plant in eighteen alternative locations, using a very detailed breakdown of the cost of inputs and transport costs to different markets. This kind of detailed pre-investment survey or cost-benefit analysis is essential for efficient planning. Apart from Mexico, the only other place in which it has been adequately developed is in Brazil, where 'executive groups' of technicians have prepared detailed operational plans for industrial expansion since the mid-1950s.

In industry, there is less of a problem of diffusing new knowledge about technology than there is in agriculture where the production units are much smaller and more scattered and producers are less well educated. Nevertheless, some governments have found it useful to create Productivity Centres for managerial and supervisory training and technical assistance to small firms. They have been particularly active in Taiwan and Mexico. It is also useful for governments to promote university education in management and to alert universities to the research problems of industry. Most governments have done rather little in this respect.

THE EFFICIENCY OF INDUSTRIALIZATION

Industrialization has been the major element in the development strategy of most countries. The concentration on industry is justified in terms of the structure of demand, and the previous backwardness of these economies was most marked in this sector. But resource allocation within industry has been inefficient and future growth could be accelerated by pressures to rectify this.

The major problems are as follows:

(*a*) Could the choice of technology be improved? Should more emphasis be given to labour intensive or small-scale industry?

(*b*) Could the product mix be improved? Has the pattern of expansion been rational? Was there a correct balance between consumer goods, consumer durables and capital goods?

(*c*) Has the degree of international specialization been appropriate? Has import substitution been carried too far? Could greater success have have been obtained in increasing exports?

(*d*) Could greater competition stimulate efficiency?

Finally, we would like to get some rough idea of how much gain in future growth rates could be obtained by eliminating present inefficiencies. Is the order of magnitude significant?

a. *Choice of Technology*

The most remarkable thing about manufacturing productivity in developing countries is that it is generally so high. The average productivity level in the twenty-two countries is about 60 per cent of that in the United Kingdom. Productivity is still low in Ceylon, Ghana, India, Pakistan and Thailand, but in these countries most industrial labour is still employed in handicrafts.

Productivity is high because of the nature of technology. Most modern techniques were developed in countries where wages are high. Consequently this technology does not provide as much employment as is desirable in countries where labour is plentiful. Often there is little effective choice about ways of producing a given item. Old labour-intensive techniques may be so inefficient that they require more capital per unit of output than modern machinery.

Table VI–7

Levels of Output Per Man in Manufacturing in 1965

$ at US 1965 relative prices

Argentina	3,157	Spain	3,984
Brazil	2,630	Taiwan	2,589
Ceylon	284	Thailand	464
Chile	4,233	Turkey	1,208
Colombia	1,588	Venezuela	6,254
Egypt	1,593	Yugoslavia	4,148
Ghana	295		
Greece	2,893	Average	2,289
India	437		
Israel	3,911		
Malaya	4,496	France	6,261
Mexico	2,380	Germany (FR)	4,938
Pakistan	590	Italy	4,916
Peru	1,430	Japan	4,359
Philippines	935	UK	3,762
South Korea	849	USA	10,182

Source: M. Shinohara, *Japan's Industrial Level in International Perspective*, Ministry of Foreign Affairs, Tokyo, 1966; UN *Monthly Bulletin of Statistics*, New York, *The National Income and Product Accounts of the United States* 1929–1965, Survey of Current Business, Washington DC, 1966 for the calculation of real output levels. Employment from *Yearbooks of Labour Statistics*, ILO, Geneva, and national sources.

However, except for India,[1] most countries have not even tried to develop a labour-intensive technology. Governments have generally *fostered* the use of capital-intensive techniques. Capital goods have been given favourable tariff treatment. Licenses have been allocated on a priority basis to importers of capital equipment. If there is a multiple exchange rate system importers of capital goods normally receive favourable rates. Rates of interest have been kept artificially low.

These influences have probably not had a big effect on the technology adopted but they have been leaning in the wrong direction.

[1] Indian efforts to encourage small-scale labour-intensive industries were not successful. See P. N. Dhar and A. F. Lydall, *The Role of Small Enterprise in Indian Manufacturing*, Asia Publishing House, Bombay, 1961. They were concentrated on hand spinning and weaving of cotton textiles, which turned out to be of low quality and high cost. However, the Indian purpose was not simply to find the most suitable labour-intensive technology, but was a politically-inspired attempt to carry out Gandhi's ideals of self-sufficient village life.

In order to adapt technology to a situation where capital is scarce and labour is cheap, governments should:

(*a*) follow price policies which value labour, capital and imports at something like their true cost to the economy;

(*b*) stimulate applied industrial research designed to produce labour-intensive technologies;

(*c*) stimulate the domestic production of simpler types of capital goods;

(*d*) promote the use of second-hand equipment. The Greek shipping industry is one of the world's biggest and works extensively with second-hand ships. Mexico started her steel industry with old US equipment, and recently bought US military surplus supplies to construct a shipyard. Brazil has also made extensive use of old equipment.[1] Unfortunately, these seem to be isolated examples, and some countries such as India and Pakistan have even prohibited the import of used equipment;

(*e*) promote intensive use of equipment through shift-working. This is done in Hong Kong and should be generally feasible in surplus labour conditions, but it is not clear whether this practice is, in fact, more widespread in developing than in developed countries.

b. *The Product Mix*

In the mid-1950s, when the second Indian five year plan appeared (for 1955–60), it gave priority to the development of heavy industry, capital goods and steel, at the expense of consumer goods and agriculture. This emphasis was continued in the third five year plan. The second plan was prepared under the influence of Professor Mahalanobis who had put forward a model based on the same kind of strategy as that adopted by Soviet planners in the Stalin epoch. Mahalanobis like other people influential in Indian plan-making at that time, was a physical scientist, not an economist, and his rationale for the choice of strategy was hardly couched in economic terms.

Mahalanobis' model was based on the assumption that the rate of

[1] See N. H. Leff, *The Brazilian Capital Goods Industry 1929–1964*, Harvard, 1968, p. 26: 'All the [capital goods] sector's foreign firms have made extensive use of used equipment which would otherwise have been scrapped as economically obsolete in their home-country plants. Such equipment available to the firm at an opportunity cost little higher than its scrap value may still have a useful economic life in the conditions of a less-developed economy. For example, equipment that has been scrapped for machinery of greater capital-intensity or larger optimal scale may be economic because of different relative factor prices or a smaller market size.'

capital formation in the economy is entirely dependent on the domestic production of capital goods. He assumed there would be no increase in exports and that normal export earnings would be earmarked for needs other than capital goods. Therefore a high rate of expansion in domestic production of capital goods was necessary to raise the rate of investment. His neglect of foreign trade reflected a political desire to be independent of the outside world as well as pessimisim about foreign markets.[1]

Neither the Mahalanobis model nor the plan itself gave an adequate explanation for the strategy in terms of likely demand patterns, and, in fact, it turned out that an important part of steel capacity was more suitable for making consumer goods than capital equipment.[2] Nor was there any overt discussion of India's comparative cost situation in the products to which such emphasis was given. The plan underestimated the capacity of the economy to create new manufactured exports and to carry out import substitution for manufactured consumer goods and food. It was largely in physical rather than economic terms, and, as the allocation of resources in many sectors of basic industry was based on rationing rather than the price mechanism, it would have been difficult, in any case, to produce convincing cost evidence.

In fact, the performance of the economy was in the planned direction. Dependence on imports of investment goods was reduced from 51 per cent to 21 per cent from 1955 to 1965.[3] However, the concentration of public-sector investment on steel and heavy industry retarded the growth of the Indian economy. The gestation period for these projects was longer than was expected, and there were technical and managerial problems in running the more com-

1 Mahalanobis' argument that India should aim to be independent of capital goods imports does not make sense as an absolute goal, but given the experience of two world wars, two closures of the Suez Canal and temporary restrictions on arms shipments, one could make a reasonably good case for a higher degree of independence than India enjoyed in 1955. It would have been no weaker than the European case for investments in coal or in oil exploration to lessen dependence on Middle East oil.

2 A third of the output of the government steel plant at Rourkela is high-grade sheets of a type suitable for making consumer durables such as refrigerators. This steel has been sold at low prices and has led to a private-sector boom in consumer durables. This is hardly a top priority use of resources in a country at Indian income levels.

3 See J. Ahmad, 'Import Substitution and Structural Change in Indian Manufacturing Industry 1950–1966', *The Journal of Development Studies*, April 1968.

plex industries which had not been foreseen. As a result the production targets for steel and heavy industry were not fulfilled, and scarcity of foreign exchange prevented some of the capacity from being fully utilized. There is little doubt that Indian growth would have been faster if more emphasis had been placed on agriculture, on consumer goods and on light manufactures for export.

Several Latin American countries, including Argentina, Brazil, and Mexico, have also built up a substantial steel industry and capital goods sector, but none of them gave heavy industry quite as high a priority as in India, and none of them has experienced such great technical difficulties as India which developed its three new steel mills simultaneously.

There have been one or two widely publicized follies, such as the small steel mill at Helwan in Egypt, but only eight of our countries have a steel output exceeding half a million tons a year, and in most of these cases natural resource endowment and size of local markets

Table VI–8

Steel Output in Developing Countries in 1967

million metric tons

Argentina	1·3	Mexico	3·0
Brazil	3·7	Spain	4·3
Chile	0·6	Turkey	1·0
India	6·4	Yugoslavia	1·8

Source: *Monthly Bulletin of Statistics*, UN, New York.

justify steel industries of this size. There is no more reason to doubt the long run rationale of their steel investment than there is for that of the USA in the 1950s and 1960s, some of which was technically obsolete and in a poor position to compete with imports.

Only a few developing countries make capital goods on any scale (Argentina, Brazil, India, Mexico, Spain and Yugoslavia) and generally they are rather efficient industries, because except in India and Argentina, they have been built up without protection. Some capital goods industries require small production runs and are rather labour-intensive, so they are quite suitable for manufacture in developing countries. Their products are built to individual specification rather than being mass-produced. Development of indigenous capital goods is also helpful because their design will tend to take some account of local labour costs and may help evolve a technology suitable for low-wage economies. Brazilian experience has shown that capital goods production can be profitably expanded without protection, and can successfully compete with imports on both price and quality.[1] Brazil has been more successful than India because it has a longer tradition of technical education and research, it has been helped by large-scale immigration of technically skilled people, since 1955 it has made extensive use of foreign direct investment, and it has generally promoted competitive conditions in the industry. There was no attempt to monopolize it for the public sector, and no protection until 1962. A recent careful study for Mexico has shown that it is also ripe for a substantial expansion of capital goods production on an economic basis.[2] Pakistan also intends to build up its steel and capital goods production, so that import dependence will be reduced from 75 per cent in 1969 to 50 per cent in 1975.[3] This is a more modest goal than India set itself in the 1950s, and it may well be that the lessons of Indian experience will enable Pakistan to expand in this area with fewer difficulties than India experienced.

More questionable than investment in steel has been the wisdom of concentrating prematurely on automobile production. In the developing world as a whole, twenty-six countries either make or assemble cars, and their total output is about 1 million automobiles. These are made by 200 firms, i.e. an average output of 5,000 a firm. When cars are simply assembled from imported knocked-down

[1] See N. H. Leff, *The Brazilian Capital Goods Industry*, Harvard, 1968. The Brazilian capital goods industry has a rather long history, and already supplied 61 per cent of domestic requirements by 1947–49. By 1965, it supplied 75 per cent of local demand. This in spite of the fact that 'In the years 1945–62, most equipment imports entered Brazil without tariff or other import restrictions, and indeed under a preferential exchange rate'. The most competitive firms in Brazil appear to be the local rather than the foreign ones.

[2] See A. S. Manne, 'Key Sectors of the Mexican Economy, 1962–72', in I. Adelman and E. Thorbeke, *The Theory and Design of Economic Development*, John Hopkins, 1966. By careful 'process analysis', Professor Manne decided that the Mexican market by 1972 could support nine out of twelve new capital goods industries which Nacional Financiera was considering and that this could be done without protection and produce a 15 per cent return on capital. The industries included as feasible were internal-combustion engines, tractors, mining and construction machinery, metal-working machinery, jigs, elevators, cranes, conveyors, power-transmission equipment, welding machinery and a variety of special products. The excluded items were turbines and generators, ships and locomotives.

[3] See *Socio-Economic Objectives of the Fourth Five Year Plan*, Planning Commission, Islamabad, November 1968.

parts, this does not have a great effect on production costs, but domestic production of cars requires quite large-scale output to be economic. The countries which have gone furthest with domestic production of parts have been Argentina, Brazil and Mexico. All these are big countries with a relatively prosperous urban bourgeoisie, and were obviously getting near to a situation where car production could be economic. This would have been the case if they had followed either the recent Soviet or Canadian model. The USSR is concentrating production in one big plant. Canada has gone in for specialized production in co-operation with the USA, and has removed tariffs under the Canada-US free trade agreement. Mexico could have followed the Canadian example, and Argentina and Brazil might either have co-operated or followed the Soviet model. Neither of these courses was followed. Instead, they created many different firms (thirteen) in Argentina, eleven in Brazil and twelve in Mexico) and a large number of models, none of which has an adequate production run. The high level of protection has permitted most of them to stay in business and as yet there have been few of the amalgamations which have characterized the recent evolution of the European industry.

In Brazil, 98 per cent of the components are now produced locally. This is a higher percentage than is the case in Western Europe, or indeed in the United States, since it made the free trade agreement with Canada. The Scania-Vabis truck plant in Brazil is more Brazilianized than the home plant company in Sweden which has a larger scale of production. As a result Brazilian automobiles cost about two-thirds more[1] (after eliminating turnover tax) than do cars produced in Europe or the USA. The most economical production line is in Volkswagen, which has half of the Brazilian market. One reason why there has been little concern about high costs is that a good deal of the investment in the industry was supplied by foreign companies. But nevertheless there are also large Brazilian resources in the industry and the high prices enable foreigners to make a profit. In 1967, competition and efficiency in the industry were greatly strengthened by the lowering of the Brazilian tariff and the abolition of import quotas. The tariff is still high, but nevertheless

[1] See N. H. Leff, *The Brazilian Capital Goods Industry*, Harvard, 1968. It has been shown by Leff that in Brazilian market conditions, the costs of local production rise steeply when the national integration quota is pushed above 80 per cent. In a smaller market, such as Chile, the rise in costs obviously accelerates at a much lower level of national integration.

the possibility of imports forced down domestic prices, and may eventually lead to some rationalization of existing production. One possible justification of the multi-plant approach is that it probably builds up local technical skills more quickly than the single plant approach and many of the foreign firms have done a great deal in this respect.

One of the worst cases of uneconomic automobile production has been in Chile, where import of fully assembled automobiles was prohibited in order to foster domestic production. Firms wishing to enter the industry were forced to locate their plants at Arica, 1,000 miles from Santiago. In 1964, twenty different firms assembled twenty-five different models there with a total production of 7,600 cars! At that time, 27 per cent of the parts had to be produced in Chile, but the percentage of domestic content was raised every year. It has been estimated that Chile paid from $2 to $4 of domestic resources for every $1 of import substitution in this industry. One curious feature of the industry is that some of the finished cars were delivered to Santiago by air, as domestic aviation is heavily subsidized and aircraft are imported at a favourable exchange rate.[1] Chile would have been much better off if she had carried out import substitution in agriculture rather than automobiles. The climate is similar to California and the land endowment is very favourable, but Chile is nevertheless importing food on a substantial scale. The extreme protection given to industry has raised farm costs and incentives are further curtailed by price ceilings on domestic food products and favourable exchange rates for food imports.

Our conclusion on product mix is really as follows. One cannot lay down any hard and fast rules. It may be economic for developing countries to produce any kind of good, whether textiles, consumer durables, steel or capital goods. A good deal depends on the size of the country and its natural resources. But the objective should be to pick items which can be produced at low cost. This leads us directly to our next point.

c. *International Specialization*

In practice, most governments have approached the question of international specialization by trying to replace all the imports which the country was physically capable of making, with little regard for cost. There has been a major preoccupation with short-term balance

[1] See L. L. Johnson, 'Problems of Import Substitution: The Chilean Automobile Industry', *Economic Development and Cultural Change*, January 1967.

of payments difficulties and with the possibility of eliminating imports of non-essential goods. There has been reluctance to relax protection once the infant industry stage has passed. The tariff structure is usually not carefully planned, but has grown inadvertently through *ad hoc* responses to requests by industrialists, or as a response to payments difficulties. This bias is a very understandable one. It is difficult to calculate costs exactly, and the creation of new export markets is more difficult than the first phases of import substitution. Developed countries originally built up their export markets for manufactures in privileged colonial markets, and the smaller European countries built up their exports in countries which were contiguous and easy of access, whereas this is not possible for the developing world. When industrialization started in Latin America in the 1930s, the outside world was one of contracting markets and heavy trade restrictions. This, together with the experience of two world wars within a brief span of thirty years provided the background for Latin American pessimism about exports in the early post-war period. This was strongly expressed in Raoul Prebisch's short essay in 1950 which was published more or less as a manifesto by the Economic Commission for Latin America and has had a powerful influence on policy throughout the area.[1] This document starts, 'reality is undermining the outdated schema of the international division of labour'. Its pessimism about exports is based partly on the experience of the 1930s and the war, but also on the US dominance of the world economy at that time, the fact that its import ratio had shown a long-term decline, and the existence of a dollar shortage which then inhibited Europe's capacity to import. However, this manifesto did not advocate import substitution and export pessimism to the degree which subsequently emerged in Latin America.

Latin American countries have generally followed a policy of successive stages of import substitution. Starting with light consumer goods, they moved to consumer durables, and aimed to eliminate capital goods imports later. At each stage the emphasis has been on more or less *complete* replacement of imports. The ultimate aim of this philosophy is to produce what is sometimes called a *fully integrated* economy, i.e. one with no international trade. This autarkic philosophy was stimulated by two world wars and the experience of the 1930s plus a feeling of revulsion against the colonial implications of the pre-1929 pattern of international trade. However,

[1] See *The Economy of Latin America and Its Principal Problems*, UN, New York, 1950.

it is rather out of keeping with today's trading possibilities and reflects a degree of nationalism which has no contemporary rationale.

There has been some attempt to provide intellectual justification for the 'integration' approach by stressing the importance of linkages between different sectors of the economy. There has been a tendency to assume that industries with a high degree of interdependence will generate economies of scale and markets for each other, and that the linkages will provide a self-reinforcing element of dynamism in the economy. But when the scale of production is small, the interdependence will *raise* costs, and rapid expansion in closely related sectors may place a strain on the supply of skills which might be avoided by a less 'integrated' approach.

Another important consequence of this approach is that investment is heavily concentrated on *new* lines. Older industries have been neglected and have declined in efficiency. This is certainly true of the textile industry in Brazil and India, both of which have faced government obstacles in obtaining new equipment. This has amongst other things, reduced their capacity to export. The concentration on new lines has also increased the strains on managerial and technical capacity.

Outside Latin America, there has been a less explicit philosophy of import-substitution, but countries have drifted into it, because it seemed the easiest way to deal with balance of payments problems. Some countries have not yet had such severe difficulties as Argentina, Brazil or India, simply because their industrial development is at an earlier stage, where the technical problems, investment requirements and skill needs are not so great. But most of the smaller countries have committed fewer errors because they never entertained the fallacy that they could achieve complete autarky, and their policies have therefore been less extreme.

There now seems to be fairly general recognition that protective policies have been pushed to extreme lengths. Many of the most obvious lines of import substitution have been exhausted, and greater emphasis is being given to export promotion.

Raoul Prebisch, in his report for the first UNCTAD meeting in 1964, stressed the dangers of excessive protection and urged greater emphasis on exports of manufactured goods.[1] High protective tariffs have:

[1] See *Towards a New Trade Policy for Development*, Report by the Secretary General, UNCTAD, 1964.

'encouraged the establishment of small uneconomical plants, weakened the incentive to introduce modern techniques and slowed down the rise in productivity. Thus a real vicious circle has been created as regards exports of manufactured goods. These exports encounter great difficulties because internal costs are high, and internal costs are high because, among other reasons, the exports which would enlarge the markets are lacking.'

In Brazil and Argentina, which are two of the biggest manufacturers in the developing world, exports were less than 2 per cent of output in 1965. It is true that these two countries are well endowed to specialize in agricultural exports, but ultimately they should aim to be exporting much higher proportions of manufacturing output if they are to achieve adequate economies of scale and bring their productivity closer to that in the developed world. The same is true of India where only 2 per cent of the increase in industrial output from 1950 to 1965 went to exports compared with 22 per cent for import substitution and 76 per cent to meet growth in home demand.[1]

In fact the market for manufactured exports has been expanding rapidly. For developing countries as a group they rose by 9 per cent a year from 1953 to 1967. This is four times as fast as exports of agricultural products and raw materials. Our definition of manufactures includes a number of processed raw materials. If these are excluded, the expansion of the market is much faster. Lary has found that exports of labour-intensive manufactures increased by 13 per cent a year in the same period.[2] The earlier pessimism about export possibilities for manufactures would therefore seem to have been grossly exaggerated, and the wide differences in the experience with manufactured exports from developing countries are largely due to reasons of domestic policy. (See Chapter VII below for an analysis of export performance.)

Export promotion, of course, involves a much greater effort to assess costs and competitiveness correctly, it involves taking greater investment risks, and it means greater emphasis on re-equipment and somewhat less on introducing new lines of production. It requires the provision of export credit, commercial representation and market

[1] See J. Ahmad, *op. cit.*, Import substitution represented 10·8 per cent of growth in consumer goods, 12·6 per cent in intermediate goods and 42 per cent in capital goods.

[2] See H. G. Lary, *Imports of Manufactures from Less Developed Countries*, NBER, Columbia, New York, 1968, p. 107.

research. It also requires a greater fiscal effort on the part of governments because in the initial stages they may have to subsidize exports, whereas they can promote import substitution simply by imposing tariffs and quantitative restrictions. In order to promote competitiveness, the protection of domestic industry will have to be reduced and this may well produce political problems with business groups whose profits will be squeezed.

It is easy to see that industrialization programmes should have given more emphasis to the benefits of international specialization. But it is difficult to advise a country on how it should make its choice. The decision is particularly difficult for small countries which will be less self-sufficient than large ones because they cannot enjoy adequate economies of scale in many products. The importance of the scale problem is clear from Table VI–9. Over a wide range of industry,

Table VI–9

Scale of Manufacturing Activity in 1965

Gross value added in $ million at US relative prices

USA	187,781	Pakistan	1,958
USSR	127,028	Taiwan	1,722
Japan	50,431	Greece	1,469
Germany (FR)	47,706	Egypt	1,354
France	34,623	Philippines	1,141
UK	34,328	Turkey	1,135
Italy	27,166	Colombia	1,094
Spain	11,466	Israel	860
India	9,663	Malaya	836
Brazil	8,216	Peru	682
Argentina	6,735	South Korea	679
Yugoslavia	5,807	Thailand	315
Mexico	4,868	Ceylon	86
Venezuela	2,151	Ghana	84
Chile	2,070		

Source: Appendix A, Table A–7.

there is no clear ground for choice because the ultimate factors in competitiveness are not location but the skill of workers and the organizing ability of managers. The problem is quite different from that in agriculture where climate and soils often indicate clearly where the pattern of specialization should lie. Comparative advantage in many industrial products is something the country can create for itself by doing things efficiently. The government should, therefore, make a careful study of potential markets and production costs, but decisions of this kind usually require special contacts or knowledge which will only be possessed by people who are actively seeking to make a profit out of the venture. There are therefore fairly strong grounds for providing protection to industry in a uniform way, and letting market forces operate in selecting particular lines for specialization.

The choice of an efficient growth pattern within industry is a very difficult technical problem for planners. There have been very useful attempts by Professor Chenery and the United Nations to provide some general guidelines, but there are no golden rules or sets of equations which provide a ready-made answer.[1] The decisions require careful investigation by accountants, engineers, and economists and they can easily make mistakes if the price system is distorted by inflation, over-valued exchange rates and subsidized interest rates. All major investment decisions involve an element of risk because of changes in demand or technology or mis-estimates of cost, and there have been plenty of big mistakes in developed countries, e.g. the Ford Motor Company's decision to make the Edsel, the Russian emphasis on hydro rather than thermal power stations, or much of the investment of the British aircraft industry. At least, in developing countries, the major decisions do not usually involve much techical novelty and should be easier for this reason, but the big distortions in their price mechanism sometimes make it necessary to supplement ordinary accounting with shadow price calculations and detailed cost-benefit studies, if investment alternatives are to be properly weighted.

d. *Competition*

Most countries have paid little attention to promoting the competitiveness of industry. As a result many producers make monopoly

[1] See *A Study of Industrial Growth*, United Nations, New York, 1963, which is based on earlier work by Professor H. Chenery, and is intended to provide a guide to the 'normal' pattern of industrialization in response to population size and per capita income. In fact, the choice will be affected by specific variations in natural resources, location and trade possibilities, the skills and economic history of individual countries. Some of the more detailed techniques of industrial programming are described in a report by a UN expert group, *Formulating Industrial Development Programmes*, ECAFE, Bangkok, 1961. An even more detailed manual for 'programming' of individual projects is provided by the *Manual on Economic Development Projects*, United Nations, New York, 1958, and more recently by *Manual of Industrial Project Analysis in Developing Countries*, OECD Development Centre, Paris, 1968–69.

profits, and inefficient firms are protected from bankruptcy. It is indeed remarkable how little objection there has been from local capitalists to programmes of state industry. Most of the state enterprises were new ventures which did not threaten established private interests, and many of the state plants have sold their products or services at low prices which helped increase the profits of the firms purchasing these goods. The local capitalists have been much more vociferous in protesting against the role of foreign direct investment. In most countries, there have been no serious clashes of interest between industrial workers and industrialists, because these workers, though badly paid by Western standards, are a privileged group in their own community. Because of this and because industrialization is such an important political symbol, there has been little attempt to examine the social and economic costs of the pampered industrial sector to the economy as a whole.

WHAT WAS THE COST OF INDUSTRIALIZATION?

Recent evidence of the overall cost of industrial inefficiency shows that it is higher than was once realized. In 1958, Professor Harberger estimated the protection in Chile raised costs to an extent which cost the economy 2·5 per cent of its annual GNP.[1] But Professor Balassa has since pointed out that Harberger understated 'effective' protection, as well as the ratio of trade to GNP. Balassa suggests that the real cost of protection could be anywhere from 7 to 14 per cent of Chilean GNP, without any allowance for the protective effect of quantitative restrictions.[2] However, it should be noted that Chile is probably the extreme case of the high costs of protection.

In a recent careful study of ex-factory prices in Pakistan with the cif. cost of imports, Professor Nurul Islam has reached some interesting conclusions.[3] Using Tariff Commission data for 359 products (which were not a random sample as they exclude textile items) he concluded that Pakistan consumer goods cost 60 per cent more than imports, intermediate goods 87 per cent and capital goods 77 per cent. In most cases the differential was higher than the

[1] See A. C. Harberger, 'Using the Resources at Hand More Effectively', *American Economic Review, Papers and Proceedings*, May 1959.

[2] See B. Balassa, 'Integration and Resource Allocation in Latin America', Instituto Torcuato di Tella, Buenos Aires, 1966 (mimeographed).

[3] See N. Islam, 'Comparative Costs, Factor Proportions and Industrial Efficiency in Pakistan', *The Pakistan Development Review*, Summer 1967.

tariff, because quantitative restrictions created a scarcity premium. Islam does not discuss the problem of quality measurement, but the average quality of Pakistani goods may well be lower than imports.

Islam suggests that these figures give a misleadingly high impression of real domestic costs for two reasons. Firstly, the official exchange rate is over-valued by about 50 per cent, so the cost differential should be corrected by an adjustment factor. (The relevant adjustment is not 50 per cent but 23 per cent as domestic products also have an import content which would rise if the currency were devalued). Secondly, domestic entrepreneurs make excessive profits and could still continue to produce at prices 10 per cent lower (this would put some entrepreneurs out of business and close down plants, many of which are now working below 40 per cent of capacity).

Thus he concludes, after making these allowances, that home costs are more than 30 per cent higher than import costs. This means that industrial inefficiency costs about 3·5 per cent of GNP. If this situation were temporary and simply represented an initial premium paid by society to nurse industry through the stage in which economies of scale were being realized and new skills learned, it might be worth paying, but in fact, Islam found that the high cost industries included both old and new firms. He also found a very wide dispersion of costs between industries, and there were quite a number of firms with costs below those of imports. Reduced protection would divert resources to more efficient firms and to drive out inefficient entrepreneurs.

In the Pakistani case, where there are extensive quantitative restrictions, the tariff margin gives an inadequate view of local cost differentials. But in Latin American countries there must be many cases where the tariff exaggerates the 'needs' of local manufacturers. In the automobile industry, domestic prices have tended to be very close to those of duty-paid imports, but this is not typical. Brazilian wool yarn has 'effective' tariff protection of 679 per cent, and it is just possible that domestic prices might be this much higher than imported goods, if local production were dominated by a monopolist or by a few producers working in collusion. But domestic costs are normally not as high as this because there is *some* internal competition. Similarly, Brazilian protection against imported alcoholic beverages is high, but local whisky and gin is of good quality and sells very cheaply. In Latin America, high tariffs are often a partial substitute for a more realistic exchange rate, and they may remain high long after the exchange rate has been corrected. These variations in the operational significance of tariffs make it difficult to derive conclusions about efficiency simply from tariff data. We really need studies of price differentials of the type which Islam has done for Pakistan before we can make a reasonable judgment.

In several of the countries under survey the level of industrial tariffs is ten times as high as in Europe or the United States. If we assume that in most cases the high tariffs are a partial compensation for overvalued exchange rates, it is probably safe to assume that the operational incidence of protection is five times as great as in Europe. In 1950–62, European trade liberalization probably contributed 0·14 percentage points a year to GNP growth.[1] In developing countries, the relative importance of the industrial sector is, on average, about half as great as in Europe, but if protection is five times as high in these countries, they could possibly raise their GNP growth by 0·35 percentage points a year by a ten year pro-

[1] It is curious, in view of the political effort involved in abolishing quantitative restrictions on European trade in the 1950s, in creating the Common Market and EFTA and in achieving the Dillon and Kennedy Rounds in GATT that many economists have considered their efficiency effects to be negligible. The special ECE study on growth factors in Europe in the 1950s never even mentioned gains from trade. In 1954, Verdoorn estimated the likely gains from an all-European customs union at 0·05 per cent of GNP (not annually, but in total). Verdoorn took account of trade diverting as well as trade creating effects, but his gross trade creation effect was a once-for-all gain of only one-seventh of one per cent of GNP. Tibor Scitovsky, *Economic Theory and Western European Integration*, Allen & Unwin, London, 1958, endorsed the general conclusions of Verdoorn's study with regard to increased specialization, but stressed that the gains from increased competition would be substantial. The most serious attempt to assess the gains is by E. F. Denison, *Why Growth Rates Differ*, Brookings, Washington DC, 1967. He has estimated that reduction of trade barriers between 1950 and 1962 contributed 0·08 percentage points to annual growth. Denison used nominal tariff levels as a basis for his calculations, whereas it would be better to use the more refined measures of 'effective tariffs' which are now available. This would probably raise his estimates by about three-quarters, i.e. to 0·14 per cent a year. Denison assumes that cost differentials are two-thirds as high as trade barriers, i.e. that domestic production behind a 15 per cent tariff wall could involve 10 per cent higher costs than free trade. It should be noted that a recent study by the Wonnacotts suggests that most of the productivity difference between the United States and Canada is due to tariff protection and the inefficiency of smaller Canadian domestic markets. Their expectation of the potential gains from free trade is about 300 times as great as Verdoorn estimated for Europe. See R. J. and P. Wonnacott, *Free Trade Between the United States and Canada: The Political Economic Effects*, Harvard, 1967.

gramme of tariff reduction. The biggest gains would probably be attainable in Argentina, Brazil, Chile, India and Pakistan. On the other hand, some countries such as Greece, Israel, Malaya, Peru and Taiwan have relatively open economies and have much less inefficiency to remove, and some such as Ceylon, Ghana and Thailand have very little industry.

Finally, we must remember that it is rational to subsidize or protect home production *temporarily* in the initial stages of industrialization. There will be internal economies of scale within individual plants as their output expands. There will be external economies for particular plants as their industry expands, because the cost of raw materials and parts will drop as the scale of production increases. There will be productivity gains which derive from the increased size of the industrial sector as a whole, as efficiency increases in repair services, transport, banking, and marketing.

Efficiency will also increase over time because of the 'learning process', which cumulates entrepreneurial experience, organizational ability, managerial and worker skills. The first generation of firms will be plagued by the difficulties of learning, but the second generation will reap the benefits. The economy will acquire a new flexibility in dealing with changes in technology and demand. It may well be worthwhile for an economy like Pakistan to sacrifice 3 per cent of GNP to cover these 'learning' costs, but it is necessary to check constantly on how much learning is being done, and it would certainly be cheaper to provide some of the learning by better apprenticeship and managerial training.

There is strong evidence that several countries have pushed import substitution to rather costly extremes where internal prices are high, too many firms have been created and capital is used well below capacity. Most of them could profitably have specialized more on their most efficient lines of production and increased exports, both to developed countries and to each other. In most cases a unilateral reduction of protection from its present high levels would increase efficiency, and would be even more beneficial if carried out by several countries in concert.

Our criticism of resource allocation within industry does not necessarily imply that too many resources were devoted to the sector. The prime need is for better allocation within industry, though in a few countries, notably Argentina, India and Pakistan, less resources should have gone to industry and more to agriculture.

Chapter VII

Foreign Markets for Goods and Services

International trade has been a major source of economic growth. In the eighteenth century, Adam Smith extolled the productivity benefits which could be derived from specialization and economies of scale. In the nineteenth century, most of the growth which occurred in developing countries was due to the stimulus of new trade opportunities. Not only did they derive benefit from specialization, but they were also able to exploit surplus resources of land and labour, which had hitherto had no economic outlet. Trade was their 'engine of growth', long before they were able to exploit the benefits derivable from technological progress and capital formation.

But since 1950 the trade of developing countries has been disappointing. Exports have grown more slowly than those of developed countries and indeed in the 1950s they actually grew more slowly than they did before 1913. The 1960s have brought substantial improvement, but export performance has still lagged well behind that of developed countries. From 1950 to 1967, our sample of twenty-two countries had an export growth of 4 per cent a year (which is representative of the experience of developing countries as a whole, except the oil producers) whereas the six big developed countries shown in Table VII–1 had an export growth of nearly 9 per cent. By contrast, in the preceding decades 1880 to 1950, developing countries did better than the developed world.

As the exports of developing countries have been rising more slowly than their GNP, they have had difficulty in financing imports in spite of large foreign aid. They have had to eliminate 'non-essential' imports by severe trade restrictions which have made resource allocation less efficient, and, in periods of extreme difficulty, sharp cuts have been necessary in imports of capital goods and raw materials as well. In several cases, the deflationary impact of import

Table VII–1

Growth in the Dollar Value of Exports 1880–1967

Annual average compound growth rate

	1880–1913	1913–37	1937–50	1950–67	1950–60	1960–67
Argentina	7·0	1·6	4·6	0·4	−2·3	4·5
Brazil	3·5	0·4	10·9	1·2	−0·6	3·9
Ceylon	4·1	2·1	7·8	0·3	1·6	−1·4
Chile	2·1	1·1	3·0	7·1	5·6	9·3
Colombia	2·6	4·1	12·5	1·5	1·6	1·3
Egypt	2·6	1·0	7·5	0·6	1·0	0·0
Ghana	9·3	3·6	9·2	2·2	4·4	−0·8
Greece	3·7	5·7	0·3	10·5	8·5	13·6
India	2·7	−0·1	3·8	1·9	1·2	2·8
Israel	n.a.	n.a.	1·1	16·8	19·0	13·7
Malaya	4·1	4·2	3·8	0·7	1·2	0·0
Mexico	4·7	1·6	6·9	4·7	3·9	6·0
Pakistan	(2·7)	(−0·1)	n.a.	1·2	−2·2	6·3
Peru	5·3	3·2	5·7	8·6	8·6	8·7
Philippines	1·8	4·9	6·1	5·4	5·4	5·5
South Korea	n.a.	11·3	−15·2	16·8	3·7	38·0
Spain	1·3	−1·4	8·5	7·7	6·4	9·6
Taiwan	n.a.	6·8	−3·9	13·4	8·0	21·0
Thailand	4·9	2·4	11·1	4·9	3·0	7·7
Turkey	2·7	0·7	6·9	4·1	2·0	7·2
Venezuela	1·3	8·0	15·3	5·5	7·7	2·5
Yugoslavia	6·3	3·6	0·8	12·9	13·5	12·0
Average	4·0	3·0	4·9	5·8	4·6	7·8
Weighted Average	3·3	1·8	6·2	4·0	3·0	5·4
France	2·1	−1·3	9·3	8·1	8·5	7·5
Germany	3·8	−0·1	−1·1	15·1	19·2	9·6
Italy	2·4	0·5	6·2	12·3	11·7	13·2
Japan	8·4	5·2	−2·9	16·1	17·3	14·5
UK	2·6	0·1	6·8	5·0	5·4	4·5
USA	3·2	1·4	9·0	6·8	7·2	6·3
Average	3·8	1·0	4·6	10·6	11·6	9·3
Weighted Average	3·0	0·6	6·0	8·8	9·3	8·1

Source: See Appendix E.

cutbacks has led economies to work below capacity, e.g. in Argentina, Brazil and India. For these reasons, many development theorists and particularly those concerned with foreign aid, consider that the balance of payments is the most important constraint on development.[1]

However, there has been a very wide variation in the export experience of different countries. In Greece, Israel, Korea, Taiwan and Yugoslavia, exports rose by more than 10 per cent a year from 1950 to 1967. On the other hand, there were eight countries where exports rose by less than 2 per cent a year (Argentina, Brazil, Ceylon, Colombia, Egypt, India, Malaya, and Pakistan). To some extent the 1950s were abnormal because most of the fast-growing countries had some element of recovery from war and post-war disturbance, and some countries appeared to perform badly because the initial year, 1950 was affected favourably by the Korean boom. But even in the 1960s, we still find the same five countries growing at more than 10 per cent a year, and five (Ceylon, Colombia, Egypt, Ghana and Malaya) growing less than 2 per cent. In view of the wide variation in performance, it is obvious that not all developing countries were ineluctably constrained by force of circumstance.[2] Their export performance has in fact been affected by two kinds of factors:

(*a*) 'Structural problems which were due to circumstances beyond the influence of domestic policy;

(*b*) their own economic policies.

'STRUCTURAL' DIFFICULTIES

The nature of the structural difficulties is fairly well known, although there is still a good deal of controversy about some of them. In our view, they are as follows:

[1] See H. B. Chenery and A. M. Strout, *Foreign Assistance and Economic Development*, AID, June 1965, for a sophisticated econometric analysis of the foreign exchange 'gap' for individual countries. They use the concepts of a savings gap and a foreign exchange gap and determine which one was dominant. They found that the export constraint was more significant than the capacity to save in the majority of the fifty countries examined. See our Chapter VIII below for further comment on Chenery and Strout.

[2] A sophisticated analysis of the export performance of twenty-nine developing countries (of which sixteen are also in our sample) is to be found in B. A. de Vries, *The Export Experience of Developing Countries*, IBRD, Washington, 1967. Devries looks at performance in specific commodity markets for traditional exports and at capacity to generate new exports. He finds big variations in performance which have to be explained by differences in national policies.

(*a*) Developing country exports are concentrated on items for which demand is growing slowly, i.e. raw materials meeting competition from synthetic substitutes, and food and beverages for which demand is inelastic. Weak demand has been compounded by agricultural protection in developed countries. The unfavourable demand situation for traditional developing country exports can be seen very clearly in Table VII–2. In 1953, 84 per cent of the exports of

Table VII–2

Structure of Developing Country Exports 1953–67

	1953	1967	Annual per cent growth 1953–67
	$ billion		
Food, Beverages and Tobacco	7·53	10·55	2·4
Fuel	4·33	13·21	8·3
Other Raw Materials	5·96	7·88	2·0
Manufactures	2·45	8·15	9·0
Total	20·41	40·00	4·9
Total excluding Fuel	16·08	26·79	3·7

Source: *Monthly Bulletin of Statistics*, United Nations, New York, November 1965 and March 1967. The first row covers SITC items 0–1; the second, item 3; the third, items 2 and 4; the fourth, items 5–8. The figures exclude Greece, Spain, Turkey and Yugoslavia. Data on SITC classifications are not available for 1950.

developing countries (except oil producers) was concentrated on these slow-growing items. The only real scope for dynamic export performance for most countries lay in expansion of manufactures which have grown four times as fast as exports of food and raw materials.

(*b*) There has been a weak price situation for most traditional exports. The majority of developing countries have lower dollar export prices now than in 1950, whereas nearly all developed countries have experienced a rise in export prices. The most notable cases in which prices fell were in Argentina, Colombia, Malaya, Pakistan and Taiwan. Only Chile and Yugoslavia were lucky enough to experience a substantial rise in prices. This is clear from Table VII–3. The fall in prices was due partly to the weak demand situation which we have already mentioned, but it is also due to the fact that developing countries have large reserves of agricultural labour for which there is no ready alternative employment. For this reason it has not been easy to adjust supply to the weak market situation. We do not support the thesis that the terms of trade of developing countries must continue to decline indefinitely, but there are powerful forces working in this direction.[1]

Table VII–3

Index of Export Prices (Dollar Equivalent) 1950–65

Initial year = 100

Argentina	88·0	Taiwan	75·2†
Brazil	93·9	Thailand	(109·6)
Ceylon	96·1	Turkey	n.a.
Chile	146·0	Venezuela	82·4
Colombia	83·0	Yugoslavia	152·0
Egypt	115·3		
Ghana	76·6	Average	100·9
Greece	98·4*		
India	115·4		
Israel	113·0	France	119·4
Malaya	84·7†	Germany (FR)	141·3
Mexico	108·0	Italy	98·3
Pakistan	84·2	Japan	101·0
Peru	107·6	UK	148·3
Philippines	93·2	USA	128·1
South Korea	n.a.		
Spain	94·5	Average	122·7

* initial year 1951; † initial year 1952.

Source: *Monthly Bulletin of Statistics*, UN, New York, February 1968, *Yearbook of International Trade Statistics 1966*, UN, New York, 1968, and *Statistical Bulletin for Latin America*, Vol. I, No. 1 and Vol. IV, No. 1. The figures refer to unit values converted into dollars. India 1950–52 derived from M. Singh, *India's Export Trends*, Oxford, 1964. Israel figure supplied by Bank of Israel.

[1] In 1950 R. Prebisch argued that the terms of trade of developing countries tended to decline in the long run because of weak demand, bias in technological progress against their products, and greater bargaining power of labour in developed countries. See R. Prebisch, *The Economic Development of Latin America*, UN, New York, 1950. W. A. Lewis, *The Theory of Economic Growth*, Allen & Unwin, London, 1955, argued that surplus labour in the agriculture of developing countries leads to poor terms of trade, though he did not claim that they would decline steadily. Prebisch has been attacked for overstating his case, which is difficult to prove on the basis of long term historical evidence. See the arguments of Gottfried Haberler in H. Ellis and H. Wallich, *Economic Development for Latin America*, New York, 1961. However, for the period since 1950, it is quite obvious that developing countries have suffered from worsening terms of trade.

(*c*) The concentration of exports on a few agricultural products has meant that export earnings were hit severely by fluctuations in world market conditions or by harvest fluctuations which were no fault of their own. The evidence for this instability is presented in Chapter IV above, and we strongly disagree with the recent tendency to understate this problem;

(*d*) The biggest individual export markets for developing countries are the UK and USA. These are the most open to developing countries' imports, but they were growing much more slowly than other developed countries over the period 1950–67. In the 1960s, US growth accelerated and so did US imports, but British growth weakened even further.

These structural difficulties with traditional exports were all the more important because developing country demand for imported capital goods and raw materials has been growing faster than GNP.

POLICY-INDUCED DIFFICULTIES

The export problems of developing countries have been compounded by important mistakes in their economic policy. Not all countries have made these mistakes but they have been so widespread that most of them can be considered characteristic. They have been as follows:

(*a*) Excess demand, which arose when countries tried to use more resources than they could produce. In this situation, manufacturers found it easier and more profitable to sell on the home market than to export. The payments deficit in this case was not structural, but simply a reflection of inadequate domestic savings in relation to their development ambitions. We have already seen in Chapter IV that political pressures strongly favoured the risk of doing too much rather than too little;

(*b*) Overvalued exchange rates. As no individual developing country has a dominant position in world trade or serves as a reserve currency, they are generally freer than developed countries to change their exchange rates. But until the early 1960s, there was considerable reluctance to do this, both for misplaced reasons of national pride and a feeling that frequent devaluation might accelerate the process of inflation. Thus Brazil made no change in the exchange rate from 1948 to 1953 though her internal price level rose by two-thirds in this period. India made no change between 1949 and 1966 in spite of stagnant exports. They were able to defend unrealistic rates only by erecting a complicated apparatus of exchange controls to check imports. The high level of prices impeded the growth of new export products. In India and Brazil, over-valuation allowed competitors to enter the market for their traditional exports of coffee and jute products. Temporary export subsidies are useful if a currency is overvalued, but most countries do not have the fiscal capacity to provide large export subsidies, and it is preferable to have a realistic exchange value even if this involves frequent adjustments or a floating rate (as in Peru). Frequent devaluation may accelerate the pace of price increase, but it will eliminate some of the distorting effects of inflation;

(*c*) Some countries tried to solve their payments problems by import substitution, but most of those which reduced their dependence on trade had considerable payments problems because excessive protection reduced both efficiency and competition and weakened their capacity to export. This happened most spectacularly in the Brazilian textile industry which was an important exporter in the early post-war years, but its exports vanished and efficiency declined behind massive tariff walls. There are still some countries such as Ceylon, Ghana and Malaya which were very open economies in colonial times, where further import substitution is still desirable. There is also scope in India and elsewhere for reducing food imports.

Table VII–4

Imports of Goods and Services as Percentage of GDP at Current Market Prices 1950 and 1965

	1950	1965		1950	1965
Argentina	8·5	7·1	Pakistan	8·8¶	9·9
Brazil	8·8	7·5	Peru	19·3	20·9
Ceylon	32·8	26·5	Philippines	13·1	19·0
Chile	9·2	13·2	South Korea	9·8*	16·2
Colombia	11·4	12·6	Spain	6·6	15·2
Egypt	28·3	23·9	Taiwan	14·9†	21·6
Ghana	28·4‖	23·8	Thailand	21·4‡	20·2
Greece	24·2	21·7	Turkey	n.a.	n.a.
India	6·7	5·9	Venezuela	24·1	20·4
Israel	28·4	34·0	Yugoslavia	16·0§	21·0
Malaya	32·4	35·9			
Mexico	14·8	10·4	Average	17·5	18·4

* 1953; † 1951; ‡ 1952; § 1956; ‖ 1955; ¶ 1959.

Source: As for appendices B and D.

On the whole, however, import substitution has not been a very successful policy as we saw in Chapter V.

(*d*) Lack of serious effort to export. Some countries took the structural problem for granted and had too pessimistic a view of world markets, and of their capacity to develop new export lines. The long-term perspective plan (1951–76) for India projected a big drop in the relative importance of exports. 'A doubling of exports is foreseen by 1975–76 as against an almost fourfold increase in national product.[1] Argentina and Brazil also made little effort to promote new manufactured exports until the mid-1960s.[2] Their industrialization policies were designed to promote ultimate self-sufficiency without any systematic regard for cost. They were not willing to embark on lines of production which depended heavily on exports. The tax structure provided disincentives in some cases. Heavy indirect taxes are levied in some countries which are not remitted on export shipments as is generally the case in west European countries. This has been a particularly important problem in India and Brazil, where these taxes are levied by state governments which would not be willing to surrender the revenue to federal government to reimburse exporters. Bureaucratic controls on foreign exchange transactions require exporters to fill in forms and obtain licences, to ensure that they are not engaged in black market currency transaction or tax evasion. Firms which might have a marginal interest in exporting are thus deterred;

(*e*) Most developing countries have pursued a nationalist and rather autarkic trade policy with very little attempt at the type of regional co-operation which has been practised in Europe since the war and which has done so much to expand Europe's trade. The only case of close regional co-operation within the developing world has been the Central American Common Market which has been extremely successful in expanding trade.

These characteristic policy mistakes have not been made by all developing countries and the encouraging thing is that there are

[1] W. Malenbaum, 'Comparative Costs and Economic Development: The Experience of India', *American Economic Review*, May 1964, p. 391.

[2] In a careful study of India's stagnant exports, Manmohan Singh attaches major responsibility to internal policies rather than world market conditions: 'In the mid-fifties, while export industries like jute and cotton textiles were denied foreign exchange for their programme of much-needed modernization a much too liberal approach was followed in India to allocating foreign exchange to many non-essential industries in the name of import-substitution.' See M. Singh, *India's Export Trends*, Oxford, 1964, p. 34.

several countries which have been very successful in increasing exports.

EXPORT SUCCESSES AND ECONOMIC POLICY

The countries which made a significant effort to expand manufactured exports had remarkable success. They include Greece, Israel, Mexico, Pakistan, Korea, Spain, Taiwan and Yugoslavia. Some of these countries benefited from propinquity to rapidly growing markets in Europe and Japan, but it seems clear that a similar effort could have been successful elsewhere. Export promotion involves vigorous and imaginative government action. Selling manufactured goods is quite different from selling food and raw materials which go to well-organized produce markets. It requires market research, strong foreign commercial representation, quality control, some degree of internal competition, provision of export credit and insurance, and temporary subsidies to new exports.

Table VII–5

Ratio of Manufactures to Total Commodity Exports 1953–65

	1953	1965		1953	1965
Argentina	10·2	9·0	Pakistan	1·1	36·2
Brazil	2·0	10·3	Peru	2·7	1·7
Chile	1·6	0·9	Philippines	7·5	10·9
Colombia	0·7	6·3	South Korea	0·0	61·1
Egypt	4·2	22·1	Spain	20·1	48·7
Greece	9·1	18·1	Taiwan	5·5	50·0
India	47·5	46·7	Thailand	2·2	3·8
Israel	58·3	73·9	Turkey	1·1	2·7
Mexico	7·5	16·5	Yugoslavia	14·0	62·8

Source: *Yearbook of International Trade Statistics 1965*, UN, New York, 1967; *International Trade, 1966*, GATT, Geneva, 1967, p. 56 and estimates applied by Mr Jan Tumlir of GATT.

The greatest success with new types of exports was achieved by the smaller countries. These countries were too small to have any pretensions to self-sufficiency and they made a sounder policy judgment than the bigger countries. To some extent it is easier for small countries to break into new markets on a scale which is significant for them and not disturbing to the market as a whole. But the success stories for manufactured exports do not represent special situations, or small quantities. Some of the small countries export more manufactures than the big ones. Hong Kong exports more manufactures than India; Israel and Taiwan export more than Brazil or Argentina. There is therefore every reason to believe that the big countries could have done better if they had really tried. This does not mean that their total exports could have grown as fast as Israel or Taiwan, which also expanded their agricultural exports considerably. Taiwan's success in exploiting the new Japanese market for bananas, or in developing exports of tinned pineapples was a special situation. However, many more countries could have *diversified* their agricultural exports.

Success in exporting manufactures was the result of vigorous policy effort. In Taiwan, export capacity was a major criterion in choosing industries for development. The government provided export subsidies in order to offset domestic indirect taxes, and it rebated import duties on materials used in exports, particularly new exports. It also provided rebates on business taxes and income tax to exporters. In the case of textiles these export subsidies varied from 15 to 25 per cent. It provided insurance on export risks, export finance on favourable terms, market information, and waivers of harbour dues. In order to promote the processing of foreign raw materials it set up tax free export zones with bonded warehouses, and made foreign currency loans to exporters to purchase foreign raw materials, e.g. for textiles, plywood and other timber products. It also promoted co-operation between exporters so that they could build up foreign markets jointly. The government sponsored export missions. Foreign investors and overseas Chinese were encouraged to invest in export industries. As a result Taiwan built up new exports in textiles, plywood, metals, machinery, chemicals, cement and timber products.

The expansion was particularly rapid in the 1960s, when the inflation ended and the exchange rates were unified.[1] Before that, Taiwan's exports had been hindered by inflation, high protection, detailed exchange control and licensing.

In Israel too, the government actively sought to make exports attractive from the early 1950s in spite of domestic inflation and a currency which has often been overvalued. One of the major instruments was export premiums for many classes of exporters, usually financed by special levies on imports. The government also provided cheap credit, insurance, and transport facilities to exporters.

[1] See Mo-huan Hsing, *The Republic of China's Industrialization and Trade Policies in Taiwan*, Academia Sinica, Taipei, February, 1968 (mimeographed).

In recent years several other countries have changed their policies to promote exports either by maintaining more realistic exchange rates or by specific export subsidies. Since 1959, Pakistan has raised manufacturing exports substantially by a bonus scheme which varied according to the category of product: 20 or 30 per cent of export proceeds could be sold to importers at premia which have ranged between 35 and 70 per cent above the official exchange rate for exports. India also had a system of export subsidies which were temporarily discarded at the time of the 1966 devaluation. This unfortunately offset the effects of devaluation to a considerable degree.

In 1964 Argentina adopted a three tier system of export subsidies of 10, 20 and 30 per cent, depending on the degree of novelty of the goods as export products, and it also started to grant rebates of internal taxes and customs duties on exports. These measures were accompanied by more frequent adjustment of the exchange rate to keep prices competitive, and the combination of these policies had a remarkably stimulating effect on manufactured exports. Between 1964 and 1967 they trebled though they are still low in absolute terms. In Brazil too there has been recognition since 1964 of the need to control internal demand and to adopt more realistic exchange rates with more frequent adjustment.

Mexico has had a better export performance than most other Latin American countries, largely because it had much less inflation but until recently it had not made any special effort to promote manufactured exports. However, it has now started to attract American investors to set up light manufacturing plants in its duty free border zone which exports components for use in the electronics industry in the USA.

The Inter-American Development Bank has helped Latin American countries to improve facilities for export credit, and the United Nations has been helping Latin America to improve its market research and foreign commercial representation.

These efforts to subsidize the initial phases of export expansion can be justified on the same grounds as protection for import substitutes, for the initial cost of breaking into foreign markets is high.

Some countries are lucky enough to have natural resources such as oil or other minerals for which foreign demand is expanding rapidly. Venezuela and Chile are the only countries in this position in our group, but others, geographically close to the developed world, have had large earnings from tourism which have strengthened their current balance of payments. This is true of Greece, Israel, Mexico, Spain and Yugoslavia. Egypt had large earnings from Suez Canal dues. Table VII–6 illustrates the relative contribution of commodity and service earnings to the balance of payments.

In the course of the 1960s, most governments came to realize that they should give greater emphasis to export promotion and that their earlier view of potential markets was too pessimistic. They are also pursuing more realistic policies with respect to the level of

Table VII–6

Earnings from Commodity and Service Exports in 1965

	$ million			$ million	
	Commodities	Services		Commodities	Services
Argentina	1,493	169	Mexico	1,146	826
Brazil	1,596	146	Pakistan	527	138
Ceylon	401	42	Peru	685	92
Chile	688	100	Philippines	769	323
Colombia	580	129	South Korea	175	115
Egypt	568	358	Spain	1,019	1,405
Ghana	295	64	Taiwan	451	72
Greece	331	341	Thailand	609	156
India	1,644	386	Turkey	479	202
Israel	404	306	Venezuela	2,436	128
Malaya	1,226	170			

Source: IMF, *Balance of Payments Yearbook*, Vol. 19, Washington DC.

domestic demand, and have adopted more realistic exchange rates. Some of them have reduced protection to stimulate competition, and are adopting measures to provide export credit and insurance or subsidies for new exports. The growth of exports in our twenty-two countries was much faster in the 1960s than in the 1950s. Thus there is some hope that they may move away from the extremely tight payments position they have had in the past. However, we must not forget the fundamental importance of their structural problems. Some of the traditional exports which they could most easily expand are blocked by trade restrictions in the developed world, and a significant increase in new export lines involves a major effort of market penetration. One must therefore expect that the payments problem will remain as a significant constraint in many countries unless they are helped by commercial policy concessions from developed countries.

COMMERCIAL POLICY OF DEVELOPED COUNTRIES

The developed countries have all increased their imports much faster since 1950 than they have historically. They have grown by nearly 9 per cent a year, and their cyclical volatility has been much smaller than in pre-war years. The more rapid growth in trade than income was due to the reduction of both quantitative and tariff barriers to commerce. In the early 1950s, quantitative restrictions on intra-European trade were removed, and controls on dollar imports disappeared in the late 1950s. Within the Common Market and European Free Trade Area, tariffs started to fall in 1959 and were eliminated in 1968. External tariffs were reduced through negotiations conducted in the framework of the General Agreement on Tariffs and Trade. The biggest of these were the Dillon Round of 1962 and the Kennedy Round of 1968. Barriers to automobile trade in the US and Canada have been eliminated. Restrictions on current payments were removed by the general advent of convertibility in 1958, and liquidity arrangements have been strengthened. Since 1958, none of the developed countries except Australia has introduced quantitative restrictions to deal with payments difficulties. The communist countries have also greatly increased the degree to which their economies are open to international trade.

This liberalization in commercial policy was not designed to provide any favours to developing countries. They gained something from general tariff reductions and abolition of import licensing, but the main beneficiaries were the developed countries themselves. At present, trade barriers bear particularly severely on imports from the developing world.

Although nominal tariff rates in developed countries are now generally about 11 per cent, the 'effective' rates are sometimes considerably higher, particularly for lightly processed goods. The effective incidence of duties on textile products or processed minerals is about three times as high as the nominal tariff levels. When the Kennedy round tariff cuts become fully effective the average nominal tariff will be 6·5 per cent in industrial countries, but the effective tariff on goods of interest to developing countries will be 22·6 per cent.

Furthermore, quantitative restrictions are directed almost entirely

Table VII–7

Nominal and Effective Incidence of Protection in Developed Countries

	USA		UK		Common Market		Japan		All industrial countries	
	(*a*)	(*b*)	(*a*)	(*b*)	(*a*)	(*b*)	(*a*)	(*b*)	(*a*)	(*b*)
Nominal tariff all commodities	11·5	6·8	15·2	9·1	11·0	6·6	16·1	9·4	10·9	6·5
Effective tariff all commodities	20·0	11·6	27·8	16·0	18·6	11·1	29·5	16·4	19·2	11·1
Effective tariff on commodities of special interest to developing countries	35·4	23·9	37·3	27·6	27·7	16·9	36·7	20·2	33·4	22·6

(*a*) pre-Kennedy; (*b*) post-Kennedy.

Source: B. Balassa, 'The Effects of the Kennedy Round on the Exports of Processed Goods from Developing Areas', UNCTAD, New Delhi, February 1968.

against developing countries and Japan. In the 1950s, there was a very rapid growth of textile exports to the UK, USA and Canada from Japan, India, Pakistan and Hong Kong. Other developed countries were not much affected as they generally had tight import restrictions. For Commonwealth countries, the UK had no protective barrier at all, and in 1959 the disruption of the local textile industry led it to make bilateral agreements with the main suppliers to restrict the growth of their exports. In 1961, the US initiated a short-term international agreement on the same lines, and started negotiations for the long-term Arrangement on Cotton Textiles which became effective on October 1962 with the blessing of the GATT. The UK and other European countries were also members. The quotas were to be steadily expanded over a five year period during which exporters restrained their own producers. In October 1967 this agreement was extended for three years. Although it allows markets to grow and is more liberal than restraints which have been imposed on imports of toys or transistor radios, it has been operated in a more restrictive sense than was originally agreed.

The impact of trade barriers on the potential manufacturing exports of developing countries is hard to assess because we know little about their capacity to supply goods at competitive prices. In the case of cotton textiles, developing countries had captured a quarter of the UK market by 1967. If they could do this in the country which used to dominate the textile market, they could probably do as well in other countries, if given the chance. But in France, restrictions are so severe that they had less than 1 per cent of the market.

For agricultural products the situation is worse than for manufactures. Protection for farm products has increased in the post-war period, and all developed countries except Denmark and the Netherlands also provide their farmers with subsidies. In 1965, subsidies which directly affected prices and production amounted to about $5·5 billion in OECD countries.[1] There were also subsidies to provide farmers with cheaper inputs and services. These policies have kept down imports from the developing world and produced surpluses which are now a general plague in continental Europe, Japan and North America. The disposal of US surpluses under P.L. 480 since 1954 has also had some adverse impact on developing country exports, though the willingness of the US to hold high stocks and its efforts to avoid interference with normal commercial channels have greatly mitigated the damage.

The abolition of agricultural protection in developed countries would lead to big imports of sugar from the developing world, but, for other products, the main gainers would be low-cost producers in the developed world, i.e. the USA, Canada, Australia, New Zealand, Denmark and the Netherlands. Professor H. G. Johnson has estimated that free trade in sugar would increase developing countries export earnings by almost $900 million, and free trade in other farm products would provide them with another $1·1 billion.[2] In addition, he suggests that US surplus disposals reduce developing country exports by about $700 million a year. The removal of protection would provide a substantial, once-for-all boost, but after this was over, agricultural exports would still grow slowly because demand is sluggish.

Mineral products and agricultural raw materials often enter developed countries with very low or zero tariffs, and revenue duties on tropical beverages have recently been reduced in response to pressure from the developing world, but the USA, which is now one of the world's high cost producers of raw materials has, at various times, imposed quotas on imports of oil, lead and zinc. European countries have also given protection to their coal industry at the expense of oil producers. In the past, the US strategic stockpile has created problems, it greatly exacerbated the Korean commodity

[1] See *Agricultural Policies in 1966*, OECD, Paris, 1967.
[2] See H. G. Johnson, *op. cit.*, pp. 88–94.

cycle and has since operated as a depressing influence on prices as stocks have been released. However, it is unlikely to have much significant influence in the future.

The few special arrangements which favour developing countries are largely a legacy from the colonial period. These include the preferences of sterling area countries in the UK market as a relic of the imperial preference system erected in 1932 at Ottawa, US sugar quotas, US tariff preferences for the Philippines, and the Common Market's Treaties of Association with countries which are ex-colonies of France, Belgium and the Netherlands. Most of these arrangements distort resource allocation and confer favours on some developing countries at the expense of others.

UNCTAD

The developing countries themselves were rather slow in forming a pressure group to put forward their own proposals for commercial policy. There were several tentative attempts to create such a group between the Afro-Asian Conference at Bandung in 1957, and the Cairo Conference of developing countries in 1962 which first put forward the idea of a UN Conference on Trade and Development.

The Conference took place in Geneva in 1964 after some opposition from the developed countries whcih preferred to discuss such matters within the traditional framework of the GATT. The preparation of the Conference was in the hands of Raoul Prebisch, the former Secretary General of ECLA who had been a leading spokesman for the Latin American countries in the post-war period, and a leading theorist on the impact of trade on development.

The document presented by the Secretary General of the Conference, whilst pessimistic about some of the inherent structural biases of the world trade system, was very positive in stressing the need for developing countries to be outward looking, to avoid excessive import substitution, to promote export earnings, and to strengthen regional co-operation.

The Prebisch suggestions[1] covered a wide field of policy including creation of a new system of preferences for the industrial goods of developing countries, a strengthening of commodity agreements to guarantee the purchasing power of primary exports, a new scheme for compensatory finance to offset the deterioration in the terms of

[1] See *Towards a New Trade Policy for Development*, UN, New York, 1964.

trade, reduced revenue duties on imports of tropical products such as coffee, cocoa and bananas, readjustment of the debt of developing countries, a change in GATT rules to favour the developing countries, and setting up UNCTAD as a permanent body.

The initiative in the Conference was taken by the developing countries, and the discussions ranged over the whole field of trade and aid. The developed countries were not very well prepared and took a variety of different positions. The UK was positive on compensatory finance, and willing to consider an extension of Commonwealth Preference. France made suggestions for discriminatory preferences and for a system of high support prices for primary products. The USA took a strongly negative line on preferences and was positive about little else. It was fairly clear that the communist countries had little to offer the developing world. In terms of practical concessions, nothing was achieved, but the developing countries did emerge as a bloc with common interests and UNCTAD was set up as a permanent UN body.

Between the first and second UNCTAD Conference little progress was made, as the developed countries were occupied with the Kennedy Round in GATT. There was some reduction in European excise duties on tropical products, and Australia introduced a system of preferences for the industrial products of developing countries.

By the time of the second conference, the USA had modified its negative stand on preferences and there was some agreement in principle by the developed countries that preferences were desirable, though no agreement as to how they should be implemented in practice, as the USA is opposed to discriminatory preferences of the type offered by the Common Market and the UK.

The second meeting in Delhi in 1968 coincided with severe balance of payments problems for the UK and the USA, and with a world monetary crisis, so that its practical achievements were negligible. The developed countries did, however, pledge themselves to devote 1 per cent of their GNP to aid, and there has since been unexpected success in creating a sugar agreement.

It looks as if progress in UNCTAD will be slow and frustrating. Unfortunately, the commercial policy outlook of developed countries is still based on the idea of reciprocal bargaining. As developing countries have not offered them anything, they have not made concessions. However, it is obvious that developing countries will not use trade concessions to hoard exchange reserves but will use their increased earnings to step up imports, so there is little real need for reciprocity. Secondly, the developing countries have structural payments problems not present in the developed world, and they deserve favourable treatment. Thirdly, trade concessions in some fields would have an impact that is almost equivalent to giving aid. The contribution of increased trade opportunities depends on the degree to which they improve the efficiency of resource allocation. In agriculture and textiles the developing countries have both idle capacity and idle labour, so the impact on resource allocation would be very favourable. The developed countries would get cheaper food and clothing and could easily find alternative jobs for their farmers and textile workers. Finally, increased trade possibilities would have a salutary influence on economic policy in developing countries, which has concentrated too much on import substitution and not enough on export promotion.

REGIONAL TRADE AGREEMENTS

More than a fifth of the trade of developing countries is that which they do with each other, and this is the part which has been moving most slowly. This is because they have pursued a much more restrictive commercial policy than the developed world, and with the exception of the Central American Common Market, they have done very little to foster effective regional preference systems with each other, either for payments or trade.[1] Regional arrangements are

[1] The case for regional co-operation in trade and payments (in the Asian context) is well put by Robert Triffin: 'These potential benefits are enormous indeed. The economic and financial infrastructure of the region was largely influenced, for more than a century, by foreign capital and entrepreneurship primarily interested in it as a provider of primary products and as an outlet for European and American manufactures. This trend was further aggravated, in later years, by the very efforts of each country to establish and develop industries of its own behind the protective barriers of tariff walls and other import restrictions. This protection of each country's "infant industries" was applied *equally* to the infant industries of its neighbours and to the fully "adult industries" of the more industrialized countries of Europe and North America. This "equal" treatment inevitably favoured the latter at the expense of the former, since the more advanced producers of the industrialized countries were better able to jump over the national barriers than the infant industries of the less developed neighbouring countries. The same is true of the further restrictions resorted to from time to time for balance-of-payments reasons. They stifle mutual ECAFE trade and are therefore mutually defeating for all concerned.

'Reciprocal commitments to trade liberalization could break this spiral for

probably the easiest way of reopening these economies to international trade and competition, but so far progress has been disappointingly slow, particularly in the Latin American Free Trade Area.

CONCLUSIONS

Our conclusion therefore is that the balance of payments has been a constraint on development partly for structural reasons and partly because of mistaken policies. The experience of several countries shows that payments difficulties can be mitigated by efficient policy measures and that trade can still be a major engine of growth by providing scope for economies of scale and specialization. However, the average developing country is still likely to suffer considerably from payments difficulties even when its economic policy is efficient. For this reason, there is a very strong case for trade concessions by the developed world.

the ECAFE countries as they did for the OEEC countries in the decade of the 1950s.'

See R. Triffin, 'Payments Arrangements within the ECAFE Region', Yale Growth Center Paper No. 114.

Chapter VIII
External Finance

External funds played an important part in accelerating post-war development. Between 1950 and 1967 the net receipts of external finance by all developing countries were probably about $120 billion plus about $20 billion of military aid. These funds helped to supplement domestic savings, to meet payments deficits, to introduce new technology and skills.

There are several different sources of external finance. Detailed figures are not available for the whole period since 1950,[1] but for the six years 1960–65 we can compare the relative importance of different sources of finance with considerable accuracy. For our twenty-two countries, economic aid from foreign governments and international agencies provided $19 billion. Private sources supplied another $15 billion; half of this was private investment of the traditional kind, $2·4 billion was trade credit and nearly $5 billion was provided by private donations and emigrants' remittances. The total flow is shown in Table VIII–1, which demonstrates the wide variation in country experience with different kinds of capital. Some countries, like Spain, get most of their external finance from private sources, whereas in India the great bulk consisted of aid. Private sources are relatively more important for our twenty-two countries than they are for developing countries generally. African countries get most of their foreign capital as aid, and private flows to Africa have probably been negative in the past decade.

Our figures on aid flows are net in the sense that loans are calculated after deducting repayments. However, we have not deducted interest and dividend payments, which are currently running at about $5·5 billion a year for developing countries as a whole compared with a net capital flow of about $12 billion a year.

[1] In Chapter II, and in Appendix D, we have presented estimates for the whole period for the total flow of external finance, but the breakdown by categories is not available before 1960.

Table VIII–1

Main Sources of External Finance 1960–65 (excluding military aid)

$ million disbursed

	Economic aid from the USA: grants and net lending	Economic aid from other Western governments and international agencies: grants and net lending	Economic aid from communist countries: grants and net lending	Net receipts of private capital	Net increase in guaranteed private export credit	Net grants received by private sector	Total
Argentina	168	34	(10)	944	176	−31	1,301
Brazil	951	201	(5)	669	234	58	2,118
Ceylon	37	52	(25)	−2	10	−38	84
Chile	519	160	—	323	118	46	1,166
Colombia	226	177	—	449	36	25	913
Egypt	851	241	(450)	9	144	102	1,797
Ghana	60	73	(65)	(189)*	197	−87	497
Greece	178	104	—	610	84	960	1,936
India	3,904	1,642	(450)	100	−116	483	6,463
Israel	251	460	—	752	73	1,730	3,266
Malaya	26	74	—	462	3	−409	156
Mexico	74	252	—	1,563	291	−69	2,111
Pakistan	1,882	585	(35)	267	31	116	2,916
Peru	36	89	—	309	177	32	643
Philippines	157	173	—	52	91	465	938
South Korea	1,273	98	—	100	53	256	1,780
Spain	245	2	—	1,166	210	1,292	2,915
Taiwan	488	1	—	87	17	77	670
Thailand	177	88	—	312	140	34	765
Turkey	910	198	(5)	183	31	48	1,375
Venezuela	122	6	—	−942	27	−503	−1,290
Yugoslavia	592	236	(−111)	0	371	271	1,359
Total	13,127	4,946	(934)	7,602	2,398	4,858	33,865

* Estimate based on 1961–65 data.

Sources: *Geographical Distribution of Financial Flows to Less Developed Countries* (*Disbursements*), 1960–64 and 1965 editions, OECD, Paris, 1966 and 1967, for government flows and guaranteed export credit. Communist aid disbursements are my estimates based on commitments data and partial information on disbursements published by the US State Department. Private capital and grants from *Balance of Payments Yearbooks*, IMF, Washington DC. The figures on private flows may involve some items already included as government payments in cases where a government in a developed country lends to the private sector in a developing country. Conversely, the figures omit lending by the private sector in developed countries to governments of developing countries.

In addition to economic aid there is a considerable flow of military aid which is not very fully documented. However, identifiable US military aid to sixteen of our countries amounted to $4·5 billion from 1960 to 1965. In addition there was US military aid to India and Pakistan, and considerable Soviet aid to Egypt and other countries.

Table VIII–2

US Military Grants, Loans, and Excess Military Stock Disposals 1960–65

$ million

Argentina	54	Mexico	10
Brazil	143	Pakistan	n.a.
Ceylon	0	Peru	77
Chile	76	Philippines	134
Colombia	50	South Korea	1,187
Egypt	0	Spain	247
Ghana	0	Taiwan	815
Greece	542	Thailand	280
India	n.a.	Turkey	779
Israel	19	Venezuela	53
Malaya	0	Yugoslavia	1

Source: *US Overseas Loans and Grants*, AID Report for House Foreign Affairs Committee, March 1967.

a. *Private Foreign Investment*

Historically, private investment played an important role in sparking off economic development. It was a major instrument for introducing new technology, in providing skills, management and entrepreneurship, in opening up new internal and export markets, as well as in supplementing domestic savings.

The UK started lending in Latin America in the 1820s and was followed by the French in the middle of the century. The flow of capital to developing countries gathered momentum in the 1870s, and rose to a peak in the decade before the First World War, when the UK was investing about 7 per cent of its GNP abroad and France about 3 per cent. By 1914, there were $24 billion of foreign assets in developing countries. The UK owned over $7 billion, France nearly $5 billion and Germany about $3 billion.

The countries which received most capital per head of population were those with rich natural resources which could be exploited by improved transport facilities. This was true of Argentina, Chile, Malaya, South Brazil and Mexico. In Argentina external finance was equal to domestic savings and financed half of investment.

Foreign investment was important in developing railways, mineral resources and plantation agriculture, and was destined mainly to open up economies to international trade, though in Latin America there was also considerable investment in light and power, which helped

Table VIII–3

Net Receipts of Private Capital and Remittances per Head of Population 1960–65

$ per annum annual average

Argentina	8·1	Mexico	6·9
Brazil	2·0	Pakistan	0·6
Ceylon	0·4	Peru	7·4
Chile	9·7	Philippines	3·1
Colombia	4·7	South Korea	2·7
Egypt	1·4	Spain	14·1
Ghana	6·4	Taiwan	2·3
Greece	32·2	Thailand	2·7
India	0·2	Turkey	1·4
Israel	166·2	Venezuela	–27·4
Malaya	1·1	Yugoslavia	5·5

Source: Fourth, fifth and sixth columns of Table VIII–1.

industrial growth. Three-quarters of the capital was in the form of bonds. In colonies, such investments were guaranteed against default by the metropolitan power, and in independent countries, default was usually prevented by military pressure. Foreign bondholders were able to establish first claim on the customs revenues of Turkey and China. Egypt was administered by the representatives of the bondholders and they tried to do the same in Mexico. The popularity of bonds was helped by the relative stability of prices in those days and the free convertibility of currencies. The effective financing of such large indebtedness depended not only on military pressure but on the steady flow of new capital and substantial reinvestment of profits.

During the First World War there was default by China, Mexico and Turkey. There was a big reduction in the real value of French financial claims because of devaluation and most German assets were confiscated. Liquidation, depreciation or default of foreign assets in developing countries probably amounted to about $4 billion.

Because of this, old sources of capital dried up, and the only significant new flow in the inter-war period was American investment in Latin America and Japanese outlays in Manchuria, Korea and Taiwan.

In the 1930s, many countries defaulted on their bond obligations and imposed exchange controls. Of the $5·3 billion Latin American securities outstanding in 1938, $3 billion were in default.[1] The proportion was also high in Greece, Turkey and Yugoslavia. Dividend transfers on equity investment were blocked, and profits were in any case very low in the 1930s. These defaults helped greatly to alleviate the balance of payments difficulties of some countries. The saving in foreign remittances of interest was about $50 million annually for Brazil and Argentina, and about $25 million for Mexico. In addition they economized on amortization.[2] Colonies such as India were not allowed to fall into default, and some of them had to follow very deflationary policies to service a fixed debt load in a period of greatly depressed export earnings.

Between 1938 and 1950 foreign assets in developing countries were probably reduced by half. During the war, a good deal of foreign property was physically destroyed in south-east Asia, southern Europe and north Africa. Between 1938 and 1948, the UK sold over $3·5 billion of foreign investments in developing countries. Japanese and German investments were confiscated, and the Dutch lost their assets in Indonesia. Argentina spent $1 billion of her accumulated wartime reserves to buy out all foreign investment in railways, meat packing and utilities in 1945–7. Most Mexican debt was written off in wartime agreements with the USA. Brazil and India bought out most foreign portfolio investment, and China and Indonesia nationalized foreign assets without compensation.

In the post-war period, there has been very little private lending to developing countries by bond issues until very recently. Nearly all investment has been of a direct character, i.e. it represents ownership of physical assets. More than half of it has been in petroleum and minerals, a fair amount has gone into manufacturing, and there has been disinvestment in plantation agriculture.

[1] See C. Lewis, *The United States and Foreign Investment Problems*, Brookings, Washington, DC, 1948, p. 42, and *The Problem of International Investment*, Royal Institute of International Affairs, OUP, London, 1937. p. 303.

[2] The average annual interest and amortization receipts of the USA and UK combined (from developed and developing countries) fell by over $800 million from 1925–28 to 1932–34. See Royal Institute of International Affairs, *op. cit.*, p. 283.

In 1965 the total book value of private foreign assets in all developing countries (excluding trade credit) was about $37 billion, compared with $23 billion in 1938 and $24 billion in 1914. If one allows for the rise in prices, the real value is probably smaller now than in 1914 or 1938,[1] and in relation to the economies of developing countries it is certainly very much smaller. In 1914, it was equal to five times the exports of the developing world, in 1938 three times, and in 1965 to less than one year's exports.

Since the creation of the Common Market and the establishment of convertibility for European currencies in 1958, the international flow of private capital has greatly increased, but most of it has gone to developed countries. Foreign assets in developing countries are now less than a quarter of the world total, whereas in 1914 and 1938 they were half. In 1965, the gross outflow of direct investment from the USA, UK, Japan, Italy and Germany was $4·8 billion, but only $1·8 billion went to developing countries, and the developing country share of portfolio and bond investment has been tiny. Several factors account for this situation. Growth prospects and investment opportunities in developed countries have greatly improved and new trade alignments have promoted heavy US investment in Europe. Secondly, circumstances in the developing countries have changed. Most of the countries which were previously colonies have become independent so that their creditworthiness is no longer guaranteed by a colonial power which has control over their revenues. Their foreign exchange policies now involve greater risks for the foreign investor, and there is also risk of expropriation with inadequate compensation, either because of nationalist policies against foreign investors, or of socialist policies against private capitalists. Confiscatory expropriation has been a greater risk than balance of payments difficulties and has occurred in Egypt, Cuba, Algeria, Burma and Indonesia.[2]

[1] $37 billion at 1965 prices is less than $15 billion at 1938 or 1914 prices (using US GNP as a deflator). However, book values understate the market value of assets by considerably more in 1965 than in 1914 or 1938, partly because of the continuous post-war rise in prices, and partly because most of the assets are direct investments and not bonds.

[2] Several other countries have taken milder action against foreign investment. A report of the Joint Economic Committee of the US Congress, which takes a rather one-sided view of the issues, remarks lugubriously: 'The melancholy list of talk or action includes nullification of oil contracts in Argentina and Peru, expropriation and the hungry eyeing of foreign-owned utilities and mining properties in Brazil, calculated confiscatory copper taxes in Chile, and utility rates frozen by decree in several countries', see *Private Investment in Latin America*, Washington, 1964.

Table VIII–4

Book Value of Foreign Private Long-Term Capital Invested in Developing Countries 1914–65

		$ million	
Capital Exporters	1914	1938	1965
UK	7,128	8,240	9,000
France	4,800	2,624	2,500
Germany	2,976	344	1,200
USA	1,911	4,996	20,000
All developed	24,000	23,000	37,000
Capital Importers			
Argentina	3,100	3,200	2,800
Brazil	2,000	2,000	3,500
Chile	n.a.	1,300	1,000
China	1,600	3,500	0
India	2,600	2,800	1,200
Mexico	2,500	1,800	2,700

Sources: UK, France, and Germany 1914 from H. Feis, *Europe: The World's Banker 1870–1914*, Kelley, New York, 1961 (reprint of original 1930 edition). USA 1914 from C. Lewis, *America's Stake in International Investments*, Brookings, Washington DC, 1938, pp. 606 and 654. Other developed countries investments assumed to bear the same relation to the four countries indicated as in 1938. France, Germany, and the USA 1938 from C. Lewis, *The United States and Foreign Investment Problems*, Brookings, Washington DC, 1948. UK 1938 from *United Kingdom Overseas Investments 1938 to 1948*, Bank of England, London 1950. Lewis gives higher figures for the UK because she includes bonds in default. Figures for other developed countries are from Lewis. For 1965 US investment see *Survey of Current Business*, September 1967. UK 1965 direct investment (excluding oil and insurance) is given in the *Board of Trade Journal*, January 26, 1968. German direct investment (for 1964) is given in the *Monthly Report of the Deutsche Bundesbank*, December 1965. For other types of investment and other countries the figures are rough estimates based on information supplied by the OECD Secretariat. 1914 figures for Argentina, *El Desarrollo Economico de la Argentina*, ECLA, Santiago, 1959; Brazil from C. Macmillan, R. F. Gonzalez and L. G. Erickson, *International Enterprise in a Developing Economy*, Michigan, 1964, p. 18; Mexico, R. Vernon, *The Dilemma of Mexico's Development*, Harvard, 1963, p. 43; India, D. H. Buchanan, *The Development of Capitalistic Enterprise in India*, Cass London, 1966 (reprint of 1934 edition), p. 154; China, Chi-ming Hou, *Foreign Investment and Economic Development in China 1840–1947*, Harvard, 1965. The 1938 figures for developing countries are from C. Lewis, *The United States and Foreign Investment Problems*, except for China which is from Chi-ming Hou, *op. cit.*, p. 13, and includes Manchuria and Hong Kong. 1965 estimates from sources given for developed countries.

Nevertheless, some countries have received a good deal of capital. Latin America has done relatively well, as have Greece, Israel and Spain. Asian countries have fared badly, but this is due largely to their recent emergence from colonialism and their initially hostile reaction to foreign capital. Mexico received more private capital than other countries, in spite of a long history of debt default, and nationalization of foreign property in oil, railways and electricity. Mexican attitudes to foreign investment changed during the Second World War after the favourable debt settlement with the USA, and Mexico has actively promoted foreign investment throughout the post-war period. After some post-war hostility to foreign capital under the Peron and Vargas régimes, Brazil and Argentina also adopted policies rather favourable to foreign investment in 1955 and have departed only briefly from these since then. As a result they have been substantial recipients of private capital.

There were several undesirable features of foreign private investment in pre-war years. In the first place, it often led to foreign political intervention and loss of independence. Secondly, it usually enjoyed monopolistic favours not open to local enterprise. Access to land and natural resources was available at low cost because of the strong bargaining position of foreign capital with colonial governments. Foreigners were usually dominant in shipping and finance. Thirdly, the attitude of foreign companies to the training of local people was usually hostile. This was the case with the Suez Canal Company in Egypt, in rubber and tea plantations in Asia, and gold, diamond or copper mines in Africa. Fourthly, in countries with an abundance of labour and no trade unions, employers were able to draw on an unlimited supply of unskilled labour at a subsistence wage, and most of the benefits of increased productivity went to profits. When the employers were foreigners, these excessive profits were siphoned abroad.

In some cases these features of investment under colonial conditions offset the benefits which normally accrue from foreign capital and know-how. This was probably true in Egypt, India and China where foreign investment was small in relation to the political and economic costs to the recipient.[1] But in many countries foreign investment was a substantial net contributor to growth. This is

[1] See M. Kidron, *Foreign Investments in India*, London, 1965, which reaches negative conclusions on its value, and Chi-ming Hou, *Foreign Investment and Economic Development in China 1840–1937*, Harvard, 1965, for an opposite view of China.

certainly true in Argentina, Chile, Brazil and Malaya, as well as the USA, Canada, Australia and Tsarist Russia. If account is taken of debt default, the cost of the foreign investment was not large for these countries.

Many of the colonial features of foreign investment have been removed in the past two decades, although they did not all disappear with the coming of political independence and they have not yet vanished completely. In the first place, the political influence of private investors over governments in independent countries is now rather weak, particularly as there are major rival powers to which they can turn for protection. Thus Mexico, Iran and Egypt were able to persist in their policies of nationalizing foreign enterprise in spite of extremely powerful opposition. Access to local resources on favourable terms has steadily decreased as the bargaining power of developing countries has improved. They have been able to exploit commercial rivalries in developed countries, and in the case of oil they have set up a powerful producers' organization in OPEC. The capacity of oil producing countries to tax foreign companies has greatly increased.[1] This is also true in the copper industry. Requirements that local personnel be given key managerial positions and adequate training have been effectively enforced. The growth of government intervention and planning has ensured that the effect of foreign investment on local resource allocation can be controlled. Thus the capacity of developing countries to benefit from private investment is not inferior to that of countries like the USA and Canada in the early phases of their growth, or of Australia today.

There is now every reason to believe that the main gainer from private investment is the recipient country, rather than that which exports capital. The strong positive features of private foreign investment on the economy of the recipient country were clearly recognized by Lenin:

'The export of capital influences, greatly accelerates the development of capitalism in those countries to which it is exported. While, therefore, the export of capital may tend to a certain extent to arrest

[1] See Z. Mikdashi, *A Financial Analysis of Middle Eastern Oil Concessions: 1901–65*, Praeger, New York, pp. 100, 177 and 248. Government revenues per ton of oil in the Middle East rose from $1·60 in 1950 to $5·40 in 1964, after stagnating from 1913 to 1950. Government revenue from oil in Iran, Saudi Arabia, Iraq and Kuwait rose from $133 million in 1950 to $1·83 billion in 1964. In 1964, the total government revenue from oil in developing countries exceeded $3·5 billion.

development in the capital-exporting countries, it can only do so by expanding and deepening the further development of capitalism throughout the world.'[1]

In fact, Lenin's theory of imperialism is not so much a theory of exploitation but simply an explanation of the large pre-1914 capital outflow as a feature of capitalism in decay. The much more dynamic capitalism we have had since the Second World War has exhibited no need for privileged colonial markets or any incapacity to employ its savings in productive investment.[2]

Some countries have been reluctant to attract foreign private capital because they consider it an expensive substitute for aid which can be obtained on more favourable terms. A country which succeeds in attracting a lot of private capital will not seem a very deserving candidate for aid. But the need for foreign funds is too large for this argument to be given a lot of weight, and the function of private investment is not simply financial. Private investment is not only a useful way of meeting a trade deficit or filling a savings gap. It is one of the most important ways of acquiring modern technology and skills. In many branches of industry, domestic firms cannot hope to start production successfully merely by buying machinery. They will need advice on the feasibility of running a plant efficiently on the scale contemplated, on foreign markets for potential exports, on site selection and factory design, on installing and servicing machinery, on organizing the flow of work and checking quality and costs. There are some lines of production where this is within the competence of local people, but in other cases more substantial foreign help is essential. It is difficult to hire foreign industrial talent without foreign investment or project aid, because the competent people will be working for firms which cannot detach them for lengthy periods under technical assistance programmes. The necessary skills and know-how can often only be attracted by offering a foreign firm an equity participation in the venture. The only country which has managed to make rapid technical progress without sizeable foreign investment is Japan, but developing countries would find it difficult to follow the Japanese strategy because they have a much

1 See V. I. Lenin, *Imperialism, the Highest Stage of Capitalism*, Moscow, 1964, p. 107.

2 The UK is perhaps an exception, but a recent careful report on British experience with the export of capital does not suggest that capital exporters get very attractive rewards; see W. B. Reddaway, *Effects of UK Direct Investment Overseas*, Cambridge, 1967.

weaker capacity to carry out research and to supply their own training. The Japanese approach also involves large payments for foreign patents and licences ($177 million in 1966, or four times the size of dividend payments on foreign direct investment in Japan.)[1]

The approach to foreign private investment which seems most appropriate for developing countries is that followed by Mexico. Mexico settled her debts amicably with the USA during the war,[2] and the favourable relations which grew up between the US Export-Import Bank and Nacional Financiera provided a favourable experience of the uses of foreign capital which reassured the Mexican government. Mexico's appeal to foreign investors has been enhanced by the stability of the exchange rate since 1954, and the absence of controls on capital movements.

The Nacional Financiera is the main development bank providing funds for Mexican industry. Created in 1933, it was relatively small until the post-war period, but it has had time to build up a first-rate staff of development bankers, engineers and economists, and is now the major instrument for attracting foreign capital. The Mexican government remains very discriminating in its use of foreign investment. Foreigners are excluded from the natural resource industries of the country, and the government has continued to nationalize foreign enterprises (with compensation) in the post-war period. All foreign investment is subject to close licensing control, and work permits for foreign personnel are difficult to get.

In the 1960s, Nacional Financiera started to take the initiative itself in seeking foreign partners for Mexican enterprise. It seeks leading foreign firms in industries it wishes to develop which are willing to engage in joint enterprises and train Mexican personnel. Foreign investors usually get a Mexican market protected by tariffs and import restrictions, though in many cases the government exercises price controls to check excessive profits. Foreign investment has been diffused over a wide range of industry and has had a far-reaching impact in furthering development. Foreign enterprises have

[1] See A. Maddison, *Economic Growth in Japan and the USSR*, Allen & Unwin, London, 1969, p. 62.

[2] In 1943, the oil companies received $24 million compensation from Mexico for the 1938 nationalization, instead of the $500 million which they had claimed. The claim of US citizens for property sequestered during the 1910–20 revolution were settled. Back interest on government debt was waived and the capital was reduced from $509·5 million to $49·6 million. In 1946, the railway claims were settled for $50·5 million instead of the $557·6 million originally demanded. These data were supplied by the Colegio de Mexico.

sometimes been bought out when Mexican firms were capable of taking over with reasonable efficiency, and the original investment agreement itself may specify foreign participation for only a limited period. Mistakes have not been entirely eliminated. Given the size of the Mexican market, there was scope for only one or two firms in the motor industry if adequate production runs were to be achieved, but under pressure from foreign firms, the original plans for the industry were modified and twelve firms were allowed to start production. The government has tried to stimulate efficiency by imposing price controls, but prices are high and are likely to remain so unless tariffs are reduced and some firms forced out of the market.

Although many foreign investors in Mexico would complain that the government is too interventionist, or in some sectors so suspicious that it has prevented potentially useful investment, it would seem that Mexico has, in fact, developed an excellent system of foreign investment control which could well serve as a model for other countries.

In 1965, about a quarter of foreign assets in developing countries represented portfolio investment, i.e. shares and bonds, and three-quarters was direct investment, i.e. ownership of physical productive assets. This is the reverse of the situation in 1914. One consequence of this changed structure is that the cost of financing foreign investment is now rather high. In the old days, investors were satisfied with 5 per cent interest on their bonds, but the average rate of return on foreign assets now seems to be around 10 per cent. As a result the outflow of interest and dividends to private foreign investors is about $4 billion a year (excluding interest on trade credit), which is higher than the net inflow of new capital.[1] The profit rate on investment in natural resources and oil seems to be well above 10 per cent. In many lines of manufacturing it is lower, because a good deal of this investment was induced by protectionist policies. Those making the investment did it for 'defensive' reasons, i.e. they were attempting to keep some presence in a market which would otherwise be closed to their products. In modern conditions of steadily rising prices 10 per cent is not an unreasonable amount to pay for equity investment where part of the cost is destined to pay for technical assistance and transfer of skills. However, 10 per cent is too much to pay for capital intended simply to provide 'finance', and if this is what the

[1] See estimates in A. Maddison, 'The Balance of Payments of Developing Countries', *Banca Nazionale del Lavoro Quarterly Review*, June 1966.

country needs it should try to raise money from bond issues rather than encouraging equity investment. When Mexico has required foreign capital for financial and not technical reasons, it has raised the money by bond issues (the same is true, incidentally, of Japan).

In recent years there has been a spectacular renaissance in the market for foreign bonds, particularly in the Eurodollar market. Argentina, Brazil, Ivory Coast, Jamaica and Mexico raised funds in this market in 1968 at a cost to them of about 8.5 per cent including commission and charges, and there is no reason why other governments and private companies in developing countries should not start to participate in this market. In the past, the only developing countries which raised substantial funds by foreign bond sales were Mexico which kept itself credit-worthy and Israel, which was in a special position because most of its sales were to the Jewish community overseas and the motives of the purchasers were not purely financial.[1] In the first half of 1968, the international bond market provided \$3·5 billion of funds of which developing countries obtained only \$161 million.[2]

There is a significant outflow of private capital from developing countries which is difficult to measure because a good deal of it is illicit.[3] Most countries have tried to restrain capital outflows by exchange control but this is not always very effective in countries with a weak administration. A good deal of the outflow is capital flight by people who are hedging against political uncertainty and risks of devaluation. Given the nature of these countries, these are likely to remain important influences. But the outflow can be reduced by more efficient policy—a simplification and rationalization of exchange rates, better exchange controls, less inflation, or better organized capital markets. The creation of favourable profit opportunities for domestic investment by protective tariffs and import restrictions has also helped a great deal.

[1] In spite of the fact that Israel has sold bonds at a nominal 4 per cent interest, the distribution costs have been so high that the effective cost to Israel was about 8 per cent, see Chaim Ben-Shachar, *Public International Development Financing in Israel*, Columbia University School of Law (mimeographed), March 1963.

[2] See World Bank, *Annual Report 1968*, p. 63.

[3] See our own estimate of the amount involved for all developing countries in 1963 was about \$1·5 billion a year. This includes the flow from oil producing countries which have no exchange controls. See A. Maddison, 'The Balance of Payments of Developing Countries', *Banca Nazionale del Lavoro Quarterly Review*, June 1966.

TRADE CREDIT

Most developing countries have had access to substantial amounts of medium-term trade credit. The total amount outstanding in 1965 was about \$6·5–7·0 billion.[1] These funds are guaranteed against political, exchange and commercial risks by government agencies in developed countries. The system originated in the 1930s when the traditional credit mechanisms broke down and developed countries provided guarantees to sustain their exports. In the 1950s there was an attempt to check competition in the supply of this kind of credit by informal agreement amongst export credit agencies in the Berne Union, but the volume of credit outstanding has grown steadily every year and maturities have tended to lengthen. The bulk of the funds are for a period around five years, and the interest cost is usually about 8 per cent a year, so the annual burden of interest and amortization is about 28 per cent on five year credit. In 1965, amortization and interest on export credit amounted to \$1·9 billion[2] and was a heavy burden on the balance of payments of developing countries. In view of this, there would seem to be strong a case for greater recourse to the bond market where issues can be made for twenty years and interest costs are no lower than for export credit. However, it is much easier to get export credit than to raise a bond issue. Many countries are not creditworthy enough to sell bonds but can get trade credit.

PRIVATE GRANTS

Until recently private grants and transfers to developing countries were usually assumed to be fairly small in relation to other sources of capital. However, for our group of twenty-two countries the flow was about \$800 million a year.[3] These grants to individuals vary greatly from country to country. A large part consists of emigrants' remittances which bring large inflows into Greece, India, Spain, the Philippines and Yugoslavia. Malaya and Venezuela, by contrast,

[1] See W. I. Thorp, *Development Assistance Efforts and Policies, 1967 Review*, OECD, Paris, 1967, p. 62. These debts are in addition to the \$37 billion of foreign assets already mentioned.

[2] See W. I. Thorp, *op. cit.*, p. 73. About \$1,350 million was amortization and \$550 million interest.

[3] A recent OECD figure gives \$1 billion as the probable magnitude for all developing countries. See W. I. Thorp, *Development Assistance Efforts and Policies 1967 Review*, OECD, Paris, 1967. However, this may still be on the low side.

have a large immigrant population and an outflow of funds. Some countries benefit from private charitable organizations abroad. The biggest beneficiary is Israel which receives large remittances from the United Jewish Appeal in the USA. Israeli private citizens have also received large restitution payments from the German Government.

The role of private capital has undergone considerable change in the past ten years, and the total size of the flow has not increased. Nevertheless for the twenty-two countries examined, private capital supplied more than a third of total external resources, and it is clear that the flow could be considerably increased by action on the part of the recipient countries. There can obviously be no general purpose strategy towards foreign private investment. The needs of different countries for foreign skills and technical assistance vary a good deal. In Ghana a successful enterprise will need a good deal of foreign skill and in Mexico much less. Policy on joint enterprise, use of management contracts, or eventual state purchase of a joint enterprise will have to be tailored to the needs of the country. The more advanced the country, the smaller will be its need for technical help. On the other hand, the wealthier developing countries are not normally suitable candidates for government aid, and they need foreign capital as a source of finance rather than of technical assistance. Countries in this situation should raise funds by bond issues rather than equity investment. In several countries, both less and more advanced, foreign capital can be particularly useful in building up new markets for exports. Whatever the situation of the country it is desirable to think in terms of a 'managed' approach to foreign capital. For this purpose it is necessary to have a powerful domestic financial institution like Nacional Financiera which is capable of intelligent bargaining with foreign interests on reasonable terms and which can decide what form of foreign borrowing is desirable. Except in special situations, it would seem dangerous simply to create favourable tax incentives and then let foreigners start up any enterprise they want (though this has worked well in Hong Kong and the Ivory Coast). It would seem even more harmful to exclude all foreign enterprise on principle. The main requisite is to establish creditworthiness by regular servicing of debts, maintaining freedom to repatriate dividends and capital, and paying adequate and prompt compensation for nationalization. If these conditions are fulfilled, a country can raise substantial amounts of capital even if it has considerable inflation and tight exchange controls, although it is better to have a convertible currency and a fair degree of price stability. One of the most powerful attractions to foreign investors is commercial policy. Creation of protected markets or customs unions can induce big increases in the capital flow. The Central American Common Market and the European Common Market have both shown this dramatically.

The flow of private capital can also be stimulated by action on the part of developed countries. Germany, Japan and the USA give considerable emphasis to the virtues of foreign investors in promoting private enterprise in developing countries, and they have therefore established schemes to provide guarantees against political and exchange control risks to their own investors overseas. Most countries provide guarantees like this for export credit and this is obviously the reason why this type of credit is so readily available. It would help greatly if developed countries were to extend guarantees of this kind to longer-term borrowing. The US AID also has a programme to provide information and to finance surveys on new investment opportunities. Germany and Japan have certain tax incentives for private capital and the US has had tax favours for Western Hemisphere Corporations since 1942 (though these favours have mainly benefited Canada and do not affect direct investment). As a by-product of its balance of payments problems, the US now discriminates in favour of investment in developing countries because its exchange equalization tax on portfolio investment and its voluntary restraints on direct investment are not applied to the developing world.

The IBRD has also done a great deal to reopen private capital markets for the benefit of developing countries, and has encouraged them to improve their creditworthiness by servicing their foreign debt without default and to make reasonable compensation for nationalization. It has also tried to promote the private capital flow by getting agreement to its convention on investment disputes and is trying to do the same for a multilateral investment guarantee scheme.

GOVERNMENT GRANTS AND LOANS

Foreign aid has been a novel and favourable aspect of post-war experience. There were earlier periods in which governments made significant grants or loans to others, such as Britain's subsidies to its allies during the Napoleonic wars, or US government loans to its allies during the First and Second World Wars, but aid for the peacetime economic development of foreign countries has no significant precedent before the Marshall Plan of US aid to Europe. Indeed there was often a drain of funds on government account to the metropolitan colonial power in pre-war years.

REASONS FOR AID

The origins of aid to developing countries are mixed. In 1950 there were only two significant donors and their motives were mainly political. US economic aid was an adjunct to military support and an effort to contain external communist pressure. The aid recipients were concentrated on the borders of the USSR and China. Greece, Turkey, Korea and Taiwan were the main beneficiaries. France's aid to its colonies was large because of the support these countries gave to the Free French movement during the war, the intention to create a very close political and cultural link with France, and because several of them had a large French population which expected the government to provide roads, hospitals, etc., of the same standard as in France. In view of previous losses in the real value of loans issued in francs, the French government gave almost all its aid in the form of grants.

British aid started in 1940, but became significant only in the last stages of decolonization and has been concentrated on Commonwealth countries. However, British methods of war finance provided developing countries with $10 billion of sterling balances. These massive drawing rights were almost as big a boon to the developing world as Marshall Aid itself.

The creation of a vast number of newly independent states in the 1950s opened the way for other aid donors. The Indian balance of payments crisis of 1958, and the conversion of Cuba to communism also created new aid incentives. Germany and Japan started to give aid and to provide reparations as part of a programme of political rehabilitation and an effort to rebuild their trade. Soviet aid started in 1954 with the purpose of acquiring political influence in newly independent countries. In the course of the 1960s, all developed countries started giving bilateral economic aid. In many cases the dominant motive was one of moral obligation to help poorer countries rather than a desire for political influence. This certainly seems true of the aid programmes of countries like Canada, Sweden, Norway and Switzerland.

VOLUME OF AID

Between 1950 and 1967, net government aid to all developing countries rose from about $1·7 billion[1] to about $7·7 billion a year. In these eighteen years the total flow was about $80 billion or about six times the value of Marshall Plan aid to Western Europe. As it was spread over 1·5 billion people instead of 250 million, the per capita amount has been about the same as Marshall Aid. However, the real value per head was smaller because prices are now higher, and the impact on the recipient economies was less sharp as it was spread over eighteen years instead of four. The burden on donors has also been smaller. In 1949–52 Marshall Aid took about 1 per cent of American GDP, but aid now represents less than 0·4 per cent of the GDP of developed countries with a range from 0·1 per cent in the USSR, 0·3 per cent in the USA to about 0·7 per cent in France. The aid flow is small in relation to some of the regional income transfers that take place within developed countries. Aid from the German Federal Republic to West Berlin is about 3 per cent of West German GDP and the tax burden of providing aid to southern Italy is about 6 per cent of the GDP of northern Italy.

TERMS OF AID

Of the $80 billion of aid, about $53 billion was in the form of grants or required no repayment in foreign currency and about $27 billion represented net lending. As loans have to be repaid with interest, they are not equivalent to grants. Government loans represent a subsidy only to the extent that they are given on more favourable terms than could be obtained by the recipient from other sources. It is difficult to assess how big the implicit subsidy may be. Some of the recipients would be able to raise funds on foreign capital markets on the strength of their own credit, but for most of them the only alternative would be medium-term export credit. In 1966, the weighted average interest rate on new loans committed by western countries was 3·1 per cent compared with a rate for export credit of about 8 per cent, and bond issues which cost the borrower about

[1] This is a rough estimate from US and OECD sources. US economic aid to developing countries was about $900 million compared with over $3 billion to Western Europe. French contributions were about $500 million, UK about $100 million, all other countries $100 million and multilateral aid about $100 million. In 1967 the distribution was as follows: USA $3·4 billion, France $800 million, UK $450 million, other countries $2·0 billion and multilateral about $1 billion.

8·5 per cent, so the loans do involve a sizeable study. The World Bank (IBRD) lends at rates in line with its own borrowing costs, which are lower than those which developing countries would incur because of its greater creditworthiness. By the end of 1967, the World Bank had made loans of $10·8 billion (though not all of them went to developing countries). From 1960 the IBRD resources were supplemented by the International Development Association (IDA) which makes 'soft loans' for long maturities (up to fifty years) at a nominal interest rate or interest free. By the end of 1967 IDA had lent $1·7 billion. Communist countries also provide loans at low interest rates, usually around 2·5 per cent.

The cost of a loan depends on its maturity and on the length of the grace period (i.e. the number of years that elapse before amortization is due) as well as the interest rate. In 1966, the average maturity period for loans from western countries was 23·5 years. The initial debt service burden for the typical government loan in 1966 was therefore about 7·1 per cent a year (4 per cent amortization and 3·1 per cent interest) if there was no grace period, and less if amortization was deferred. This compares with 28 per cent for a typical five year export credit and 13·5 per cent on a typical twenty-year bond issue.[1] Several writers have calculated the concessionary element in loans by measuring the difference between actual terms and theoretical market costs. Such estimates are bound to be rough as we do not really know what 'market' terms might have been if countries had attempted to borrow on this scale commercially. For the period 1950–67 as a whole, the grant-equivalent of government lending was probably about $7 billion.[2] The total 'gifts' received by developing countries were therefore about $60 billion, i.e. $53 billion in grants and a $7 billion grant element in concessionary loans.

[1] Details on average loan terms for 1962–66 are shown in W. I. Thorp, *Development Assistance Efforts and Policies, 1967 Review*, OECD, Paris, 1967, p. 76.

[2] Methods of calculating the grant element in concessionary loans are described in G. Ohlin, *Foreign Aid Policies Reconsidered*, OECD Development Centre, Paris 1966. Using Ohlin's method, and taking an 8 per cent export credit as the typical alternative, the average concessionary element in loans appears to have been about 25 per cent, i.e. about $7 billion at its value to the recipient. For the donors, the cost of the grant element is smaller because their borrowing rate is lower than that of developing countries. However, the cost to the lender must also include some allowance for the risk of default: there has been little of this in the post-war period, but several countries have had to be given moratoria.

As the grant element in loans is only about a quarter of their total value, there is a strong case for making this clearer to parliaments which are voting aid funds. In most cases the immediate budgetary commitment for a loan is no different from a grant so that the very real difference in the transaction may pass unnoticed and the burden of aid is exaggerated. Mr Horowitz, the Governor of the Bank of Israel, has made an ingenious suggestion to meet this problem in the context of multilateral aid. It was to the effect that governments should provide some of this aid not directly as loans, but as guarantees against default and interest subsidies to issues in private markets. Thus the aid appropriation would be smaller and correspond to the real transfer cost, but the benefit to recipients would be the same. The government guaranteed bond issues could be tied to purchases in the country of issue, or better still, the balance of payments burden of the commercial loan component could be transferred to the markets most able to bear it, e.g. from the USA or UK to Germany. Such a scheme would probably require government underwriting of the private issues to ensure that the funds actually became available on the intended scale. The Horowitz scheme was rejected by the World Bank in 1965 because it considered that it would impose too great a strain on the capacity of private capital markets, but it would seem that this was a rather pessimistic view by present market standards. In any case it is worth examining whether a system of government guarantees for bond issues would not serve a more useful purpose than the present rather indiscriminate support for short-term export credit.

By 1965, developing countries had accumulated debts to foreign governments and international agencies of about $30 billion (excluding guaranteed export credit).[1] The 1965 interest on this was about $840 million. In itself, this did not constitute too alarming a burden for countries with annual exports of goods and services of more than $50 billion, and gross capital receipts of $14 billion a year. However, they also had to pay $550 million interest on export credit, $4 billion in dividends and interest on private capital, and $2·76 billion in amortization. Thus it is clear that the servicing of foreign loans and investment is a serious problem. Argentina, Brazil, Ghana, India, Indonesia and Turkey have avoided default

[1] See W. I. Thorp, *op. cit.*, pp. 62 and 71, which gives a figure of $40 billion for all types of debt and export credit. We know that export credit was $7 billion of this, and we have assumed that there was about $3 billion of debt to non-governmental creditors.

only by rescue operations by their creditors who have rolled over some of the loans. A good part of aid is designed simply to avoid default on previous debt. In view of this, there has been a considerable effort to ease the terms of official loans in the 1960s. In 1962, Germany was charging 4·4 per cent interest on these, Italy 6·1 per cent, Japan 6 per cent and the UK 5·8 per cent. The USA put heavy pressure on these countries to be more generous, because in 1962 it was lending at 2·5 per cent interest and felt that its loans were being used to pay off more onerous debts to other countries. Since then US interest rates have been raised and all the other countries have lowered their rates substantially and many other countries give loans with long maturities and substantial grace periods, so that there is no longer such a wide disparity.[1] The terms of lending still vary considerably for individual borrowers. In general they are tailored to the debt servicing capacity of the recipient. Canada, for instance, has made interest free loans to India for fifty years with a ten-year grace period (which is equivalent to a gift of 90 per cent of the amount), but its loans to Mexico have been 6 per cent export credits with grace periods of two years on which the gift element is only about 15 per cent of the value.

The 'harmonization' of loan terms has been one of the main achievements of the Development Assistance Committee of OECD in which aid donors have attempted some degree of co-ordination of aid policy. The terms now are geared more closely to the need of the the recipient rather than to the administrative tradition of the lender. However, the debt service problem remains very big and there is a strong case for substantial debt cancellation. Debt cancellation would often be legislatively easier to attain than an equivalent amount of additional aid funds, but the benefit to the recipient would normally be bigger than an equivalent amount of new money, because new money is usually tied to purchases in the donor country, whereas funds released from debt servicing would be available for purchases anywhere.

TIED AID

Although government loans are given on favourable terms, they may have some disadvantageous characteristics which are not shared by private loans. In most cases, concessional loan contracts specify how

[1] Loan terms are not, of course, identical and some countries now have more generous terms than the USA, e.g. Canada, Denmark, Sweden and the UK, which give interest-free loans.

the proceeds will be spent. Sometimes, resource allocation is distorted by the lender's insistence on large or demonstrative projects or highly capital intensive projects are adopted which may be inappropriate to a labour surplus economy. However, this kind of problem is less important than it used to be. The main problem now is that about three-quarters of aid is 'tied' to purchases in the aid-giving country. This does not matter if the things which are bought are items which would in any case have been purchased from that source. But there is an increasing tendency by some aid donors to see that tied aid is devoted to 'additional' exports which it would not otherwise have supplied. Sometimes the borrower may be forced to use loans to buy goods from the lending country which are more expensive than they would be from alternative suppliers, either because the supplying country is not the most competitive in this particular line, or because contractors in that country may attempt to raise prices in the knowledge that outside tenders cannot be accepted. A careful analysis of these cost disadvantages of 'tied credit' has been made for Pakistan where the average effective difference between tied procurement and free international bids on big investment projects seems to have been about 12 per cent. In other countries with less diversified aid receipts and less sophisticated programming, the extra cost would probably have been greater.[1]

Generally speaking, the divergence between the nominal and 'market' value of aid is smaller for industrial commodities or products for which there is a well established world price than it is for investment projects. However, some observers have claimed that there is a wide divergence between nominal and market values in the case of food aid. US surplus food disposals were about a quarter of the total grants received by developed countries from 1950 to 1967. Some of these were valued at their cost to the US government rather than at world market prices, which were lower. The world market price would itself have been lower if US surpluses were marketed normally.[2] In some cases these transactions have had harmful

[1] See M. ul Haq, 'Tied Credits—A Quantitative Analysis', in J. H. Adler, ed., *Capital Movements and Economic Development*, Macmillan, London, 1967.

[2] J. A. Pincus has tried to assess what the value of US surplus food disposals would have been if they had been sold on the world market. His estimate shows a value to the recipient of less than half of the official figure. See J. A. Pincus, 'The Cost of Foreign Aid', *Review of Economics and Statistics*, November 1963. To the donor the cost of such aid is practically zero as the US would have bought the food in any case, and would have had to destroy most of it, if it had not been given away.

effects on agricultural policy in recipient countries, as we have seen in Chapter V. Furthermore, the US was, until recently, required by Congress to receive payment in 'local currency' for most of these shipments. This does not involve the recipient in any foreign exchange burden[1] but it gives the US some influence over the recipient country's budget. This system of 'counter-part' funds is administratively cumbersome and politically embarrassing for the US. In one or two cases, the attempt to use these funds as 'double-duty dollars' may have had harmful inflationary effects.[2]

Technical assistance is another form of aid where the purchasing power of a dollar may vary a good deal according to the source of supply. A dollar of aid from the US, spent on providing the services of a school teacher, will supply only a third of the man-years which could be obtained from Europe with the same money.[3] However, the USA supplies very few teachers compared with France and countries usually concentrate technical assistance on the fields in which they have special expertise, so there should not be too great a divergence between the real and nominal value of funds made available for experts. In any case, the 'market' in personal services is very imperfect, and if developing countries set out to purchase the services they get through technical assistance it would probably cost them a good deal more. In the case of grants for foreign study there will be a divergence between the nominal and real value of the funds if the students do not return home afterwards. In 1967, technical assistance amounted to about one fifth of all Western aid; it provided training for 80,000 students and trainees, and provided 110,000 experts or volunteers for work in developing countries. In addition many students from developing countries received indirect aid as they studied abroad in institutions subsidised by governments.

One consequence of aid tying is that it may create a large gap between aid commitments and disbursements. This 'pipeline' problem of accumulated unspent funds is greatest in the case of project assistance, and is most severe in countries with a poor administration. Thus we may find that a country has quite a lot of aid to its credit,

[1] Some of the 'local currency' is earmarked for local US Embassy expenditure. This is really no different from repayment in dollars, and is therefore not considered as aid by the US. But this practice also has undesirable features for these funds are used more lavishly than dollars and tend to swell the size of US embassy staff unnecessarily.

[2] See J. Lewis, *Quiet Crisis in India*, Brookings, Washington, pp. 315–26.

[3] See A. Maddison, *Foreign Skills and Technical Assistance in Economic Development*, OECD Development Centre, Paris 1965, p. 64.

but is desperately short of funds for 'maintenance' imports, i.e. imports which are not needed for construction but simply to keep its industrial capacity and labour force employed. For this reason, some tied aid is now supplied in the form of maintenance imports and this can greatly relieve balance of payments pressure as it has done in India.

The tying of grants and loans is now pretty universal. About three-quarters of all aid is 'tied' and this probably knocks about 10 to 15 per cent off the real value of the total flow. However, if aid were not tied there would probably be much less of it, and one can hardly expect it to have the same characteristics as a commercial transaction. To some extent, aid tying is due to balance of payments problems in donor countries, but it is also due to the fact that people who make gifts prefer them to be personal. Not many people give cheques for birthdays or Christmas, and one could hardly expect the USA, France or the UK to give aid on the same scale if it were spent largely on German or Japanese goods. In the early post-war years, the US actually encouraged aid recipients to use the money for 'offshore purchases', but the political and economic strength of the US was then overwhelming and the US was in fact usually the cheapest source of supply. The Development Assistance Committee of OECD has made continuous efforts to reduce aid tying, but its efforts have had no success. Bilateral aid is tied much more now than it was in 1960.

METHODS OF AID ALLOCATION

Table VIII–5 shows average annual receipts of aid by country in the period 1960–65. The table includes both grants and loans and should really be adjusted to exclude the non-concessional element in loans. However, even in this crude form it is clear that there is an extraordinary range in aid receipts per capita. At the bottom end of the scale we find seven countries getting $2 per head or less, whereas Israel got $46 and Chile $13. It is therefore worth analysing how aid is allocated and whether the present allocation is rational.

Curiously enough, most donors have avoided explicit statements of their allocation criteria. In the 1950s, French aid was usually given in the form of grants for general budgetary support with no substantial constraints on the way it was used, or any explicit justification for the total amount allocated to a particular country, except historical and administrative accident. This approach was feasible, (*a*) because aid was very large and concentrated on a rather

Table VIII–5

Net Receipts of Economic Aid per Head of Population 1960–65

$ per annum annual average

Country	$	Country	$
Argentina	1·6	Mexico	1·3
Brazil	2·4	Pakistan	3·6
Ceylon	1·6	Peru	1·8
Chile	13·2	Philippines	1·7
Colombia	3·7	South Korea	7·7
Egypt	8·7	Spain	1·3
Ghana	4·3	Taiwan	6·3
Greece	5·5	Thailand	1·4
India	2·0	Turkey	5·9
Israel	46·2	Venezuela	2·5
Malaya	2·1	Yugoslavia	6·1

Source: First three columns of Table VIII–1 divided by six and by 1965 population. Aid is the total of government grants and loans. Strictly speaking only the concessional element in loans should be treated as aid in the same way as grants.

small group of countries; (*b*) aid involved no balance of payments problems as the trade of these countries was practically all with France; (*c*) French experts and administrators remained an important part of the civil service in many of the recipient countries (where this changed, as in Guinea, French aid ceased immediately); (*d*) there was no detailed parliamentary discussion of the aid programme, no feeling that it might put a burden on the French balance of payments or be too large for France to afford. In fact, even within the administration there was no clear knowledge of the total cost of aid.

At the other extreme, the IBRD practice in the early 1950s was to make loans on market terms only to meet the foreign exchange cost of particular projects. By concentrating on projects, the Bank believed that it was ensuring that the loans were being used efficiently and it also felt that the discipline of careful scrutiny was helpful in educating officials in the recipient country. The Bank was not required to evaluate the general economic policy of the recipient and this avoided delicate political problems. Its only concern with the general economic policy of the country was with its capacity to service loans and its previous debt record.

In a situation in which aid was inadequate to meet total needs, neither approach provided adequate criteria for allocating funds. The French system was too *ad hoc* and lacked adequate accountability, so that some countries and projects got more than they deserved, but non-francophone countries were not even considered. The Bank method also did not ensure the right *countries* were getting priority. It was easier to find good projects in countries which were rich and prosperous than in those which were poor, but it was also possible to find a good project in a country whose general fiscal and financial policies were poor. In many cases the Bank picked projects which would have been financed anyway so that its loans were really not financing their ostensible purpose, but enabling the recipient country to use its own resources on other more marginal objectives.

In fact, France has not followed these criteria in the extreme form in which we have presented them and IBRD policy has evolved considerably. The French Finance Ministry and the Cour des Comptes make sure that there is some check on priorities and use of resources, and the familiarity with the problems of the relatively few recipient countries ensures an enlightened approach and helps avoid waste. The World Bank policies changed after the Indian balance of payments crisis in 1958. It sent broad programme review missions to India and Pakistan at the end of the 1950s and has done the same for many more countries since then. It now gives considerable weight to both general economic need and to success criteria.

In the USA the situation has always been somewhat different. The detailed accountability of the administration to Congress is traditionally greater than in European countries, and there is more suspicion of the possibility of corruption. The relationship between the US and the recipient countries was more varied and less traditional than in the case of France with her colonies. Finally, US interests were global, aid was so large and involved so many projects that it could hardly follow the casual French approach. The US was therefore much more in need of an aid philosophy and of articulate criteria for aid allocation than other countries. For these reasons there were eight Presidential committees on foreign aid and several reorganizations of the aid agency, in an attempt to improve aid allocation, whereas in France there was no serious questioning of the old approach until the Jeanneney Report of 1963. The UK approach has been something between that of France and the USA, whereas Germany and Japan have been more concerned with commercial and political issues and have given less attention to performance.

The aid philosophy which emerged in the USA evolved over a

number of years from the work of the MIT group of Rostow, Millikan and Rosenstein-Rodan, and of Professor Chenery when he was Programme Director of AID. The solution was 'the programme approach' under which aid was allocated not on the basis of need or income level, but on potential performance. This meant that the recipient country had to prepare an overall development plan, showing that it was pursuing a self-help strategy and that aid would be a catalyst leading to self-sustained, i.e. self-financed, growth in a reasonable period of time. Performance was to be judged by several macro-economic criteria—the growth rate achieved, the rise in the domestic savings ratio, the increase in exports, the improvements in skills and administrative capacity, the wisdom of fiscal and monetary policy—rather than success in implementing individual aid projects. This strategy involved concentrating aid on a limited number of countries which were considered good risks. The follow-up procedure required regular country reviews. In return, recipients were supposed to get aid up to the limits of absorptive capacity, i.e. up to the point at which it ceased to yield reasonable returns.

There were substantial advantages in this approach. The development plans provided some idea of the comparative efficiency with which aid might be used. The proposed measures of performance provided guidelines for crosschecking and following up. The stress on performance helped ensure that resources were not wasted. The discussion of the general strategy of development was likely to be even more educational to recipients than technical discussions on single projects. The programme approach also provided assurance to recipients over a number of years, and enabled them to gear aid to their plans rather than rely on year to year decisions.

However, there are political snags in a bilateral application of the programme approach which is intended to reward virtue and to impose sanctions for poor performance. Formulation of a mutually agreeable programme requires involvement in the recipient country's central policy problems, ones which affect every political interest group in the country. Most countries resent giving foreigners this much say in their affairs, particularly when they have only just won their independence. In general they will only agree to programmes which they would have followed anyway, and they may often have little compunction in breaking agreements. The US (understandably enough) has been sensitive to charges of interfering too far on basic issues of policy and has usually been reluctant to apply strong sanctions for inadequate performance, or even to appear in public as a strong critic. Thus programme surveillance when applied bilaterally is an obvious target for charges of neo-colonial interference by critics of the recipient government, but paradoxically enough, is too embarrassing a relation for really strong pressures to be applied.

There are also delicate personnel problems. On the US side, the aid decision involves high level officials in Washington for only a brief period. Most of the detailed surveillance is carried out by large numbers of lower level US aid officials in the recipient country, who are continually asking for statistics and progress reports. In the recipient country such matters are too important to delegate, and the few key officials who run the country's economic policy spend a disproportionately large amount of their time meeting these requests and listening politely to advice. This problem could be reduced by scaling down the size of AID missions, but the real need is to provide surveillance and policy review arrangements which will be useful enough to survive the aid period.

For small aid donors, the US approach to country surveillance is simply not feasible unless they concentrate on very few recipients. As the US spends over $3 billion a year on aid, it can afford to maintain several thousand aid officials, but smaller donors cannot afford such overheads. There is therefore a fairly strong case for multilateral surveillance.

The procedures for multilateral policy review created in Europe in the Marshall Plan period within OEEC were so effective and useful that they are still carried on today within the OECD, where the economic policies of the US itself are now also subjected to regular, frank and articulate scrutiny by other countries. When governments subject themselves to this kind of discipline, it provides responsible and objective analysis which is often not available at home. Apart from its technical and educational value, this external view can be of great help to governments in persuading domestic opinion to accept the more painful aspects of their policies. There are occasions when governments know what should be done, but hesitate to do it because it is politically unpopular. It is easier to act if they seem to be bowing to outside pressure, particularly if it is accompanied by financial help. Most countries are initially reluctant to engage in this kind of co-operation and aid is obviously a useful lever of persuasion. However, the aid lever should be used with long-term goals in view, and the policy review procedure must be divested of any conceivable tutelary features if its usefulness is to be genuinely accepted. Policy reviews should cover the whole range of factors affecting growth, and should be held every two years. There is no need to examine the impact of aid year by year and dollar by dollar. If overall policy is reasonably sound, the aid will be properly used. Unless a reasonably long time horizon is used for policy assessment, there will be a tendency to emphasize crash programmes and other wasteful ventures.

The World Bank and OECD consortia arrangements designed to assess the aid needs of India, Pakistan, Greece and Turkey are a first approximation to multilateral surveillance, and have been meeting regularly for several years. There are also World Bank consultative groups for Ceylon, Colombia, East Africa, Korea, Malaysia, Morocco, Nigeria, Peru, Sudan, Thailand and Tunisia. However, these meetings do not normally involve regular and articulate scrutiny of the recipient country's general economic policy. They are usually joint pledging sessions which look at aid programmes as a whole and at major projects. In the case of India, where a big change in economic policy was obviously required in the mid-1960s, the consortium does, however, apperar to have exercised some pressure to move in lines which were eventually followed.

Mutual surveillance in developing countries has been developed furthest within the framework of the Alliance for Progress. At first, the guidelines for allocation of aid were laid down by a committee of 'wise men', i.e. a group of nine independent experts of different nationalities. Their surveillance functions were later taken over by an OAS committee, the CIAP, which makes regular reports on the performance of participating countries. These meetings are regular, and all member countries of the OAS are participants. They have contributed something to the improvement in policies in Latin America in the 1960s but the process of policy analysis still has major deficiencies. First of all, the basic aid relation is a bilateral one between the USA and the individual country being examined. Other recipient countries participate, but usually consider it bad form to criticize a Latin American neighbour too severely in front of the USA. The active discussions in CIAP are therefore largely confined to the country under review, the US delegates and the secretariat. There is not the same degree of participation of member countries which characterizes OECD country reviews. If CIAP is to work as effectively as OEEC it would be useful to give the Latin American countries collective control over allocation of part of the aid funds, such as European countries obtained in EPU. It need not be a large part, but unless they have some material interest of this kind, most countries will not treat the mutual policy review very seriously. It might also help if CIAP country reviews were held in Latin America rather than in Washington, and if the US status in the committee were reduced to that of an observer, as it was in OEEC.

On the whole, there is a keen awareness amongst aid donors of the problem of assessing aid priorities correctly so that it is fairly distributed and waste is avoided. The creation of aid ministries with a unified aid budget has sharpened public awareness outside the USA and there is now quite a respectable quantity of European literature on problems of aid allocation. France had the Jeanneney Report and the UK has had a series of studies by the Overseas Development Institute. Within the OECD Development Assistance Committee, there has been very thorough exploration of the different methods of approach which have had an educational value for all aid donors. The existence of this Committee has also helped guide some of the new donors, and encouraged them to build up their own programmes to very sizeable proportions. However, the scope for real co-ordination of aid policy is limited, as the motives of the USA, France, Germany and Japan in the aid field are often as divergent from each other as they are from those of the USSR.

There are also more fundamental analytical problems in allocating aid on the basis of performance. The Chenery approach[1] involves considerable sophistication in the detailed analysis of performance but all rigorous models are necessarily rather simple and may give misleading conclusions. Our own analysis in Chapter II provides an alternative analytical framework for measuring policy performance which could also be used in allocating aid. Our model is different from that of Chenery in several important respects. It segregates the spontaneous from the policy element in growth, it recognizes differences in income level as a factor influencing savings capacity, it takes explicit account of differences in labour supply and makes allowance for the retarding effects of initially unfavourable economic structure and of low educational levels on the effectiveness of labour inputs. On the other hand it places less emphasis on structural constraints in the balance of payments. Our model therefore gives considerable weight to the initially unfavourable

[1] The AID approach is set out in H. B. Chenery and A. M. Strout, *Foreign Assistance and Economic Development*, AID, Washington, 1965. This is mainly concerned with savings and export performance and makes no attempt to identify growth due to domestic policy efforts, e.g. it does not distinguish between autonomous and policy-induced savings.

factors which weaken the growth potential of the poorest countries. Thus it gives similar performance marks to India and Israel, in spite of the enormous difference in their growth rates. By our criteria the present per capita allocation of aid between countries does not reflect very rational decision-making either in terms of need or policy performance. Israel got $46 of aid per head and India only $2.

Another serious shortcoming in present aid doctrine is that aid is conceived as a temporary proposition, and its supposed objectives are only obliquely related to the abolition of poverty. Aid is to be given only for the period in which a country achieves its take-off to self-sustained growth. It is supposed to provide countries with extra resources to use for investment and other development purposes so that they can break out of a situation of economic stagnation and set off a process of cumulative growth, i.e. a steady rise in real income per head. In fact, all of the countries we have examined have made significant progress in this respect in the past twenty years. In spite of temporary setbacks, as in India in 1965–66, and in spite of accelerated population growth, it seems clear that domestic economic policy alone is now adequate to achieve continued increases in per capita income in future. The take-off has therefore been achieved, but is growth self-sustaining?

The concept of self-sustaining growth has been used in two rather different senses. In the first place it is used to describe a golden age in which the spontaneous growth forces in the private sector will be strong enough to propel the economy forward to higher income levels and the need for deliberate policy action would wither away. This situation is different from that during the take-off in which government policy will have to drag the economy forward and break down the institutional obstacles and inertia of a stagnant economy. However, there has been a great increase in the degree to which even highly developed countries depend on active government policy and close inter-governmental co-operation in order to sustain their growth. All private enterprise economies now depend heavily on both spontaneous and on policy-induced growth, so that self-sustaining growth in this sense is no longer a very meaningful goal for any kind of country.

Self-sustained growth is also used to describe a situation in which a country can attain its full growth potential without balance of payments support, i.e. when it can finance all the imports it needs from its own export earnings and private capital receipts. Although a good many indicators have been devised which help to determine whether a country is moving towards this goal, it is doubtful whether any country will ever actually reach a position in which foreign aid could not increase its growth rate. The UK for instance, has not been in a state of self-sustained growth in the post-war period, and the USA has also had a long-standing balance of payments deficit. This criterion is therefore so vague that it permits almost any country to make a case for aid.

The desire of both aid donors and aid recipients to foresee an end to aid had led both sides to attach importance to self-sustaining growth as the ultimate goal. The trouble with this is that it makes no distinction between levels of income. The US has attempted to help both Chile and Pakistan towards self-sustained growth, and Pakistan has made good progress in this direction. But it is surely an odd strategy which plans to stop aid to Pakistan in 1985 when the per capita GDP will be $280 if the targets are reached.[1] In Chile, by contrast, the aid programme was started when the income level in real terms was more than $800, and policy has been much less efficient.

The present criteria for allocating aid funds are not very satisfactory either in identifying which countries should be helped or in demonstrating when aid should be ended. We can improve the situation by setting up improved procedures for policy review by developing countries themselves and by continuing to improve the analytical quality of performance models, and the data on which they are based. However, there is another major step which can be taken to make aid distribution fairer. The primary purpose of aid should be to help countries which are poor to get richer. We should define potential aid recipients in terms which are objectively measurable and keep on helping them until they pass the poverty line. Our own suggestion for the poverty line is a per capita income of $500 when measured at 1965 US prices. This is a lower definition of poverty than would be acceptable inside the USA itself, but it is near

[1] The target figure is derived from our own estimates of the 1965 level and Pakistani aspirations on growth up to 1985. The chief economist of the Pakistan planning commission has produced a 'Rostow' model for the 25-year period 1960–85, assuming that aid will disappear by 1985 and that domestic savings will be raised from 6 to 24 per cent of GDP. In this model aid reaches a maximum of 6·4 per cent of GDP within the period, but would be less (about 4 per cent) for the period as a whole. This gives aid a more modest role than in Taiwan. In fact Pakistan was getting aid equal to 4 per cent of its GDP in 1960–65. See M. ul Haq, *The Strategy of Economic Planning*, Oxford University Press, Karachi, 1966.

the income level in Taiwan to which the USA has ceased giving economic aid. The purpose of foreign aid is, of course, very different from domestic anti-poverty programmes. Foreign aid is not relief intended to bring up incomes to a minimum $500 level in order to boost consumption. On its present scale, aid is only big enough to provide an income supplement of around $4 a head and it must therefore be channelled into uses (mainly investment) which will raise production.

Hitherto, the definition of an underdeveloped country has been largely a matter of pragmatic convenience for aid statisticians. But now that the statistics do exist, we can see that some countries are much less underdeveloped than others. It would be sensible to take some of the richer countries out of the underdeveloped world and treat them as developed. The change in the definition might break the continuity of aid statistics, but it would be a tangible demonstration that there has been progress within the developing world and that aid has been a successful operation. There is also a precedent for such a transition in the case of Italy. Countries above the $500 level need not have achieved self-sustaining growth in the sense that they ceased to be capital importers. Between $500 a head and $1,000, they should remain eligible for World Bank Loans and the harder type of government loans, but not for grants or concessional loans. This would highlight the need to make private capital markets function better in allocating funds to deserving borrowers which had just passed the $500 level. It would force countries to prepare themselves for developed country status, whose advent would be much more predictable. It might be desirable to give countries some kind of reward or consolation prize when they reach this turning point. The most obvious present would be cancellation of government debt which they had acquired during the aid period. $500 may seem an arbitrary figure and it may seem harsh to require a sharp transition from one status to another. However, past experience shows that clearly defined obligations of just such an arbitrary character have been very useful e.g. the percentage quotas laid down for trade liberalization by OEEC, the percentage tariff cuts in the Common Market, or the IMF requirements for countries with convertible currencies. The trouble at the moment is that there is no clear way of telling whether a country is still underdeveloped.

If this criterion were applied to the twenty-two countries under review, nine of them would no longer be candidates for aid, i.e. Argentina, Chile, Greece, Israel, Malaya, Spain, Taiwan, Venezuela and Yugoslavia. In none of these cases would there be major political or economic difficulty in cutting out further aid, and several of them are star examples of how successful it has been. It is also desirable that countries beyond the $500 income level should behave like developed countries in their commercial policy, or at least remove the restrictions they presently apply to imports from developing countries.

For countries below the $500 level we still have a problem of aid allocation for which there are no simple solutions. The programme approach can be further refined, but is still too rough to be a very firm guide. A good deal will also depend on common-sense political judgements on whether the country can use aid efficiently. A third crosscheck would be a regular flow of data on the per capita aid receipts of different countries. This is useful prima facie evidence of the fairness of aid allocation and equity considerations are of some relevance when we consider the weakness of our analysis of policy performance.

Although it is clearly possible to improve the allocation of aid, it is more difficult to estimate what the aggregate amount should be. In the 1950s there were several efforts to make global estimates of requirements. Most of these estimates involved remarkably small amounts, considering that they assumed (or said they assumed) that there would be no constraint on the total supply, and that aid would be supplied up to the limit of absorptive capacity.

On the whole, the advocates of aid whose models are cited in Table VIII–6 have reason to be satisfied with the results achieved. Our twenty-two countries increased their per capita income by an average of 2·8 per cent a year from 1950 to 1967 instead of the 1·8–2·0 per cent which was forecast, and external finance reached $11 billion a year compared with the $6·5–7·5 billion they projected. The average investment-output ratio for the twenty-two countries was in fact 3, as most of the estimates postulated. However, these earlier estimates of what could usefully be spent on aid were too modest. They assumed that most of the developing countries would start from a position of more or less complete stagnation and would face many institutional barriers to growth. Hence the emphasis on the limits of absorptive capacity (which was not defined in any detail). Some idea of what absorptive capacity might have been is provided by the experience of countries which got a lot of aid. In four countries, external resources averaged 10 per cent of GDP, and their GDP grew by an average of 8 per cent a year. In the eighteen other countries,

Table VIII–6

Estimates of Aid Requirements

	Reference year	Projected growth of GNP per capita (per cent) (per annum)	Projected ratio of gross investment required for a unit increase in GNP	Existing foreign capital flow assumed ($ billion)	Additional foreign capital required ($ billion)
M. F. Millikan and W. W. Rostow	1953	2·0	3	3·0	3·5
J. Tinbergen	1959	2·0	3	4·0	3·5
Paul Hoffmann	1959	2·0	3	4·0	3·0
P. N. Rosenstein-Rodan	1961	1·8	2·8	4·0	2·4

Source: See G. Ohlin, *Foreign Aid Policies Reconsidered*, OECD Development Centre, Paris, 1966, for a summary of the different estimates.

external resources averaged only 1·2 per cent of GNP and income grew by 5 per cent a year. There is no doubt that the superior performance of the first group was due largely to foreign aid. Our own calculation in Table II–12 suggests that external finance accounted for 2·8 per cent a year of growth in the first group and 0·5 per cent in the second. Greece, Israel, Taiwan and South Korea did not run into technical bottlenecks. A good deal of their growth was due to inreased efficiency. They all increased their marginal rate of domestic savings appreciably. All of them managed to rid themselves of galloping inflation, and in the first three countries there was a clear move to self-sustaining growth and a steady decrease in the relative importance of external resources. It is true that Israel and Taiwan both had an unusual 'absorptive' capacity because of the skills of their immigrants and the dedication and strength of their governments, but much of this was devoted to military purposes, and there is really no reason to doubt that if aid had averaged 10 per cent of GDP of all developing countries that the average growth rate would have been much higher.

In our view, the limitations of absorptive capacity have been exaggerated. The inventors of the concept were cautious because they did not want to frighten Congress about the potential size of the aid flow, but, at present, developing countries are getting on average about $4 of aid per head each year and it is clear that this volume of aid has come nowhere near the limits of absorptive capacity for developing countries as a whole, though it may have done so in individual cases. Aid has been limited to what the developed countries thought they could afford to give in the light of their own public opinion, the urgency of other claims on public finance, their balance of payments situation, etc. As aid is unlikely to reach absorptive capacity there is all the more reason for distributing it as efficiently and as fairly as possible.

The absolute level of aid has risen steadily since 1950, but the really big increase occurred from 1959 to 1961 and the overall burden of aid in relation to the GNP of donor countries has remained unchanged since 1964 at about 0·4 per cent. It is even smaller if we eliminate the non-concessional element in loans. At the UNCTAD Conference in Delhi, the OECD member countries accepted the obligation to raise their total net capital exports to developing countries to 1 per cent of GNP. However in 1968, US aid appropriations were cut to their lowest level since the programme began. To some extent the faltering in US aid is due to payments difficulties, to disillusion with the fact that aid does not win friends, and to impatience that the process of development takes so long. But there is also a strong feeling that aid has been a failure, that resources have been wasted, and that instead of increased prosperity the developing countries are getting closer to famine conditions. In our view, this latter judgement is quite mistaken. But it is understandable that it should have arisen. There was a dramatic harvest failure in India for two years running. This, in itself, was an act of God, but it helped to dramatize some of the real failings of development policy in India. There has been a sharp increase in military spending in several developing countries. The administrative and technical limits to African absorptive capacity have been illuminated by the political chaos in that continent. Population growth is accelerating in most developing countries and reducing the income benefits of many of their development efforts. In spite of this, the case in favour of aid remains strong. The output performance of most developing countries has been surprisingly good since 1950, and in countries which received a lot of aid it has been outstanding. Economic policies have been far from perfect, but have certainly been no worse than those of the United States. To some extent, the present scepticism about aid may be a backlash reaction to some of its gloomier advocates. Estimates of an ever-widening foreign exchange 'gap' have been put forward by UNCTAD which are based on a deep pessimism about the self-help capacity of the developing world. The 'world food problem' has often been presented as if it were a Malthusian spectre, and UN reports usually give greater emphasis to the failures than to the basic fact that the Development Decade target is being fulfilled.

Chapter IX

Population Control and Economic Growth

There is now a fundamental difference between the demographic situation of rich and poor countries. In the developing world, population grew by 2·6 per cent a year from 1950 to 1967 and the rate is still increasing. In developed countries, the average rate was just above 1 per cent and is declining. This is the major reason for the slower growth of income per head in the developing world even though its total output is actually increasing faster than that of rich countries.

The problem is often presented as if it were essentially a desperate race between population and food supply with serious danger of world famine. We have seen in Chapter IV that this is incorrect and anachronistic as an analysis of the contemporary world. The countries in which agriculture has performed inadequately are those in which economic policy was wrong, and there is no evidence that agriculture has come near to its productive ceiling. Furthermore, the famine-mongers underrate the progress already made in living standards. In India and Pakistan a significant portion of the population is living at bare subsistence levels in the sense that a little less food would lead to death. But in most developing countries the situation is less apocalyptic. Not only is the *average* standard well above subsistence, but in all the countries we have examined total output is increasing faster than population. Because the crude Malthusian view of the problem is so obviously inapplicable in Latin America or Africa, politicians in those countries have not taken the population question seriously. If the choice were as sharp as that posed by Malthus,[1] more governments would have taken

[1] Malthus wrote his famous essay on population 170 years ago, and based his argument on assumptions which had some applicability to eighteenth century conditions but which are no longer valid: (*a*) that population has a natural

vigorous steps to foster birth control. But the real point in population policy in most countries is not to avoid starvation, but to eliminate poverty more quickly. Population control would make it possible to raise output per head much faster and would even accelerate the growth of total output. Its benefits are particularly great in the first generation. If we are to convince politicians to take action in this field, real issues must be stated clearly.

There have been three main phases in demographic history in the 2,000 years of our era. Until about 1700, world population increased extremely slowly at about 0·04 per cent a year. It took seventeen centuries for world population to rise from 300 to 600 million. There was little change in technology,[1] and no improvement in living standards. Birth and death rates were both about 35 per 1,000 population. Gravestones in ancient Athens and in seventeenth-century London tell the same story—an average life expectation of about thirty-five years.[2] Population expanded only where the area of cultivation could be increased. It was in this era that there was sharp pressure of population on food supplies, and most people lived at levels of bare subsistence. Population moved in cycles. As agriculture expanded to more marginal soils, the likelihood of bad harvests increased and there were more serious famines. Poor transport limited trade in food. Poor nutrition and lack of medical knowledge led to a widespread incidence of disease and particularly of epidemics. The worst of these was the Black Death (bubonic plague) which wiped out a fifth of the European population between

tendency to grow faster than output; (*b*) that most people have a living standard which provides only for bare subsistence.

As a result he argued that population would have to be limited either by natural checks such as famine and epidemic, or by sexual continence.

[1] The main changes of economic significance between Roman times and 1700 were the development of harness for horses (which improved their traction power about threefold), the development of windmills and water wheels and improvements in navigation. Until Watt invented the steam engine in 1775, the most powerful machine in the world was a series of water wheels at Marly, 'built for Louis XIV by the Liege carpenter Rennequin in 1682. It had a potential capacity of 124 h.p. and delivered at least 75 h.p. in actual work, but owing to faulty maintenance it had less than one-fortieth of its original capacity by 1796', see C. Singer, *et al.*, eds., *A History of Technology*, vol. IV, Oxford, 1958, p. 155. The average eighteenth-century water wheel had an energy output of only 5 h.p.

[2] The life expectation of those who could not afford gravestones was obviously lower. It has been suggested that average life expectation in this period was less than thirty years, see L. I. Dublin, A. J. Lotka and M. Spiegelman, *Length of Life*, Ronald, New York, 1949, p. 42.

1347 and 1351. After such catastrophes the standard of living rose temporarily because there were fewer people in relation to the land available and there was often a switch from crop to livestock production as diets improved. However, as population recovered, there was renewed pressure on productive capacity.

The second phase of demographic progress lasted from 1700 to about 1950. In these 250 years, world population quadrupled and growth was ten times as fast as in the earlier period. The production potential was raised because improved transport permitted settle-

Table IX–1

Estimated World Population by Region AD 0–1965

Millions

	World	Africa	US and Canada	Latin America	Asia	Europe including USSR	Oceania
AD 0	300	—	—	—	—	—	—
1700	600	—	—	—	—	—	—
1750	750	100	1	12	480	150	2
1800	960	100	6	20	630	200	2
1850	1,240	100	26	35	810	265	2
1900	1,650	150	81	65	930	423	6
1950	2,517	222	166	163	1,381	572	13
1965	3,285	310	214	243	1,825	675	18

Table IX–2

Growth Rates of World Population, AD 0–1965

Annual average compound rate

	World	Africa	North America	Latin America	Asia	Europe including USSR	Oceania
AD 0–1700	0·04	—	—	—	—	—	—
1700–1750	0·4	—	—	—	—	—	—
1750–1850	0·5	0·0	3·3	1·1	0·5	0·6	0·0
1850–1900	0·6	0·8	2·3	1·2	0·3	1·0	2·2
1900–50	0·8	0·8	1·4	1·9	0·8	0·6	1·6
1950–65	1·8	2·3	1·7	2·7	1·9	1·1	2·2

Sources for Tables IX–1 and 2: Derived from Goran Ohlin, 'Historical Outlines of World Population Growth', UN World Population Conference, Belgrade, 1965; and J. D. Durand, 'World Population Estimates, 1750–2000', same conference; and, *Demographic Yearbook*, 1965, UN, New York, 1966.

ment of new lands. There was also a diffusion of existing agricultural knowledge between continents. America provided the rest of the world with new and highly productive crops—potatoes, sweet potatoes, cassava, maize and peanuts. Potatoes yielded three times as much food per acre as previous crops and became a staple food in Europe, and cassava played the same role in Africa. Similarly, the introduction of horses to America greatly increased its population potential. Famines became rarer; the last one in Europe was in Ireland, in 1845; in Asia, the last one was the Bengal famine of 1944. All continents benefited from these changes, but this second phase was already one in which there was divergence between the rich and poor countries. Living standards increased very substantially in developed countries, but much less in the developing world. Europe and America created a new agricultural technology based on research, seed selection and fertilizer; they developed industry, benefited from bulk transport of food, and from improvements in medical knowledge and facilities which greatly reduced the incidence of disease. In the eighteenth and first half of the nineteenth century these advantages of Europe and America led them to faster demographic growth than Asia and Africa, but in the 1870s their fertility began to fall with the spread of birth control.

Since 1950, most of the world has had access to the technological advantages which were largely confined to Europe and America in the second phase. The world production potential is expanding much more rapidly, public health technology has been greatly improved and many diseases have been conquered quickly. As a result world population has again accelerated, but the acceleration has been greatest in the developing world.

Nearly all developing countries were affected by the post-war upsurge in population. The highest natural growth rate was in Mexico where population is expanding by 3·3 per cent a year and is still accelerating (the higher rates in Israel and Venezuela were due to immigration). At current Mexican rates of growth the population will quadruple every forty years. The rapidity of the increase has taken most governments unawares and consciousness of the problem really dates from the early 1960s when the population censuses of 1960 and 1961 became available. In India and Pakistan the plans for the second half of the 1950s forecast a population growth rate of 1·4 per cent a year, whereas the actual out-turn was over 2 per cent in both cases.

The post-war acceleration in population growth has been primarily

Table IX–3

Growth Rates of Population 1870–1967

Annual average compound growth rates

	1870–1913	1913–50	1950–67		1870–1913	1913–50	1950–67
Argentina	3·4	2·2	1·8	Taiwan	—	1·9	3·1
Brazil	2·1	2·1	3·1	Thailand	—	2·3	3·0
Ceylon	1·3	1·6	2·5	Turkey	—	(1·2)	2·7
Chile	—	1·5	2·4	Venezuela	—	1·6	3·8
Colombia	—	2·3	3·2	Yugoslavia	—	0·6	1·2
Egypt	—	1·4	2·5				
Ghana	—	2·6	2·7	Average	(1·5)	1·6	2·6
Greece	—	1·2	0·8				
India	0·4	0·9	2·2				
Israel	—	—	4·5	France	0·2	0·0	1·1
Malaya	—	2·1	3·0	Germany (FR)	1·1	0·8	1·2
Mexico	1·4	1·4	3·3	Italy	0·7	0·7	0·7
Pakistan	(0·4)	(0·9)	2·4	Japan	1·0	1·3	1·1
Peru	—	1·6	2·6	UK	0·9	0·4	0·5
Philippines	—	2·1	3·2	USA	2·1	1·2	1·6
South Korea	—	(2·1)	2·8				
Spain	—	0·9	0·8	Average	1·0	0·7	1·0

Source: See Appendix C for developing countries. Developed countries from A. Maddison, *Economic Growth in Japan and the USSR*, Allen & Unwin, London, 1969.

due to drastic reductions in death rates, particularly in infants and children. Health programmes have eliminated infectious diseases and malaria, and have improved water supplies and drainage. Better nutrition has also contributed. As a result, the average expectation of life at birth has risen to about fifty-five years in developing countries. This is similar to the situation in the UK in 1900, but much lower than the present figures of seventy years in Western Europe and the USA. Death rates are now about 10 per 1000, but birth rates are still about 40–50 per 1000.[1] The only historical parallel for this combination of very high birth rates and low death rates is the situation of the new settlers in the USA and Canada in the eighteenth century.

The decline in death rates is a great improvement in human welfare, better health and nutrition have increased the working

[1] See papers by H. Gille and G. J. Stolnitz in *World Population Conference 1965*, vol. II, UN, New York, 1967.

capacity of the labour force, and the rapid growth of population is itself a major source of political pressure and personal initiative for faster growth. Population pressure may act as a stimulus to economic growth if labour is scarce or immobile, or it may tend to push a society out of its natural torpor in order to defend its living standards. However, developing countries do not have a shortage of labour and the need for development is already apparent.

In Europe and North America the fall in death rates was more gradual than in the developing world and there was also a gradual reduction in fertility. The birth rate fell in France in the eighteenth century. In Germany and the UK it fell from 35–40 to about 15 per 1000 in the period between 1875 and 1930.[1]

The reduction of fertility in the developed world occurred through several mechanisms. Late marriage is one of the main characteristics which has distinguished Europe from the rest of the world since the seventeenth century. The extreme cases are Ireland, where a quarter of women are unmarried at age forty-five and India where only one per cent of women are in this situation. Until recently there was also small scope for premarital intercourse in the puritanical societies of many Western countries. Abortion, coitus interruptus and traditional methods of birth control also played a significant role, but in the twentieth century modern methods of birth control have come to be widely used. It is quite likely that the population of developing countries will also spontaneously seek to reduce fertility now that death rates have fallen so drastically[2], but as this fall in death rates has been so sudden, there is a much greater need for government sponsorship of birth control to accelerate the process than there ever was in developed countries.

The economic case for birth control is extremely strong in developing countries. The major consequence of high fertility is that a very large part of the population are children, and most adult women are fully occupied looking after them. We can see this quite clearly by comparing the situation of Japan and the Philippines (see accompanying chart). In Japan it has been official policy since the war to check population growth by abortion and birth control. In

[1] In the UK, the birth rate fell from 35·3 per 1000 in 1876–80 to 15 in 1931–35. In Germany it fell from 39·2 to 16·6 in the same period, see D. V. Glass 'World Population 1880–1950', in H. J. Habakkuk and M. Postan, *The Cambridge Economic History of Europe*, Cambridge, 1966, pp. 68–9.

[2] Argentine fertility has been declining since the nineteenth century, Chilean fertility since the first world war.

1963 only 27 per cent of the population were under fifteen years of age. In the Philippines, 47 per cent of the population were children. In Japan 36 per cent of females were in the labour force, and in the Philippines only 16 per cent. As a result there were two dependents for every worker in the Philippines, but in Japan there was only one dependent. The Philippine case is typical of the situation in

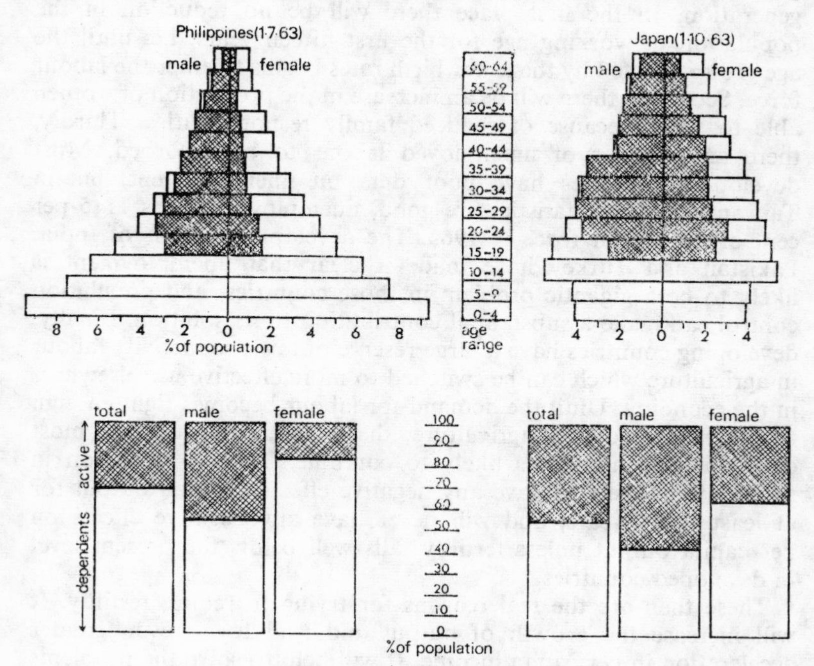

Distribution of Population by Age, Sex, and Activity Rate

developing countries. Japan shows what can be achieved by birth control.

In Japan, one-third of GNP is saved. This is about twice as high a proportion as in the Philippines. Japan's higher capacity to finance productive investment owes a good deal to the higher ratio of workers and the fact that it has fewer dependents to be fed, housed, clothed and educated. Thus higher capacity to invest is one of the biggest positive effects of population control. At the same time, a higher proportion of investment is available for raising per capita income.

A recent World Bank study estimated that 65 per cent of investment in developing countries goes to maintaining per capita income at a constant level, whereas the corresponding figure for a sample of developed countries was less than 25 per cent.[1]

In the very long run, a reduction in birth rates will reduce the growth in labour supply, but this is unlikely to happen for at least a generation. In the first place there will be no reduction in the population of working age for the first fifteen years, i.e. until the age group affected by the lower birth rates begins to enter the labour force. Secondly, there will be an increase in the proportion of women able to work because of reduced family responsibilities. Thirdly, there are reserves of unemployed labour to be absorbed. Most developing countries have poor data on unemployment, but in Taiwan where the statistics are good, unemployment was 11·5 per cent of the labour force in 1965. The development plans of India, Pakistan and Turkey have made it clear that unemployment is likely to be a gigantic problem in those countries, and population control can make a substantial contribution to its solution. Finally, developing countries have a large reserve of low-productivity labour in agriculture which can be switched to more effective use elsewhere in the economy. Until the demand for labour becomes tight enough to pull people out of agriculture, the dualistic character of most developing economies is likely to continue. Thus, a reduction in fertility is unlikely to have any negative effects on total output for at least thirty years, and will never have any negative effects on per capita output unless fertility falls well below the present level in developed countries.

These then are the real reasons for trying to reduce fertility. It will increase the growth of output and lead to an even greater acceleration in per capita income. It will help to solve the problems of unemployment, liberate women from domestic burdens, and speed up the assimilation of depressed agriculturalists into the modern sector of the economy.

The potential gains from lower fertility apply to almost all developing countries except those rare ones (like Greece or Spain) where population growth is already fairly low. It is only in very special cases that rapid population growth seems desirable. One case is Kuwait which has enormous oil resources, and where rapid population growth has helped to accelerate total growth of the

[1] See G. C. Zaidan, 'Population Growth and Economic Development', *Finance and Development*, No. 1, 1969.

economy. But Kuwait's population needs were solved largely by immigration. This was necessary because the shortage of labour was also a shortage of skills. Kuwait has, in fact, provided a valuable migration outlet for people elsewhere in the Arab world, but unfortunately cases like this are very rare.

It is only in very recent years that governments have recognized the need to alleviate the population problem by intensive programmes of birth control. It has become obvious that the autonomous development of contraception by private individuals and firms would procede rather slowly, and that government aid was required to accelerate progress. A considerable change has taken place both in developing countries and in those giving aid. Until 1965, the only sources of birth-control aid were private organizations like the Ford Foundation, the International Planned Parenthood Federation (IPPF), the Population Council, and the programmes of the Swedish government. Since then other countries have decided to give such aid and the United Nations has been permitted to start operations in this area. However, technical assistance in this field is still rather small, because of the shortage of people with adequate training and experience. The biggest programme is that of the US AID which rose from $2 million in 1965 to $50 million in 1969. The Swedish programme cost $9 million in 1969, and the British programme about $300,000. In 1968, the UN programme cost about $2 million, and private agencies spent about $25 million.

Intensive research in the past decade has produced a number of remarkable technical advances which have made effective family planning programmes a more realistic proposition. The biggest innovations have been oral contraceptive pills and intra-uterine devices. These were important advances in contraceptive technology. The cost of a woman-year of protection via the pill (thirteen cycles) now ranges from $1·25 to $2 a year in AID programmes,[1] and intra-uterine loops cost only 3 cents each and $2 for medically supervised insertion.

However, the early hopes that these methods were the final answer, were exaggerated.[2] In the first place they are not ideal

[1] See *Population, International Assistance and Research*, OECD Development Centre, Paris, 1969, p. 35.

[2] 'It has become apparent with the experience of the last few years that the oral pill and the IUD, while far superior in many respects to contraceptive methods available previously nevertheless have serious drawbacks which limit their effectiveness. We are faced with the danger that within a few years these two

medically. 'The present generation of contraceptive pills interferes with the central nervous system—pituitary—ovary circuit and is theoretically less desirable than, for example, a method which selectively affects one or more lower circuit links without systematic effect."[1] Secondly, they have not proved so universally acceptable as was first hoped. The immediate response to these devices was very encouraging because they were used by people already strongly motivated. In fact each new device is likely to bring in a new wave of users because in the intimate business of birth control, people have a wide variety of inhibitions and preferences and need as wide a range of choice as possible, including abortion. At the present time, most of the research on contraceptive technology and reproductive biology is carried out in the United States and even there the expenditure is only $50 million a year. It has recently been suggested that this amount should be trebled. The most rewarding lines of research seem likely to be in the field of twice-yearly injections of progestin to suppress ovulation, better intra-uterine devices, morning-after pills, and non-surgical abortion (luteolytic drugs).[2]

There is also a great need for developing suitable retail channels for the distribution of contraceptives. At the present time, most countries which run official programmes make them available only through clinics to which many people are reluctant to go.

Even more necessary is the use of modern advertising techniques and market analysis.[3] In India, for instance, official birth control propaganda is still excessively bureaucratic and medically oriented. This is quite evident from advertising of public facilities which we quote in the following extract from an advertisement (which appeared in *The Hindu*, of Madras on December 15, 1968).

methods, for which such high hopes have been held, will in fact turn out to be impracticable on any mass scale'; see J. Maier, 'Population Programme of the Rockefeller Foundation', in OECD Development Centre, *op. cit.*, p. 188.

[1] See O. Harkavy, 'Current Research in Technical Methods of Control of Human Reproduction', in OECD, *op. cit.*, 1969.

[2] See Harkavy, *op. cit.*

[3] Swedish technical assistance gives considerable emphasis to motivational analysis. In Pakistan 'the new emphasis on motivational work in 1963 was indeed a result of past experience. Between two and three thousand family-planning clinics had been established throughout the country. But there were hardly any customers. Obviously, a major educational effort aiming at a maximum dissemination of birth control information to the general public was long overdue.' See OECD Development Centre, *op. cit.*, p. 108.

FAMILY PLANNING

ADVANTAGES OF THE INTRAUTERINE CONTRACEPTIVE DEVICE METHOD

1. The Lippes Loop may be used for spacing or limitation of pregnancies.
2. The loop may be inserted in married Women of Child-bearing age for control of conception.
3. The number of pregnancies a woman has had before insertion makes no difference.
4. When the Loop is IN SITU, neither the husband nor wife is conscious of its presence.
5. This is a 'One time' method. Once it is inserted by the physician the woman does not need to return for supplies as with previous methods.
6. The procedure is reversible; therefore, a signed consent is not considered necessary from either the husband or wife.
7. When a woman wishes to have another child, the physician removes the loop. Pregnancy may occur within a month or so. The loop has no effect on future childbearing or on future offspring.
8. The loop is inexpensive, and it is available free of cost to every woman in the country.
9. One of the great advantages is the diagnostic and curative service available to every woman coming for a loop, Gynaecological disorder such as vaginitis erosion of the cervix cancer of the cervix, tuberculosis of the reproductive organisations, metropathio and adnexal infections can be detected and treated.
10. Published reports agree that the Lippes Loop is one of the most effective methods known today.

ANY FURTHER INFORMATION CAN BE HAD FROM:

1. The Deputy Director (Family Planning), 81 Mount Road Madras-6.
2. Hospital for Women and Children, Egmore, Madras-8.
3. Government Kasturba Gandhi Hospital for Women and Children, Triplicane, Madras-5.
4. Kilpauk Medical College and Hospital, Madras-10.

DIRECTOR OF HEALTH SERVICES AND
FAMILY PLANNING, MADRAS-6

India started research and experimentation in family planning in 1951 and its nation-wide programme began in 1956. But it had a very limited success and was concentrated on traditional methods.[1] By 1960, advice had been given to only 1·4 million women out of 75 million families in the country. In the third five-year plan, greater emphasis was placed on the programme and 600,000 people were sterilized from 1961–4. However, these operations cost an average of $8 each, and India was still not manufacturing contraceptives. In 1965, the first UN mission on birth control recommended a greatly increased programme, with major emphasis on intra-uterine loops. The programme involved an expansion in medical auxiliaries from 10,000 in 1965 to 170,000 in 1971, 400,000 village radio sets to diffuse information on the programme, provision of jeeps for rural family planning workers, and incentive payments to midwives and to new users of the loops. Thus the administrative cost of the programme was much bigger than the contraceptives themselves, which are now made in India. Nevertheless, the total cost is only a small part of the development budget and is obviously one of the cheapest ways of raising per capita income.

In Pakistan, the family planning effort started much later than in India, but the programme adopted in 1965 was more ambitious, partly because fertility is higher. The programme envisaged a per capita expenditure in the plan period of 12 cents a year as compared with 5 cents in India, South Korea and Taiwan, and 4 cents in Turkey.

In Taiwan, the national programme was adopted in 1964 after a period of experimentation and has had greater success than in India because of the higher education level and greater accessibility of the population. Already in 1965 loop insertions were at the rate of 10 per 1000 head of population, which is the Indian target for 1975, and it is hoped to reduce the population growth from 3 per cent in 1964, to 1·8 per cent a year in 1970.

In South Korea, the programme was also started in 1964 and has been accepted almost as readily as in Taiwan. Other countries which have started national programmes within the past few years are Hong Kong, Turkey, Malaya, Ceylon, Egypt, Tunisia, and

[1] Budget allocations for family planning purposes were 6·5 million rupees in the first five year plan, 50 million in the second, and 162·2 million in the third plan. Actual spending was 1·6 million, 22·9 million, and 70·1 million respectively. See T. J. Samuel 'Why Family Planning has had no Impact', *Economic Weekly*, Bombay, October 17, 1964.

Thailand. Even China has undertaken a programme of population control, although Marxist economists have in the past denied that there could be a population problem under socialism. In Latin America, unfortunately, the only countries which have done anything to sponsor birth control officially are Chile and Puerto Rico.[1]

In Latin America there is still religious opposition to birth control which has prevented governments from official sponsorship of family planning, and it is most unfortunate that Papal policy in this respect has proved so conservative. However, Latin America enjoys a higher income and educational level than much of Asia, there is growing evidence of increased use of the more expensive contraceptives, and several governments have permitted the opening of family planning clinics by private groups.

These various efforts at birth control may well take a decade before they do more than check the present rate of population growth in the developing world as a whole. But there is reason to hope that they will ultimately have a very much bigger effect and make a major contribution to the growth of per capita income. They will greatly reduce the investment cost of a given per capita income growth, and their efficiency should increase as experience accumulates.

[1] The references to country programmes are derived from G. Ohlin, *Population Control and Economic Development*, OECD Development Centre, Paris, 1967.

Chapter X

Conclusions

It is easy to be pessimistic about economic development. Three-quarters of the world's population lives in a degree of poverty which rich countries have not known for generations, and the income gap has widened in spite of $80 billion of foreign aid. In the past twenty years, many panaceas have been suggested and found inadequate. Land reform, community development, planning, creation of social overhead capital, technical assistance, a take-off engendered by foreign aid, development of human resources and education, a 'green revolution' in agriculture have all inspired hope and enthusiasm. Each in turn has led to some degree of disillusionment. Since the mid 1960s, there has been a new wave of pessimism. India, which was so often regarded as a test case for the success of aid and development policy, has been in a mess. The harvests failed in 1965 and 1966 on a massive scale, and the country came close to famine. The balance of payments crisis was so severe that an important part of the industrial sector was left idle for lack of supplies. The investment rate dropped as the government diverted resources to military purposes. Faith in planning was shaken as a series of government inquiries, and IBRD reports showed the inefficiency of the control mechanism and of government enterprises. The Fourth Plan was three years late in appearing and is still very tentative. The whole of Indian economic policy is undergoing an agonizing reappraisal and the political system is showing dangerous cracks. Another disturbing feature is that nearly all the wars of the past twenty years have taken place in the developing world, and their incidence and violence has been particularly severe since 1965 in Vietnam, in the Middle East, in India, Pakistan and Nigeria. Rates of population growth have steadily increased and the Malthusian spectre of large-scale famine has claimed increasing public attention. Foreign aid appropriations have been cut substantially in the US and none of the ambitious aid targets of UNCTAD has been met.

Discouragement is compounded by some of the propagandists for the developing world. Some are so gloomy about past achievements that they argue as if the living standards of developing countries were decreasing in absolute terms. This is as false as the now discarded Marxist doctrine of the absolute pauperization of the workers under capitalism. But it is repeated so often that it comes to be believed. Secondly, the blame for the alleged lack of progress is often laid entirely at the door of the developed world. It is true that developed countries could do a good deal more to help both with aid and trade, but continuous public castigation is not the best way to win concessions and this approach discourages an objective assessment of the real achievements of domestic policy.

Our own view of the development process and of future prospects is more cheerful. Even a brief survey makes it clear that the developing world has moved decisively into a new era. Political independence has permitted experiment with a wide variety of growth policies. Colonial types of exploitation have virtually disappeared. Aid has been outstandingly successful in countries where it was given in large quantities. If post-war performance is measured in the light of economic history, the acceleration of growth has been remarkable almost everywhere. Per capita income has risen about three times as fast as in the past, and progress has been significant enough for this generation to have experienced very tangible evidence of change for the better. Improvements in health, nutrition and sanitation have lowered death rates dramatically. In a short leap the people of the developing world have jumped from a medieval to a modern life expectation. It is not possible to quantify this gain in economic terms but its importance is obvious when we recall how medieval Europe was haunted by ghoulish and macabre imagery—with images of death lavishly embellished on every cathedral door. There has also been a big improvement in education. The idea that these countries are predominantly illiterate is no longer true. The majority of working adults are now literate and although the content of schooling leaves a lot to be desired, it has contributed greatly to enrich the lives and social mobility of those who received it.

There has been genuine progress in development policy. Twenty years ago it was not at all clear how one should go about promoting economic development, and there was certainly no idea that such substantial results could be achieved. There was very little information about the economies of these countries and very few economists and statisticians to provide it. Most economists in the developed world (including Keynes) had never given their problems serious thought. But the urgency and immensity of the problems has provoked a whole series of new models and ideas for policy. Some of these were ineffective or dangerous, but the ferment of controversy has created new dimensions in economic analysis and a much more realistic view of the policy problems.

On the political level there is increased sophistication, more pragmatism, and less emphasis on ideology. There also has been some convergence of views. In the 1950s, many of the new political leaders in Asia and Africa disliked capitalist solutions, curbed their own private sector, rejected foreign private capital, and pursued a 'socialist' course with emphasis on planning and state industries (though none of them used Stalinist techniques of resource mobilization). In Latin America there was disillusion with the international economy, and with liberal capitalism which had broken down so decisively in 1929 and showed little sign of recovery during or immediately after the war. Therefore Latin America tended to follow inflationary and autarkic economic policies on the lines developed in Europe in the 1930s, particularly by Dr Schacht.

Public discussion of basic economic policy issues in the 1950s tended to be bitter, particularly when it involved confrontation between the developing world and Western countries or international organizations. Within the developed Western countries there had been a remarkable revival of economic liberalism and a dismantling of the controls and trade barriers erected in the 1930s. The stabilizing role of government was of course powerful, but the general tenor of policy was completely different from that of Latin American populism and Afro-Asian socialism.

As a result there was no possibility of dialogue between an old-school liberal economist like Jacobsen, as head of the IMF, and the archetypal Latin American populist Kubitschek as President of Brazil. Similarly the USA, although it was the major aid donor to India, refused to finance any of its 'socialist' inspired state steel plants, even though it had earlier helped to finance state steel works in Brazil and Mexico—countries which in practice are no less 'socialist' than India. There were also violent clashes between the USA and developing countries on questions of commodity stabilization and trade policy in the first session of UNCTAD.

By the end of the 1960s there were some notable changes in the situation. In Latin America, the deliberate attempt to promote growth by inflation has been abandoned. Three of the most inflationary countries, Argentina, Brazil and Chile have made major efforts (not too successful as yet) at stabilization and more realistic exchange rates. They have also abandoned the extreme emphasis on import substitution and have made more of an effort to promote exports. In India there has been a slow conversion to the need to use the price mechanism more, to rely less on stifling controls and to run nationalized industries efficiently. There is also a clearer recognition of the potential role of the private sector and foreign capital. The so-called crisis in planning which has caused so much heart-searching amongst Indian economists, is in reality a move towards a more sophisticated policy mix in which the price mechanism is being restored to a more realistic role. It is a milder form of the same crisis which has affected Soviet planning and it is being resolved more successfully. The past two decades have been a period of *Sturm und Drang* for development policy and though this period is by no means concluded we are now in a position to put the achievements in perspective, and to assess the scope for further improvements.

In order to assess the actual and potential contribution of policy to growth we constructed a model and applied it to our sample of twenty-two countries. In spite of the crudeness of statistics and the necessarily simplified treatment involved in any model, it puts the performance of all countries within the same frame of reference and brings out clearly some of the major characteristics of post-war growth.

The average growth of our countries was 5·6 per cent a year, which is better than the 5 per cent target set by the United Nations for the development decade of the 1960s. The model suggests that about 2 percentage points of the annual growth since 1950 can reasonably be attributed to the domestic policy effort of governments. The rest is due to spontaneous growth forces of the type which operated in pre-war years, and foreign aid has also made a significant contribution. The policy effort of most countries has been concentrated on resource mobilization, i.e. investment in physical capital and in human skills and training. There are a few countries where policy led to significant gains in efficiency, and many where resource allocation was inefficient. The model also shows that the growth potential depends on the level of development. The poorest countries have greater difficulty in raising savings and government revenue than the richer ones, and this must be borne in mind when assessing the success of policy.

There are three ways in which domestic policy can contribute to accelerate the growth of income, i.e. by increased resource mobilization, increased efficiency and population control.

The effort of resource mobilization has already been vast. The average proportion of income devoted to investment is now as high as in the USA and proportion collected in government revenue is close to Japanese levels. There is still scope for increased effort, particularly in the longer run, but the most promising prospects for higher growth lie in more efficient resource allocation.

If the effort of investment and taxation is to bear its proper fruits, there must be better management of the general level of demand with more attention to the dangers of inflation, better allocation of scarce capital resources, better provision for diffusing new inputs and technology to farmers, more regard to comparative advantage in choice of industries for development, and much more attention to export promotion. Increased efficiency will require more careful planning. There is need for better and more topical statistics, closer scrutiny of costs, better choice of technology, more attention to the economic value of research and education, better management of public enterprise and a closer link between the public and private sectors both in planning and implementation. A better mix of fiscal and monetary policy is required for stabilization purposes. There is need for greater use of the price mechanism to reinforce other weapons of policy. Efficiency is difficult to achieve if the rate of interest is too low, if the exchange rate is overvalued, if farm prices are set so low that farmers do not find it profitable to sell food to the towns, and if public enterprise sells electricity, transport, steel and other products at a loss.

Efficient policy also requires a bigger effort to deal with payments problems. Developing countries are hampered because half of their exports consist of food and raw materials for which demand is expanding slowly and prices are weak. Their export earnings are much more unstable than those of developed countries. But, some payments difficulties have been self-inflicted. Inflation, overvalued exchange rates and highly protected home markets have discouraged exporters, and in several countries there have been disincentives due to government price controls, the tax system and other bureaucratic impediments. This is true of Argentina, Brazil, and India. A few countries have had great success in building up exports and have achieved a remarkable transformation in their structure. This is the case in Israel, Korea, Taiwan and Yugoslavia. Trade performance is therefore capable of substantial improvement simply from domestic efforts.

Finally, per capita income growth can be accelerated by family planning. As a result of better health and nutrition, the death rate has fallen sharply. This is a major improvement in welfare as parents no longer see most of their children dying at birth or in infancy. However, it is difficult to employ so many people given the shortage of capital, and the increased proportion of dependants reduces the capacity to save and invest. It is therefore necessary to match the decline in death rates by a reduction in birth rates. In the long run, the benefits of slower population growth will be enormous, but Asian countries are only just beginning to take effective action in this field, and in Africa and Latin America, most governments have done nothing. It is unlikely therefore that we will see any significant drop in population growth in developing countries as a whole until the 1980s.

Although there is considerable scope for improvement in economic policy in developing countries, it is also true that some of the criticism of their policy has been misplaced, and some of their mistakes were due to policy in developed countries.

There is a popular illusion that there has been widespread neglect of agriculture in developing countries, and that there is a Malthusian crisis of world hunger. In fact, agriculture has shared in the general post-war acceleration of growth, and most countries have consumption levels well above subsistence. We found only four cases where there was a serious failure of agricultural policy, i.e. in Argentina, Chile, India and Pakistan. But the agrarian policy of these countries did not fail on the same scale as that of the USSR in the 1930s, and was no worse than the opposite failings which have plagued the post-war policy of developed countries. Pakistan has demonstrated quite clearly that, with a change in policies, rapid increases in output can now be achieved by some of the poorest and most tradition-bound farmers in the world. The more recent change in Indian policy confirms this conclusion.

Almost all governments have given heavy emphasis to industrialization. In the mid-1960s, this strategy came in for a good deal of criticism, because it was felt that money had been wasted on costly ventures which were symbols of modernization whilst agriculture was neglected. But the basic strategy of concentrating on industry was justified on four main grounds. Firstly, the demand for industrial products is growing much more rapidly than that for food. Average food consumption in developing countries is almost half of that in the United States, whereas consumption of industrial goods is only a tenth of the US level. Secondly, industrialization transforms the character of an economy, makes it more flexible, creates new skills and momentum for development. Its initial costs are high but are offset by economies of scale and learning which should make themselves felt at a later stage. Thirdly, industrialists have a high propensity to save, and a large part of profits are reinvested. Fourthly, it is easy for government to help industry. As developing countries are all large net importers of industrial products, rather simple measures of import restriction can create new markets for local entrepreneurs.

The real problem with industry is not that it received too high a priority over agriculture. This was true in Argentina, Chile, India and Pakistan. But in practically all countries there has been substantial misallocation of resources *within* industry.

Protectionist weapons have been too crude and have given far too much emphasis to import substitution in all lines which the countries were physically capable of making. As a result there has been a proliferation of new high-cost industries and little competition. It is difficult to estimate the scale on which resources have been wasted, but a carefully documented study for Pakistan, where industry is still relatively small, suggests that it might be over 3 per cent of GNP. Most countries need to reduce and rationalize their protective barriers, so that domestic industry is subjected to more competition. Export promotion needs much greater emphasis. A greater and more sophisticated use of foreign direct investment would help in solving technical problems, and in several countries the management and pricing policy of public enterprise need to be overhauled.

Some of the past errors in resource allocation have been fostered by policies of the developed world. Agricultural protection in developed countries is now more extreme than it has ever been before. European protection plus US surplus food disposals deprive developing countries of export markets worth $2·7 billion. In the case of manufactured goods, protection blocks a smaller amount of trade at present, but if all countries were as liberal with their textile imports as the UK, the developing world would probably sell another $1 billion worth of exports. The restrictions thus apply specially to goods in which developing countries have a strong comparative advantage. This protectionism of the developed world has reinforced the autarkic prejudices of developing countries and made them cynical about criticism of the way they allocate resources.

In this situation, action by developed countries to remove trade barriers could well be more useful than increased aid. It would, by itself, bring a considerable improvement in resource allocation and efficiency, but it would also encourage developing countries to reduce some of their own trade barriers and open their economies to the winds of competition. Financial help towards the creation of regional trade and payments arrangements would provide a very useful spur to co-operation between developing countries.

The allocation of aid has also been inefficient. The fact that a good deal of it has been given in the form of surplus food has weakened incentives to increase farm output. The earlier refusal of aid donors to help with programmes of birth control and family planning and the attitude of the Vatican on this issue have retarded action. Aid donors have tended to prefer large-scale capital projects, some of which, particularly in the field of irrigation have had a low rate of return. They were reluctant to help current developmental expenditures on education or to provide general purpose funds for imports to keep the capital stock working. They have not been notably helpful in providing aid to strengthen export capacity or regional co-operation. Technical assistance to atomic energy has encouraged diversion of indigenous scientific resources away from more useful lines of research. Uncertainty about the size and duration of aid have contributed to the problem of instability and payments equilibrium.

In the post-war period, developing countries have received about $80 billion in official aid. This is about six times as big as the Marshall Plan for Western Europe. There has been disappointment that it has not had more dramatic results and that the need for funds shows no sign of drying up. However, the aid flow is not as impressive as it appears at first sight. It has been distributed among 1·5 billion people instead of the 250 million who received Marshall Aid, and prices have risen, so that in real per capita terms it has been smaller. Secondly the recipients of aid have an income level ranging downwards to a twentieth of that in the United States, whereas the income gap between Western Europe and the USA was about 1 to 3, so the magnitude of the task is much greater. Thirdly aid has not been used as a spur to improved resource allocation. It is now so hamstrung with restrictionist clauses that it tends to foster a philosophy of autarchy and dirigisme. The genius of the Marshall Plan was that it acted as a catalyst to open up Europe's trade, free its payments and improve efficiency. Thus its indirect contribution to growth was greater and more permanent than its direct effects.

On average, aid has been equal to 1·5 per cent of the income of developing countries and less than 0·5 per cent of the income of the developed world. For most developing countries, it has been less important in the acceleration of their post-war growth than improvements in their own policy. The biggest beneficiaries have been Greece, Israel, South Korea and Taiwan. In these countries external finance averaged about 10 per cent of GDP and was a major reason for rapid growth. Their real output grew by 8 per cent a year compared with 5 per cent elsewhere, and most of the difference was due to bigger aid.

There have been a number of attempts to develop allocation criteria to determine aid 'needs'. The theory has been that developing countries should be supplied with aid up to the limits of their 'absorptive' capacity, i.e. they should get as much as they could usefully invest. However, there is little evidence that the overall volume of aid has come close to these limits.

As aid is smaller than the amount which could usefully be absorbed, there is a strong case for allocating it more efficiently and for stimulating a bigger flow of private capital.

There are serious shortcomings in present aid doctrine and practice. The most obvious defect is that aid is conceived as a temporary proposition, and its supposed objectives are only obliquely related to the abolition of poverty. Aid is to be given only for the period in which a country achieves its take-off to self-sustained growth. It is supposed to provide countries with extra resources to use for investment and other development purposes so that they can break out of a situation of economic stagnation and set off a process of cumulative growth, i.e. a steady rise in real income per head. In fact, all of the countries we examined have made significant progress in this respect in the past twenty years. In spite of temporary set-backs, as in India in 1965–66, and in spite of accelerated population growth, it seems clear that domestic economic policy alone is now adequate to achieve continued increases in per capita income in future. The take-off has therefore been achieved, but is growth self-sustaining?

The concept of self-sustaining growth has been used in two rather different senses. In the first place it is used to describe a golden age in which the spontaneous growth forces in the private sector will be strong enough to propel the economy forward to higher income levels. This situation is different from that during the take-off in which government policy will have to drag the economy forward and break down the institutional obstacles and inertia of a stagnant economy. However, there has been a great increase in the degree to which even highly developed countries depend on active government policy and close inter-governmental co-operation in order to sustain their growth. All private enterprise economies now depend heavily on both spontaneous and on policy-induced growth, so that self-sustaining growth in this sense is no longer a very meaningful goal for any kind of country.

Self-sustained growth is also used to describe a situation in which a country can attain its full growth potential without balance of payments support, i.e. when it can finance all the imports it needs from its own export earnings and private capital receipts. Although a good many indicators have been devised which help to determine whether a country is moving towards this goal, it is doubtful whether any country will ever actually reach a position in which foreign aid could not increase its growth rate. The UK for instance, has not been in a state of self-sustained growth in the post-war period, and the USA has also had a long-standing balance of payments deficit. This criterion is therefore so vague that it permits almost any country to make a case for aid.

The present criteria for allocating aid funds are not satisfactory either in identifying which countries should be helped or in demonstrating when aid should be ended. The primary purpose of aid should be to help countries which are poor to get richer. We should define potential aid recipients in terms which are objectively measurable and keep on helping them until they pass the poverty line. Our own suggestion for the poverty line is a per capita income of \$500 when measured at 1965 US prices. This is a lower definition of poverty than would be acceptable inside the USA itself, but it is near the income level in Taiwan to which the USA has ceased giving economic aid. The purpose of foreign aid is, of course, very different from domestic anti-poverty programmes. Foreign aid is not relief intended to bring up incomes to a minimum \$500 level in order to boost consumption. On its present scale, aid is only big enough to provide an income supplement of around \$3·50 a head and it must therefore be channelled into uses (mainly investment) which will raise production.

This approach involves a commitment to aid for an indefinite period of time. It will take several decades to raise all countries above the poverty line. But most rich countries have very extensive domestic welfare programmes for their poorer citizens and the indefinite continuation of aid should be easier to accept now than it was in an era of more rugged individualism.

A major difficulty in aid allocation is to devise a system of rewards and penalties to ensure that it bears some relation to performance as well as to need. However, past experience suggests that attempts to scrutinize closely the use of aid have been cumbersome for both donors and recipients and they have only had a limited success. Aid is not the only element in development programmes, and over-detailed scrutiny of these particular resources may detract attention from overall growth strategy. The best way to ensure that it is used efficiently is to provide a mechanism for assessing whether overall economic policy is successful. But it is not politically acceptable that surveillance should be carried out by individual aid donors or even by aid donors acting collectively. The experience of developed countries themselves within OEEC and OECD has shown that the most effective check on the efficiency of economic policy is by a procedure of regular international review and consultation in an organization where countries do not feel any tutelary constraints. It is highly desirable that similar regional organizations be built up within the developing world, and these organizations should themselves be used as a channel for aid in order to get them started successfully.

The definition of a poverty line at $500 per capita will leave an intermediate group of countries between this level and the $1400 level which presently constitutes the threshold of the 'developed world'. Countries in this position will generally still be capital importers, but they should get their capital on commercial terms. The knowledge that they are no longer candidates for aid should help sharpen their efforts to make better use of the international capital market and to follow sounder economic policies. The experience of Greece, Israel and Spain demonstrates that countries in this position can attract a good deal of foreign private capital and enjoy fast rates of growth. However, a good deal still remains to be done to foster their access to private capital markets, and more serious attention should be given to the Horowitz plan for using public guarantees to support loans issued on the private market, particularly where this enables the financing burden to be shifted to countries with payments surpluses, like Germany.

Finally, there is need for greater precision about the content of aid. An appreciable part of 'aid' has been given in the form of loans. Loans are aid only to the extent that the terms are more favourable than those on private capital markets. It is necessary that this be made clearer to legislators who vote on aid programmes. In cases where legislatures falter in their commitment to new aid funds, it is also desirable to explore the possibilities for debt cancellation. In this way, past loans can be converted into aid which is often more useful to the recipient than new funds.

Appendix A
Levels of Real Output

The most useful way of measuring a country's economic welfare or productivity is in terms of average output per head of population. Statisticians in most non-communist countries have now accepted the United Nations standardized system of national accounts which defines the boundaries of economic activity, and produce their figures in conformity with this system.

If we compare the gross domestic product[1] per head of population in 1965, converted into US dollars at official exchange rates, we find an income range within the developed world from $3,179 in the United States to $801 in Japan, i.e. from 4 to 1. In the developing world the range is much wider, from $1,229 in Israel to $90 in Pakistan, i.e. over 13 to 1. Over both groups of countries the range is as wide as 35 to 1.

The range between the highest and lowest incomes is indeed so wide that we are led to question their meaning. The average American may get thirty-five times as much income as a Pakistani, but is he really thirty-five times better off? In fact, the figures are misleading as an indicator of real income differences, because the figures in Pakistan rupees, French francs, etc., have been converted into dollars at the official exchange rate and this does not make adequate allowance for price differences between countries. The exchange rate reflects the purchasing power of the currency in terms of items entering international trade whereas the purchasing power parity (or real exchange rate), for which we are seeking, is one which will correct for the average difference in price level for all goods and services produced in the economy.

It is obvious that the concept of an average real exchange rate is a very complex one, for it has to take a representative account of all goods and services sold in the economy. Several hundred items must be selected if the sample is to be representative, and there is obvious room for argument on how big the sample should be, how products should be defined,

[1] Gross domestic product is the total income originating or produced in the country. Gross national product is the total income accruing to the residents of a country (before deducting an allowance for depreciation of capital). The two differ because of remittance of interest and dividends to foreigners, In developing countries, GNP is therefore generally smaller than GDP.

or whether the items have been priced in representative shops or markets. Furthermore, there will be no unique set of purchasing power ratios because we can choose the price structure of any one of the countries as a basis for the calculation. Such comparisons are often made in US relative prices, and for many purposes this is the best measure. The USA has much better statistics than most countries; it is more of a free market economy with fewer distortions arising from government controls, and the price structures of other countries tend to converge towards that of the USA, as economic development proceeds, because there is a basically similar trend in the pattern of consumer demand and productive technology. For very poor countries, however, where the pattern of output and consumption is very different from that in the United States, it would be better to use a poorer country's price system, if only because the USA will have no price for many of the commodities (because it does not consume or produce them). For a comparison involving the whole range of incomes from Pakistan to the USA, it would probably be better to use the price weights of a country in the middle of the range rather than those of the highest income country.[1] However, it is not possible to find a country in the middle of the range whose price system is not distorted by tariff protection or controls of one type or another, and most of the studies which we can use as a check on our own estimates have used USA prices as a basis for their weighting system.

Detailed attempts, to correct exchange rates for differences in purchasing power by systematically pricing several hundred items, have been made for eight European countries and the USA by OEEC,[2] and for Latin America and the USA by the UN Economic Commission for Latin America.[3]

These studies show that the *real* GNP per head of all the countries is considerably higher compared with the United States than is suggested by estimates at official exchange rates.

The relationship between the purchasing power of the currency and the exchange rate normally varies inversely with the level of income per head, because in rich countries the cost of non-traded services is high, and in poor countries, they are cheap relative to goods entering trade. As a country becomes richer, the relative price of services rises, because people

1 C. Clark, in *The Conditions of Economic Progress*, Macmillan, London, 3rd edition, 1957, tackles the problem by measuring real output in both US prices (international units) and in Indian prices (oriental units).

2 See M. Gilbert and Associates, *Comparative National Products and Price Levels*, OEEC, Paris, 1958. Estimates for these countries and for Canada, Japan and the USSR are presented in A. Maddison, *Economic Growth in Japan and the USSR*, Allen & Unwin, London, 1969.

3 See *A Measurement of Price Levels and the Purchasing Power of Currencies in Latin America, 1960–62*, Economic Commission for Latin America, E/CN. 12/653, March 1963, (mimeographed), and S. N. Braithwaite, 'Real Income Levels in Latin America', *Review of Income and Wealth*, June 1968.

who are servants, barbers, schoolteachers, civil servants or soldiers manage to increase their wages more or less parallel with those of the rest of the community, but their productivity does not rise very perceptibly. As these services do not enter international trade, the difference in their price does not affect the competitiveness of the economy, which is determined largely by the price level for tradeable goods.

However, the relationship between the exchange rate and the purchasing power of the currency is affected by differences in the degree of tariff protection, quantitative restrictions on trade, multiple exchange rates, controls on agricultural prices, etc. Developing countries are often prone to extreme balance of payments problems. Devaluations of 30 or 40 per cent are a common occurrence and, if a year is chosen in which Argentina has just done this and has an undervalued currency, and in which Brazil has not yet done it and has an overvalued currency, the picture may be quite different from that which emerges in the following year. Apart from short term variations in the degree of exchange disequilibrium, there may be longer run factors which enable a country to maintain an exchange rate which seems too high in terms of its general price level. This can occur if the country has very large receipts of aid, foreign capital, and emigrants' remittances, if it is very favourably placed for tourism or has huge natural resources. For these reasons, Israel, Venezuela and Mexico are likely to be able to maintain more favourable exchange rates relative to the overall purchasing power of their currencies than India or Pakistan, which are less favoured in terms of aid, foreign capital or tourism.

Because of the great interest of the problem, a number of attempts have been made to provide systematic short-cut estimates of purchasing power and real national product for countries where detailed comparisons are not available.[1] Professor Ruggles of Yale University is trying to exploit the work of OEEC and ECLA in order to devise a short-list of price comparisons of forty or fifty key items instead of several hundred, but has not yet come up with his results. Other writers, such as Professor P. N.

[1] There have been some more detailed efforts to compare China, India and Thailand with the developed world. Unfortunately, these studies have used different methods so that their results are not comparable. See W. W. Hollister, *China's Gross National Product and Social Accounts 1950–57*, Free Press, Glencoe, 1958, p. 146, who estimates China's national product in dollars to have been 20·6 per cent of US levels in 1952, or about 5·4 per cent of US per capita levels. S. J. Patel, 'The Economic Distance Between Nations: Its Origin, Measurement and Outlook', *Economic Journal*, March 1964, p. 126, estimates Indian per capita net output in 1959 as 8·5 per cent of US levels. D. Usher in an unpublished paper, 'A Comparison of Real National Income per Head in Thailand and the UK' has shown Thai national income per head in 1963 to be 36·2 per cent of the UK level (at UK prices), i.e. about 22·6 per cent of US levels. Usher's high figure for Thailand is due to allowance for different 'needs' in the two countries, a concept which most national income accountants would consider undefinable.

Rosenstein-Rodan,[1] have drawn on the evidence of the OEEC studies to derive an inverse relationship between the purchasing power of currencies and the level of real income.

An alternative method of measuring real product is to compare output levels directly from production statistics rather than attempting to deflate figures on expenditure by a price index. As the production structure is usually relatively simple in developing countries, the data on output may be more reliable and more readily available than figures on expenditures and prices. Furthermore, it is easier to define quality in a homogeneous way if one is dealing with goods as they are produced rather than with final expenditure.

In the past, this approach has not been used much. The OEEC used it in a study by Bombach and Paige[2] which covered only the UK and USA, and there is a Soviet study on these lines for the material product of East European countries.[3] For developing countries there are various estimates based on partial indicators, of which the most recent is that of W. Beckerman, who used only seven items (steel and cement output, letters posted, the stock of radios, telephones and automobiles and meat consumption). Beckerman has also surveyed attempts by other people to use partial indicators.[4] Most of these proxy measures cover only a small part of economic activity or are weighted together in a way which has no very clear economic rationale, and the results are not very reassuring.

We have therefore made our own estimates of real output for the twenty-two developing countries and seven developed countries, using US prices as weights, and using US levels of output as our basic reference

[1] See P. N. Rosenstein-Rodan, 'International Aid for Underdeveloped Countries', *Review of Economics and Statistics*, May 1961, who presents guesses for all underdeveloped countries, with a range of purchasing power readjustment up to 100 per cent. E. E. Hagen, 'Some Facts about Income Levels and Economic Growth', *Review of Economics and Statistics*, February 1960, had earlier suggested upward adjustments of up to 200 per cent, but his figures refer to groups of countries. More recently, Simon Kuznets in *Modern Economic Growth, Rate, Structure and Spread*, Yale, 1966, Chapter 7, has derived an estimating equation from OEEC estimates for developed countries, and applies this to make estimates by continents for the developing world. His adjustments range up to 200 per cent for the poorest countries (in Asia). Kuznets applies a price corrective of 2·2 (i.e. 120 per cent) to the figures for Latin America converted into dollars at official exchange rates in 1958.

[2] See D. Paige and G. Bombach, *A Comparison of National Output and Productivity of the UK and US*, OEEC, Paris 1959.

[3] See *Sopostavlenie Urovnei Ekonomicheskovo Razvitia Sotsialisticheskikh Stran*, Moscow, 1965.

[4] See W. Beckerman, *International Comparisons of Real Incomes*, OECD Development Centre, Paris, 1966. Beckerman's estimates have been criticized by V. Stoikov, 'International Comparisons of Income Levels', *Economic Journal*, December 1967.

point. These estimates are fairly crude, but they do provide a set of methodologically consistent figures for the countries we want to cover, and the possibility of checking the results for some of the countries with the estimates of OEEC.

AGRICULTURE

Farming

Detailed information on farm output is given for many commodities in the FAO *Production Yearbook 1966*, Rome, 1967. This gives figures for about 80 crop items as well as for all livestock products. Items which involved duplication were omitted. The same source shows the price of the different commodities for 1952–56 in the main regions of the world, relative to the price of wheat.[1] We have used the price relatives for the North American region to value the output of all countries. In the few cases where North American prices were not given, we used the price relative for the region in which the production is dominant. For coconuts we used the export price of Ceylon which is the major exporter. As there was no way of pricing hides and skins, these were left out of the calculation.

The FAO *Production Yearbook* omits some of the fruit and vegetable production of some countries, and these data were added from the FAO *Food Balance Sheets*.[2] The latter source also provided information on use of farm output for feed and seed. The food balance sheet information was generally available for 1960–62, and in most cases the ratios for those years were applied to the production figure for 1965. For non-food items like cotton and linseed, the seed ratios prevailing in the United States were used.

After adding together the detail for individual commodities, we get the results shown in Table A-1. The last column shows the amounts available from domestic production after deducting farm inputs. In order to estimate the value added by agriculture it is also necessary to deduct non-farm items purchased by farmers.

For non-farm inputs there is detailed information on purchases only for a few countries. Fertilizer consumption was therefore used as a proxy for these items in most cases. The FAO *Production Yearbook* gives data on the consumption of the three main kinds of fertilizer, which were weighted at US relative prices. There were some countries where fertilizer consumption appeared to be a misleading indicator, and for Argentina,

[1] The derivation of the price relatives is explained in an article by M. I. Klayman, in the FAO *Monthly Bulletin of Agricultural Economics and Statistics*, March 1960.

[2] Apart from FAO, *Food Balance Sheets 1960–62 Average*, Rome, 1966, we used *Food Consumption Statistics 1954–64*, OECD, Paris, 1968, and *Food Balances for 12 Countries in the Far East and Oceania 1959–61*, Foreign (Economic Research Service), 88, US Dept. of Agriculture, Washington, August 1964.

Egypt, Ghana, South Korea, and Taiwan, information on farm machinery and insecticides was used as well.

In order to convert the estimates into dollars at US 1965 prices it was necessary to rebase the figures on estimates derived from US national

Table A–1

Gross Value of Physical Farm Output and Deduction for Feed and Seed in 1965

Million FAO wheat units at 1952–56 North American prices

	Gross value of physical farm output	Feed and seed	Gross value of output after deducting feed and seed
Argentina	5,487	372	5,115
Brazil	11,159	896	10,263
Ceylon	1,216	9	1,208
Chile	773	59	714
Colombia	1,757	55	1,702
Egypt	2,338	87	2,251
Ghana	524	22	502
Greece	1,902	148	1,754
India	21,499	1,191	20,308
Israel	393	17	376
Malaya	925	19	906
Mexico	3,857	234	3,623
Pakistan	6,157	334	5,823
Peru	1,039	40	999
Philippines	2,125	72	2,052
South Korea	1,349	79	1,270
Spain	4,797	552	4,245
Taiwan	1,494	242	1,253
Thailand	2,651	69	2,583
Turkey	4,296	674	3,621
Venezuela	733	11	722
Yugoslavia	3,242	580	2,663
France	13,653	2,477	11,176
Germany (FR)	8,925	2,103	6,822
Italy	8,868	1,304	7,564
Japan	6,971	731	6,240
UK	6,638	398	5,306
USA	55,000	8,121	46,880
USSR	40,213	5,472	34,741

Detail may not add to total because of rounding.

accounts statistics. *The National Income and Product Accounts of the United States 1929–1965*, Supplement to the *Survey of Current Business*, August 1966, shows (p. 29) that US gross value added in farming was $21,991 million in 1965 (after deducting the rental value of farm homes). The *Statistical Abstract of the United States 1967*, US Dept. of Commerce, Washington, 1967, p. 617 shows that in 1965 non-farm purchases amounted to $9,304 million (excluding interest payments on mortgage debt and

Table A–2

United States Gross Domestic Product at Factor Cost by Industry of Origin 1965

$ million

	Net domestic product at factor cost	Depreciation	GDP
Farming	17,297	4,694	21,991
Fisheries	1,357	239	314
Forestry			1,282
Mining	6,432	1,349	7,781
Manufacturing	170,408	17,373	187,781
Utilities	11,605	3,146	14,751
Transport and Communication	34,078	5,708	39,786
Construction	28,328	1,545	29,873
Services	289,515	25,535	262,950
Ownership of Dwellings			52,100
Total	559,020	59,589	618,609

Source: *The National Income and Product Accounts of the United States, 1929–1965*, Survey of Current Business, Washington DC, 1966. First column from p. 21; the gross rental value of farm homes ($2,374 million, see p. 29) was deducted. The breakdown into fisheries and forestry is a rough estimate from other sources. Second column is the total of non-corporate and corporate depreciation (pp. 115 and 141). Depreciation is at market prices, so the last column is not strictly at factor cost. US sources do not show ownership of dwellings separately, and this figure was derived (at market prices) from *National Accounts of OECD Countries* 1957–66, OECD, Paris, 1968.

rents paid to non-farm households). It was therefore assumed that the sum of these two figures, i.e. $31,295 million was equal to the US figure in the last column of Table A–1, i.e. 1 FAO unit equalled 66.76 US cents. This enables us to convert the figures for the other countries into dollars and to deduct non-farm inputs in terms of dollars. Thus we are able to estimate the contribution of the farm sector to GDP at factor cost. This same procedure was used for other sectors of the economy as well, and the basic estimates are shown in Table A–2.

Table A–3

Derivation of Gross Value Added in Farming 1965

$ million at 1965 US relative prices

	Gross value of farm output after deducting feed and seed	Non-farm inputs	Gross value added after deducting non-farm inputs
Argentina	3,415	154	3,261
Brazil	6,851	193	6,658
Ceylon	806	60	746
Chile	477	122	355
Colombia	1,136	133	1,003
Egypt	1,503	267	1,236
Ghana	335	3	332
Greece	1,171	251	920
India	13,557	816	12,741
Israel	251	42	209
Malaya	605	60	545
Mexico	2,419	192	2,227
Pakistan	3,887	158	3,729
Peru	667	93	574
Philippines	1,370	108	1,262
South Korea	848	153	695
Spain	2,834	724	2,110
Taiwan	836	103	733
Thailand	1,724	31	1,693
Turkey	2,417	148	2,269
Venezuela	482	46	436
Yugoslavia	1,778	451	1,327
France	7,461	2,205	5,256
Germany (FR)	4,554	2,298	2,256
Italy	5,049	893	4,156
Japan	4,166	530	3,636
UK	3,542	949	2,593
USA	31,295	9,304	21,991
USSR	23,191	3,750	19,441

FISHERIES

Estimates of fish production are available in the FAO, OECD and US Department of Agriculture food balance sheets, and were updated where necessary from the *Statistical Yearbook 1966*, UN, New York, 1967. Quantities were converted into values at US prices from price data in the

Statistical Abstract of the USA 1967, US Department of Commerce, Washington DC, 1967, broken down as follows: shell-fish $546 a ton, other fish for human consumption $134 a ton, and fish for industrial use $55 a ton. As there are no data on inputs into fisheries, it was assumed that they bore the same relation to gross value as the non-farm inputs did to the gross value of farm output in the countries concerned. Thus we get the results shown in Table A–4 for the value of fish output.

Table A–4

Derivation of Gross Value Added in Fisheries in 1965

$ million at 1965 US relative prices

	Gross value of fish catch	Gross value added after deducting assumed inputs		Gross value of fish catch	Gross value added after deducting assumed inputs
Argentina	63	60	South Korea	150	123
Brazil	157	153	Spain	413	308
Ceylon	20	19	Taiwan	121	106
Chile	87	65	Thailand	414	407
Colombia	19	17	Turkey	63	59
Egypt	58	48	Venezuela	41	37
Ghana	15	15	Yugoslavia	12	9
Greece	40	31			
India	453	426	France	192	135
Israel	6	5	Germany (FR)	211	104
Malaya	101	91	Italy	99	81
Mexico	82	76	Japan	1,803	1,574
Pakistan	126	121	UK	321	235
Peru	362	312	USA	446	314
Philippines	130	120	USSR	1,021	856

FOOD PRODUCTION AND CONSUMPTION

In order to estimate food production levels it is necessary to deduct the non-food items from column 1 of Table A–3. The main non-food items to be deducted are fibres such as jute, cotton and wool; tobacco; and certain oil seeds. Coffee, tea and cocoa were also classified as non-food. In most countries the fish catch is destined entirely for human consumption but in Chile and Peru this is not the case, and the fish catch must be adjusted to allow for non-food uses in these two countries.

We can get a rough estimate of food consumption by adjusting the production figures for international trade. Unfortunately the information

Table A–5

Food Production and Consumption in 1965

	Food production	Fish catch for human consumption	Food and fish production	Net imports of food and fish $ million at 1965 exchange rates	Apparent consumption $ million	Apparent consumption per head $
	$ million at US relative prices					
Argentina	3,005	63	3,068	−1,172	1,896	84·8
Brazil	5,281	157	5,438	−56	5,382	66·6
Ceylon	253	20	273	95	368	32·8
Chile	439	54	493	60	553	64·4
Colombia	830	19	849	−12	837	46·4
Egypt	1,083	58	1,141	130	1,271	42·9
Ghana	199	15	214	49	263	34·0
Greece	995	40	1,035	60	1,095	128·1
India	11,902	453	12,355	962	13,317	27·2
Israel	233	6	239	−19	220	85·8
Malaya	296	101	397	111	508	63·2
Mexico	1,807	82	1,889	−333	1,556	36·4
Pakistan	3,241	126	3,367	157	3,524	30·5
Peru	531	46	577	−115	462	39·7
Philippines	1,289	130	1,419	−94	1,325	41·0
South Korea	836	150	986	39	1,025	36·1
Spain	2,706	413	3,119	59	3,178	100·6
Taiwan	798	121	919	−171	748	57·5
Thailand	1,542	414	1,956	−279	1,677	54·5
Turkey	1,978	63	2,041	−156	1,885	60·0
Venezuela	427	41	468	139	607	70·4
Yugoslavia	1,666	12	1,678	−50	1,628	83·5
France	7,317	192	7,509	110	7,619	155·7
Germany*	4,529	211	4,740	2,679	7,419	125·7
Italy	4,950	99	5,049	767	5,816	112·8
Japan	3,817	1,803	5,620	1,044	6,664	68·0
UK	3,485	321	3,806	3,698	7,504	137·4
USA	27,890	446	28,336	−2,221	26,115	134·2
USSR	20,291	1,021	21,312	669	21,981	95·3

* The production figures refer to the Federal Republic, but as the trade figures for Germany include West Berlin, we have divided the total apparent consumption by the population of the Federal Republic and West Berlin to get per capita consumption. Agricultural output in West Berlin is small.

is not available in quite the same detail as for production.[1] Imports and exports were measured at the values recorded in the trade returns converted into dollars at the prevailing exchange rate. The sources used were the *Trade Yearbook 1966*, FAO, Rome, 1967, the *Yearbook of International Trade Statistics 1965*, UN, New York, 1967, with some slight adjustments from the *Monthly Bulletin of Statistics*, UN, New York, May, 1968. The SITC items 0 (except 07) and 4 were used. Imports were recorded c.i.f. (except for Venezuela and the Philippines) and exports f.o.b. For India the trade returns appear to exclude receipts of US food shipments, and we have added $415 million to the Indian import figure to cover these.

The results are shown in Table A–5. The column on consumption includes actual consumption, changes in inventories and wastage, and for this reason is referred to as 'apparent' consumption.

FORESTRY

To complete the figures for agriculture, it is necessary to make an estimate of the output of forest products. The *Yearbook of Forest Product Statistics 1966*, FAO, Rome, 1966, provided information on production of coniferous

Table A–6

Gross Value Added in Forestry 1965

$ million in US relative prices

Argentina	29	South Korea	2
Brazil	119	Spain	32
Ceylon	2	Taiwan	6
Chile	25	Thailand	26
Colombia	42	Turkey	12
Egypt	1	Venezuela	7
Ghana	25	Yugoslavia	87
Greece	3		
India	55	France	175
Israel	0	Germany (FR)	122
Malaya	38	Italy	60
Mexico	12	Japan	258
Pakistan	14	UK	21
Peru	6	USA	1,282
Philippines	115	USSR	930

[1] The FAO food balance sheets include information on foreign trade in the same detail as production, but they are not available for 1965 for most countries. As the foreign trade ratios will not be stable from one year to another, it is not possible to apply the ratios for the years available to the 1965 data.

and broadleaved timber for industrial uses and fuel. The different types of output were weighted by US export prices. The total value of US output was taken from the US national accounts statistics, as a residual after deducting farming and fisheries from the total for agriculture.

Table A–7

Gross Value Added in Industry 1965

$ million at US relative prices

	Mining	Utilities	Manufacturing	Industry
Argentina	150·7	307·5	6,734·8	7,193
Brazil	174·5	354·3	8,216·1	8,745
Ceylon	0·0	3·3	85·7	89
Chile	171·6	81·3	2,070·1	2,323
Colombia	84·0	71·8	1,094·2	1,250
Egypt	124·0	56·0	1,354·0	1,534
Ghana	n.a.	3·3	84·4	(90)
Greece	8·6	57·1	1,469·4	1,535
India	446·1	450·2	9,663·0	10,560
Israel	2·1	38·5	860·4	901
Malaya	7·1	14·7	836·2	858
Mexico	255·0	197·5	4,867·5	5,320
Pakistan	17·6	40·2	1,958·2	2,016
Peru	69·6	39·2	682·1	791
Philippines	33·0	36·7	1,141·4	1,211
South Korea	60·0	36·6	679·4	776
Spain	110·0	351·8	11,466·3	11,929
Taiwan	30·3	72·0	1,721·7	1,824
Thailand	6·6	22·5	314·9	344
Turkey	57·3	72·5	1,135·2	1,265
Venezuela	1,391·5	100·0	2,151·5	3,643
Yugoslavia	121·0	156·9	5,807·0	6,085
France	380·2	1,592·4	34,622·6	36,598
Germany (FR)	901·3	3,217·5	47,705·9	51,826
Italy	88·9	990·3	27,165·9	28,246
Japan	316·3	2,426·4	50,431·1	53,178
UK	898·3	2,832·2	34,327·7	38,062
USA	7,781·0	14,751·0	187,781·0	210,313
USSR	4,271·1	7,418·3	127,027·5	138,847

Source: Derived from M. Shinohara, *op. cit.*, with our own rough estimates for Ghana.

INDUSTRY

The industry estimates are based on the research of Professor Miyohei Shinohara of Hitotsubashi University.[1] Shinohara's figures were based on a sample of about seventy commodities, of which fifty-three were for manufacturing and the rest for mining and utilities. The basic source for most of the items was the *Statistical Yearbook* of the United Nations. The estimates do not have the same coverage in all countries, e.g. in Greece output in firms with less than ten employees is omitted, so that the estimates for developing countries are rather crude. The items were weighted by value added at US valuation as derived from the 1958 US Census of Manufactures. Shinohara also presents alternative estimates at Japanese and British value added valuations, based on Census data for those two countries. For mining he gives only Japanese weights. Shinohara's estimates are for 1958 were updated to 1965 with the indices of production for mining, manufacturing and utilities given in the UN *Monthly Bulletin of Statistics*. In order to convert the figures into dollars we used the value of US output as recorded in the US national accounts statistics in the same way as for agriculture (see Table A–2).

One problem with Shinohara's estimates is that they overstate production in countries which import industrial items for intermediate use in greater proportion than in the USA. Unfortunately we do not know the size of industrial imports for intermediate use, but we have tried to make a rough correction by assuming that 20 per cent of the value of each country's imports of manufactures was used for such purposes. Manufactured imports (SITC items 5, 6, 7, and 8) were derived from *Yearbook of International Trade Statistics 1966*, UN, New York, 1968.

TRANSPORT, COMMUNICATION AND CONSTRUCTION

In the absence of suitable data for transport, communication and construction it was simply assumed that the output in these sectors bore the same relation to the rest of commodity output (i.e. industrial and agricultural output combined) as in the USA.

SERVICES

It is difficult to measure the output of many service industries directly. Usually we can only measure inputs of labour with some assumption about the relative productivity of labour.

[1] See M. Shinohara, *Japan's Industrial Level in International Perspective*, Ministry of Foreign Affairs, Tokyo, 1966. Earlier results were presented by Professor Shinohara in 'Relative Production levels of Industrial Countries and Their Growth Potentials', *Weltwirtschaftliches Archiv*, Band 86, Heft 1, 1961, and 'International Comparison of the Levels of Industrial Production in 1958' *The Developing Economies*, March 1965.

Table A–8

Calculation of Output in Services in 1965

	Combined employment agriculture and industry 000's	Productivity in agriculture and industry $	Absolute difference from Indian productivity level in agriculture and industry $	Productivity differential over India as per cent of that of France	Productivity in services $	Output in services $ million
Argentina	3,784	2,786	2,647	61·9	3,472	12,360
Brazil	16,480	951	812	19·0	2,141	15,317
Ceylon	2,006	427	288	6·7	1,759	1,685
Chile	1,305	2,121	1,982	46·3	2,988	3,191
Colombia	3,236	714	575	13·4	1,967	3,189
Egypt	5,824	484	345	8·1	1,802	4,330
Ghana	2,121	218	79	1·8	1,607	1,028
Greece	2,486	1,001	862	20·1	2,175	2,064
India	171,382	139	0	0·0	1,551	50,938
Israel	353	3,159	3,020	70·6	3,742	1,699
Malaya	1,575	973	834	19·5	2,156	1,906
Mexico	9,137	836	697	16·3	2,057	6,634
Pakistan	32,437	181	42	1·0	1,582	8,648
Peru	2,185	770	631	14·7	2,007	2,055
Philippines	7,323	370	231	5·4	1,719	4,456
South Korea	5,898	271	132	3·1	1,647	4,570
Spain	7,242	1,986	1,847	43·2	2,891	9,451
Taiwan	2,585	1,032	893	20·9	2,200	3,370
Thailand	10,463	236	97	2·3	1,622	3,932
Turkey	10,816	333	194	4·5	1,691	3,617
Venezuela	1,238	3,330	3,191	74·6	3,866	4,628
Yugoslavia	6,419	1,170	1,031	24·1	2,299	3,405
France	9,546	4,417	4,278	100·0	4,654	34,416
Germany (FR)	13,500	4,023	3,884	90·8	4,369	39,395
Italy	10,738	3,031	2,892	67·6	3,649	21,062
Japan	24,330	2,410	2,271	53·1	3,199	55,375
UK	11,058	3,700	3,561	83·2	4,132	46,146
USA	24,112	9,701	9,562	223·5	6,205	262,950
USSR	58,131	2,754	2,615	61·1	3,447	107,929

In some service occupations, there will be little difference in potential productivity between rich and poor countries. This is true of many teachers, doctors, dentists, civil servants, soldiers, lawyers, actors, cooks, waiters and domestic servants. There is more underemployment in poor countries than in the developed ones, many more lawyers who spend their days in coffee shops, listless shoe-shine boys waiting for customers, and many supernumerary servants; for this reason it can be assumed that the average effective productivity of these people is lower in developing than in developed countries, even if their potential output is similar. About half of the employment in the service sector in the USA consists of such people. In other service occupations such as trading and banking, productivity is likely to be much higher in rich countries. Detailed comparable data on service employment are not available for many countries, so crude assumptions have to be used. It was assumed that productivity in services was a quarter of the US level in the country where productivity in the commodity sector (i.e. agriculture plus industry) was lowest and three-quarters of the US level in the country where the commodity sector productivity was highest.[1] The two extremes were India and France. For

Table A–9

Employment in Services per 1,000 Population

Country		Country	
Argentina	159	South Korea	98
Brazil	89	Spain	103
Ceylon	85	Taiwan	118
Chile	124	Thailand	79
Colombia	90	Turkey	68
Egypt	81	Venezuela	139
Ghana	83	Yugoslavia	76
Greece	111		
India	67	France	151
Israel	177	Germany (FR)	158
Malaya	110	Italy	112
Mexico	79	Japan	177
Pakistan	46	UK	205
Peru	88	USA	218
Philippines	80	USSR	136

[1] See M. Gilbert and Associates, *Comparative National Products and Price Levels*, OEEC, Paris, 1958, where a good deal of the output in the service sector was based simply on employment comparisons, i.e. it was assumed that productivity in services was identical in the countries compared. However, the countries covered in that study were much less dispersed in income level than those considered here, and the portion of GNP for which this assumption was made was smaller than that covered by our productivity assumptions.

the other countries, it was assumed that productivity in services varied *pro rata* with productivity in the commodity sector. The estimate of service productivity can then be multiplied by service employment to provide the estimate of service output (see Table A–8). It can be seen from Table A–9 that the relative importance of service employment varies broadly with the level of income. In the richest country, the USA, it is nearly five times as high as in Pakistan, the poorest country.

Although the estimate of service output may appear to be fairly arbitrary, it should be realized that this is not due simply to lack of information, but also to conceptual difficulties in measuring some kinds of service output which would be present even with perfect knowledge.

OWNERSHIP OF DWELLINGS

Income (actual and imputed) from the ownership of dwellings is different from that arising from other service activities, because labour is not needed to produce it. Hence it can hardly be measured by imputing a productivity to its non-existent labour force. There are no data for housing in developing countries, so it was simply assumed that housing amenities bear a fixed relationship in real terms to real GDP, i.e. that the availability of housing varies directly with income, and that it is the same relation as in the USA. This will overstate income in Japan and the USSR, where housing facilities are poor for the level of income, but it is not clear whether there will be any bias for other countries.

GDP

We are now in a position to add up the estimates for the different sectors of the economy to get a figure for total GDP at factor cost. This is done in Table A–10.

Table A–11 compares the real GDP estimates at US relative prices with official estimates in national currencies converted into dollars at average 1965 exchange rates. In every case the estimate at US prices was higher than at official exchange rates for reasons explained earlier. In the case of Taiwan, the very large difference between real GDP and the estimate at official exchange rates is due in part to the very large size of the armed forces. 17 per cent of the figure for GDP at US relative prices represents the 'output' of the armed forces, whereas their value at Taiwan prices would be much lower. However, even if the military item were completely eliminated, Taiwan would still be left with a more 'competitive' exchange rate than any other country. This is probably one of the major reasons why it has been able to do so well in exporting.

In some cases there is difficulty in defining the official exchange rate because there was a multiple exchange rate system in 1965. In these countries (Brazil, Chile and Colombia), we have taken an average of the different rates.

Table A–10

Sectoral Breakdown of Real GDP at Factor Cost in 1965

$ million at 1965 US relative prices

	Agri-culture	Industry	Con-struction, transport and communi-cations	Services	Housing	GDP
Argentina	3,350	7,193	3,140	12,360	2,395	28,438
Brazil	6,930	8,745	4,668	15,317	3,279	38,939
Ceylon	767	89	255	1,685	257	3,053
Chile	445	2,323	824	3,191	624	7,407
Colombia	1,062	1,250	688	3,189	569	6,758
Egypt	1,285	1,534	839	4,330	735	8,723
Ghana	372	90	138	1,028	150	1,778
Greece	954	1,535	741	2,064	487	5,781
India	13,222	10,560	7,083	50,938	7,523	89,326
Israel	214	901	332	1,699	289	3,435
Malaya	674	858	456	1,906	358	4,252
Mexico	2,315	5,320	2,274	6,634	1,521	18,064
Pakistan	3,864	2,016	1,751	8,468	1,480	17,579
Peru	892	791	501	2,055	390	4,629
Philippines	1,497	1,211	806	4,456	733	8,703
South Korea	820	776	475	4,570	611	7,252
Spain	2,450	11,929	4,282	9,451	2,585	30,697
Taiwan	845	1,824	795	3,370	628	7,462
Thailand	2,126	344	736	3,932	656	7,794
Turkey	2,340	1,265	1,074	3,617	763	9,059
Venezuela	480	3,643	1,228	4,628	918	10,897
Yugoslavia	1,423	6,085	2,236	3,405	1,209	14,358
France	5,566	36,598	12,556	34,416	8,197	97,333
Germany (FR)	2,482	51,826	16,173	39,295	10,095	119,871
Italy	4,297	28,246	9,691	21,062	5,821	69,117
Japan	5,468	53,178	17,465	55,375	12,091	143,577
UK	2,849	38,062	12,183	46,146	9,126	108,366
USA	23,587	210,313	69,659	262,950	52,100	618,609
USSR	21,227	138,847	47,670	107,929	29,029	344,702

Table A–11

Comparative Levels of GDP at Official Exchange Rates, at US Relative Prices, and the Purchasing Power of Currencies in 1965

	GDP at factor cost converted at official exchange rate $ million	GDP at factor cost converted at US relative prices $ million	Official exchange rate (units of national currency per dollar)	Ratio of purchasing power to exchange rate	GDP per head at official rates	GDP per head at US relative prices
Argentina	15,894	28,438	188·50	1·79	711	1,272
Brazil	16,614	38,939	(1553·00)	2·34	206	482
Ceylon	1,531	3,053	4·77	1·99	136	271
Chile	4,251	7,407	(3·85)	1·74	495	863
Colombia	3,673	6,758	(13·45)	1·84	204	375
Egypt	4,796	8,723	0·43	1·82	162	295
Ghana	1,426	1,778	1·17	1·25	184	230
Greece	5,057	5,781	30·00	1·14	593	676
India	46,624	89,326	4·78	1·92	95	182
Israel	3,145	3,435	3·00	1·09	1,229	1,340
Malaya	(2,343)	4,252	3·06	1·81	291	528
Mexico	(17,740)	18,064	12·49	1·02	415	423
Pakistan	10,388	17,579	4·78	1·69	90	152
Peru	4,021	4,629	26·82	1·15	345	397
Philippines	4,890	8,703	3·88	1·78	151	269
South Korea	2,772	7,252	271·00	2·62	97	255
Spain	19,962	30,697	59·99	1·54	634	975
Taiwan	2,473	7,462	40·10	3·02	190	573
Thailand	3,557	7,794	20·83	2·19	116	254
Turkey	7,967	9,059	9·04	1·14	254	289
Venezuela	7,974	10,897	4·46	1·37	923	1,264
Yugoslavia	7,261	14,358	1250·00	1·98	372	736
France	79,551	97,333	4·90	1·22	1,631	1,990
Germany (FR)	97,500	119,871	4·00	1·23	1,715	2,109
Italy	50,126	69,117	624·70	1·38	975	1,345
Japan	78,288	143,577	360·90	1·83	801	1,466
UK	85,241	108,366	0·36	1·27	1,563	1,985
USA	618,609	618,609	1·00	1·00	3,179	3,179
USSR	325,824	344,702	0·91	1·06	1,410	1,495

Source: First column from *Yearbook of National Accounts Statistics 1966*, UN, New York, 1967, *National Accounts of Less Developed Countries 1950–1966*, OECD Development Centre, Paris, 1968 (for Argentina, Brazil, Chile, Colombia, India, Pakistan, Peru, Philippines, Taiwan, Thailand and Venezuela). Spain from *National Accounts of OECD Countries 1957–1966*, OECD, Paris, 1968. Soviet GDP derived from A. Maddison, *Economic Growth in Japan and the USSR*, Allen & Unwin, London 1969. Exchange rates from IMF, *International Financial Statistics*, Washington; the figures in brackets are averages of the main rates used by countries with a multiple exchange rate system.

The first thing to note about Table A–11 is that the dispersion of income between the richest and poorest country is still very wide, though it is now 21 to 1 instead of 35 to 1 when converted at exchange rates. Secondly, we can see that all the developing countries have a real income per head lower than those in the developed country group. The gap between income in the poorest rich country, Italy, and the richest poor country, Israel, is negligible, but the distinction between developed and developing countries is clearer than at official exchange rates, where Israel appears with a higher income than Italy or Japan. Thirdly, it is clear that the dispersion of income levels in real terms is much wider in the developing countries than in the developed world. The poorest country, Pakistan, has a real income level which is only a ninth of that in Israel, whereas the poorest of the developed countries, Italy, has an income level nearly half of that in the USA.

Appendix B
Growth of Total Output

The sources for Table B–1, for 1950 and earlier are as follows:

Argentina: 1900–50, GDP at 1960 prices supplied by CONADE, Buenos Aires, These figures are a re-weighted version of the earlier estimates at 1950 prices in *El Desarrollo Economico de la Argentina*, ECLA Santiago, 1959 (mimeographed annex). The estimate of the growth rate from 1870 to 1913 is the 5 per cent suggested by C. F. Diaz-Alejandro, *Essays on the Economic History of the Argentine Republic* (mimeographed), 1967; the same order of magnitude is suggested by A. Ferrer, *The Argentine Economy*, University of California Press, Berkeley, 1967.

Brazil: 1920–50 estimates supplied by the Fundacao Getulio Vargas, Rio de Janeiro. There are some rough estimates for earlier years by C. Furtado, *Formacao Economica do Brasil*, Fundo de Cultura, Rio de Janeiro, 1959, who suggests that GNP rose by 3·5 per cent a year in the second half of the nineteenth century and per capita income by about 1·5 per cent a year. But this would imply impossibly low levels of income per head in the middle of the nineteenth century.

Ceylon: 1938–50 rough estimates derived from D. R. Snodgrass, *Ceylon: An Export Economy in Transition*, Irwin, Illinois, 1966, pp. 72 and 240.

Chile: 1913–50 from M. Mamalakis and C. W. Reynolds, *Essays on the Chilean Economy*, Irwin, Illinois, 1965, p. 384, estimate B for 1913–25, estimate A for 1925–50.

Colombia: 1929–50 supplied by the Statistics Division, ECLA; Santiago. 1913–29 derived from L. J. Zimmerman, *Arme en Rijke Landen*, Albani, The Hague, 1964. There are some rough unpublished estimates for 1870 by W. P. McGreevey of the University of California at Berkeley, who has also surveyed early estimates for other Latin American countries; see W. P. McGreevey, 'Recent Research on the Economic History of Latin America'. McGreevey suggests that 1870 per capita income was 40·3 per cent of that in 1960.

Egypt: 1913–50 GDP at 1954 prices derived from B. Hansen and G. A. Marzouk, *Development and Economic Policy in the UAR (Egypt)* North Holland, Amsterdam, 1965, p. 3.

Ghana: 1911–50 derived from R. Szereszewski, *Structural Changes in the Economy of Ghana*, Weidenfeld & Nicolson, London, 1965. On page 149 he gives estimates for 1891, 1901 and 1911 at 1911 prices, and on page 92 an estimate for 1911 at 1960 prices. These were linked, and the difference between 1950 and 1960 was taken from our Table B–2.

Greece: 1938–50 from *Statistics of National Product and Expenditure, 1938 and 1947 to 1955*, OEEC, Paris, 1957; 1913–38 from C. Clark, *Conditions of Economic Progress*, third edition, Macmillan, London, 1957, pp. 148–9.

India: 1870–1949, national income at 1948–49 prices of the Indian Union supplied by M. Mukherjee of the Indian Statistical Institute, Calcutta. This was linked to 1950, with a calendar year adjustment from *Economic Survey 1964–65*, Government of India, Delhi. 1870 is an interpolation from M. Mukherjee's per capita figures for 1867 and 1873. There are also detailed estimates of national income at 1938–39 prices by S. Sivasubramonian, *National Income of India 1900–01 to 1946–47*, Delhi School of Economics, 1965 which show a slightly slower rate of growth, i.e. an increase of 79·6 per cent from 1901 to 1946, compared with 88·2 shown by Mukherjee.

Israel: There are no estimates linking the whole of the present Israeli economy with pre-war years. However, R. Shershevsky, *Essays on the Structure of the Jewish Economy in Palestine and Israel*, Falk Project for Economic Research, Jerusalem, 1968, shows 1936 GNP for the Jewish sector to have been 19·6 per cent of 1950, and GNP per capita at 67·1 per cent of 1950.

Malaya: 1913–52/4 from L. J. Zimmerman, *op. cit.*, adjusted to 1913–50 from our table B–2.

Mexico: 1877–1907 estimated from *Estadisticas Economicas del Porfiriato, Fuerza de Trabajo y Actividad Economica por Sectores*, El Colegio de Mexico, 1964; the figures cover only agriculture and industry so the estimate refers only to material product. 1910–50, GNP at 1950 prices, from *La Economia Mexicana en Cifras*, Nacional Financiera, Mexico, 1966. It was assumed that growth from 1907 to 1910 was at 3·7 per cent a year, i.e. the average for 1897–1907.

Peru: As for Malaya.

Philippines: As for Malaya.

Spain: 1913–50 derived from *La Renta Nacional de Espana 1940–1964*, Consejo de Economica Nacional, Madrid, 1965, pp. 112 and 164.

Taiwan: 1913–38 taken from quinquennial averages for 1911–15 and 1936–40 in N. H. Jacoby, *US Aid to Taiwan*, Praeger, New York, 1966, p. 78. On p. 89 Jacoby states that pre-war per capita income was only regained in 1956. We presume that he is referring to the pre-war peak, i.e. 1940. In 1950 per capita income was only 76·2 per cent of that in 1956. It was therefore assumed that 1950 per capita income was the same as that in 1940.

Thailand: There is an estimate for 1938–50 in *Statistics of National Income and Expenditure*, Statistical Papers, Series H, No. 8, UN, New York, September 1965. This shows 1938 as 45·4 per cent of 1950 which seems to imply an unrealistically large growth.

Turkey: 1938–50 GNP at constant market prices from *Statistics of National Product and Expenditure, 1938 and 1947 to 1955*, OEEC, Paris, 1957.

Venezuela: 1938–50 supplied by the Statistics Division, ECLA, Santiago.

Yugoslavia: 1909/12–1950 from I. Vinski, 'National Product and Fixed Assets in the Territory of Yugoslavia 1909–59', in P. Deane, ed., *Studies in Social and Financial Accounting*, *Income and Wealth*, Series IX, Bowes & Bowes, London, 1961.

Table B–1

Growth of Gross Domestic Product 1870–1950

1950 = 100

	1870	1900	1913	1920	1929	1938	1950
Argentina	4·18	16·2	34·1	38·6	63·1	67·1	100·0
Brazil	—	—	—	25·8	38·4	50·5	100·0
Ceylon	—	—	—	—	—	65·6	100·0
Chile	—	—	45·8	45·9	69·8	71·0	100·0
Colombia	—	—	25·7	—	47.1	64·2	100·0
Egypt	—	—	54·8	—	63·0	73·7	100·0
Ghana	—	16·0*	25·1†	—	—	—	100·0
Greece	—	—	66·8	—	113·7	128·8	100·0
India	40·4	49·9	65·1	69·9	82·8	90·4	100·0
Israel	—	—	—	—	—	—	—
Malaya	—	—	21·3	—	47·9	—	100·0
Mexico	15·6‡	—	36·2§	39·2‖	44·8	52·2	100·0
Pakistan	—	—	—	—	—	—	—
Peru	—	—	31·7	—	52·8	—	100·0
Philippines	—	—	45·1	—	65·6	—	100·0
South Korea	—	—	—	—	—	—	—
Spain	—	—	81·1	—	115·0	—	100·0
Taiwan	—	—	38·0	—	72·7¶	103·1**	100·0
Thailand	—	—	—	—	—	—	—
Turkey	—	—	—	—	—	80·6	100·0
Venezuela	—	—	—	—	—	42·4	100·0
Yugoslavia	—	—	55·4††	51·8	76·8	86·6	100·0

* 1901; † 1913 extrapolated from 1901–11 growth rate; ‡ 1877; § 1910; ‖ 1921; ¶ 1928; ** in the last pre-war year, 1940, the figure was 108·7; †† 1909–12.

In Table B–2, GDP for 1950–66 is derived from *National Accounts of Less Developed Countries 1950–1966*, OECD Development Centre, Paris, July 1968, except Ceylon 1950–59 where the figures were taken from the 1967 edition of this publication. In Peru, the figures refer to GNP and in Egypt to net national product. The movement 1966–68 is taken from the GNP figures given in *Gross National Product: Growth Rates and Trend Data*, RC-W-138, AID, Washington, April 1969. Figures for the early 1950s are not given by OECD for Malaya, South Korea, Taiwan and Thailand, and these were taken from the following sources:

Table

Growth of Gross Domestic

1950 =

	1950	1951	1952	1953	1954	1955	1956	1957	1958
Argentina	100·0	104·0	97·4	104·3	108·2	115·6	117·5	124·0	132·9
Brazil	100·0	105·1	111·0	114·6	123·4	131·8	134·3	143·5	153·0
Ceylon	100·0	108·4	112·2	111·2	114·4	121·4	115·0	122·5	127·3
Chile	100·0	104·3	110·3	116·0	116·5	116·4	117·0	129·3	132·8
Colombia	100·0	103·1	109·6	116·3	124·3	129·2	134·4	137·4	140·8
Egypt	100·0	110·6	110·0	110·6	117·6	123·7	126·9	130·4	146·6
Ghana	100·0	103·7	101·8	115·9	130·5	122·0	129·3	133·5	131·3
Greece	100·0	108·4	108·7	123·7	127·5	135·5	145·8	157·1	162·3
India	100·0	102·7	106·7	113·1	115·8	118·1	123·9	122·8	131·5
Israel	100·0	136·4	143·9	142·1	169·7	192·7	210·0	228·5	246·4
Malaya	100·0	102·7	85·3	79·8	81·1	103·4	106·5	109·2	109·8
Mexico	100·0	107·7	111·9	112·1	123·9	134·7	143·6	154·5	163·0
Pakistan	100·0	100·0	103·0	109·5	109·9	109·7	116·2	117·0	118·7
Peru	100·0	110·5	113·7	116·1	127·4	133·6	139·7	141·1	145·8
Philippines	100·0	104·7	113·9	122·8	129·4	139·5	146·6	153·1	159·4
South Korea	100·0	92·3	98·3	126·8	135·8	143·8	145·5	157·3	167·6
Spain	100·0	124·7	133·1	131·7	147·5	154·0	168·0	173·7	181·9
Taiwan	100·0	107·1	120·3	133·3	144·8	150·8	156·8	167·9	180·2
Thailand	100·0	108·6	114·7	128·3	127·2	140·6	144·7	146·3	147·1
Turkey	100·0	115·1	125·0	138·9	126·6	136·0	145·3	154·6	162·5
Venezuela	100·0	111·7	119·8	127·2	139·4	151·8	167·9	179·6	189·9
Yugoslavia	100·0	104·0	95·6	110·1	116·2	130·8	130·9	155·5	158·1

Malaya, 1950–55 GDP from Lim Chong-Yah, *Economic Development o Modern Malaya*, Oxford University Press, London, 1967, p. 317.
South Korea, 1950–53 GDP at 1955 factor cost from UN, *The Growth of World Industry, 1938–61*, New York, 1963, p. 484.
Taiwan, 1951 GNP at 1964 prices from N. H. Jacoby, *op. cit.*, p. 273; 1950 is our own estimate.
Thailand, 1950 is our own estimate.
For Yugoslavia, GDP 1950–59 is from I. Vinski, *op. cit.*, p. 221.

B–2

Product 1950–67

100

1959	1960	1961	1962	1963	1964	1965	1966	1967	1968
125·2	135·2	144·7	142·0	137·0	148·0	160·7	159·9	162·8	170·4
164·3	175·2	188·0	198·1	201·2	207·5	215·5	225·0	237·4	252·6
135·3	142·6	145·8	152·5	155·0	161·6	164·1	166·9	178·7	189·2
132·1	140·8	149·5	157·0	164·4	171·3	179·9	191·7	194·8	201·0
150·6	156·8	164·6	172·9	178·6	189·3	195·4	204·2	210·1	222·9
161·2	170·0	175·9	191·6	208·3	219·7	223·5	226·3		
148·9	160·1	165·8	173·9	179·9	183·8	186·3	188·3	192·8	199·2
168·3	173·9	193·5	200·6	216·9	236·4	254·5	274·0	287·2	305·0
134·0	144·0	150·7	154·7	162·9	175·0	167·5	171·3	189·3	197·1
277·4	296·4	328·1	361·5	400·5	442·0	477·4	480·2	493·6	562·7
114·7	126·0	130·5	137·6	147·1	156·0	166·9	176·9	189·6	204·8
167·7	181·0	187·4	196·6	209·1	230·4	242·6	260·8	277·8	297·4
123·9	130·6	138·7	143·9	156·6	164·5	172·2	181·1	194·1	205·7
151·0	164·7	178·2	194·7	202·0	217·8	227·2	240·8	251·9	256·8
153·9	159·3	167·0	173·4	191·9	194·4	207·8	219·6	232·8	247·4
175·7	180·3	188·4	194·8	212·7	230·5	247·4	279·1	303·9	343·4
179·9	189·6	207·7	227·7	254·5	273·8	295·4	319·6	329·8	343·7
196·9	209·2	225·8	242·2	265·9	301·7	339·7	371·5	408·3	450·3
162·3	179·5	187·1	197·2	216·5	231·9	250·3	271·6	284·9	309·1
169·0	175·2	172·3	182·7	196·5	206·2	214·7	235·4	249·5	263·7
204·8	207·7	211·7	224·0	232·4	252·0	265·2	271·1	285·2	300·9
183·6	195·3	206·2	215·0	241·2	271·8	281·1	305·2	308·3	

Appendix C
Population and Employment

POPULATION

Population figures for 1950 and 1967 from *National Accounts of Less Developed Countries 1950–1966*, OECD Development Centre, Paris, 1968 (for Taiwan the armed forces were added to the OECD figures). For earlier years, the figures were derived from the same source as the GDP figures wherever possible. The following sources were also used: A. Ferrer and E. L. Wheelwright, *Industrialization in Argentina and Australia: A Comparative Study* (mimeographed), Buenos Aires; *O Brasil em Numeros*, IBGE, Rio, 1960; *Malaysia Yearbook, vol. 4, 1964*, Government Printer, Kuala Lumpur, 1966; D. R. Snodgrass, *Ceylon: An Export Economy in Transition*, Irwin, Illinois, 1966; Yhi-Min Ho, *Agricultural Development of Taiwan 1903–1960*, Vanderbilt, 1966; E. Kirsten, E. W. Buchholz and W. Kollmann, *Raum und Bevolkerung in der Weltgeschichte*, Ploetz, Wurzburg, 1956; *Statistisches Handbuch der Weltwirtschaft*, Statistisches Reichsamt, Berlin, 1936.

EMPLOYMENT IN 1950

Activity rates derived from census or other survey data for the years indicated, and applied to 1950 population. For Peru the activity rates are an average of those for the census years 1940 and 1961. Wherever possible the census year nearest to 1950 was chosen unless there was some marked incomparability with the methods used in later years. Census data derived from *Yearbook of Labour Statistics*, various issues, ILO, Geneva. Ceylon from D. R. Snodgrass, *Ceylon: An Export Economy in Transition*, Irwin, Illinois, 1966. The Greek estimates were adjusted to allow for undercoverage of female agricultural employment. Israel from A. L. Gaathon, *Capital Stock, Employment and Output in Israel 1950–1959*, Bank of Israel, Jerusalem, 1961 (it was assumed that there were 40,000 in the armed forces). Pakistan figures adjusted upwards to make comparable with 1961 census which had a wider coverage of females and juveniles. India adjusted upwards for similar reasons. Taiwan from ECAFE, *Economic Bulletin for Asia and the Far East*, June 1963 (assuming 600,000 in the armed forces), and from *Taiwan Statistical Data Book*, Executive Yuan,

Table C–1

Population 1870–1967

000's at midyear

	1870	1900	1913	1938	1950	1960	1965	1967
Argentina	1,796	4,543	7,653	13,725	17,070	20,669	22,352	23,031
Brazil	9,797	17,984	23,660	39,480	51,395	69,730	80,766	85,655
Ceylon	2,382	3,521	4,220	5,826	7,678	9,896	11,232	11,741
Chile	—	—	3,463	4,915	6,073	7,689	8,584	9,137
Colombia	—	—	4,885	8,431	11,334	15,397	18,020	19,215
Egypt	—	—	12,170	16,190	20,461	25,832	29,600	30,907
Ghana	—	—	2,042	—	5,186	6,777	7,740	8,143
Greece	—	—	4,820	6,778	7,554	8,327	8,551	8,716
India	208,240	235,300	250,920	308,230	357,455	433,968	489,747	514,195
Israel	—	—	(689)	—	1,258	2,114	2,563	2,669
Malaya	—	—	2,443	4,235	5,190	6,909	8,039	(8,580)
Mexico	9,666*	13,607	15,160†	18,991	26,282	6,046	42,689	45,671
Pakistan	—	—	—	—	80,590	101,450	115,440	121,109
Peru	—	—	4,400	—	7,969	10,025	11,650	12,385
Philippines	—	—	9,384	—	20,275	27,410	32,345	34,656
South Korea	—	—	—	—	18,570	24,695	28,377	29,784
Spain	—	—	20,200	—	27,868	30,303	31,604	32,140
Taiwan	—	—	4,042	6,493	8,219	11,212	13,009	13,742
Thailand	—	—	8,492	—	19,635	26,392	30,744	32,680
Turkey	—	—	—	16,906	20,800	27,755	31,391	132,710
Venezuela	—	—	2,749	3,534	4,962	7,349	8,618	9,352
Yugoslavia	—	—	13,023‡	15,875	16,346	18,402	19,508	19,958

* 1877; † 1910; ‡ 1909–12.

Table C–2

Employment by Sector in 1950

000's

	Total	Agri-culture	Industry	Construction, transport and communica-tions,	Other
Argentina	6,736	1,746	1,603	3,387	
Brazil	16,960	9,802	2,068	5,090	
Ceylon	2,493	1,525	208	142	618
Chile	2,207	663	543	203	798
Colombia	3,786	2,041	538	265	942
Egypt	6,977	4,444	740	342	1,451
Ghana	n.a.	n.a.	n.a.	n.a.	n.a.
Greece	3,171	1,917	469	209	576
India	153,634	120,602	11,215	3,379	18,438
Israel	439	65	96	278	
Malaya	2,015	1,313	191	78	433
Mexico	8,437	4,922	1,114	447	1,954
Pakistan	27,207	20,814	1,745	4,648	
Peru	2,845	1,588	469	148	640
Philippines	7,674	5,470	528	299	1,377
South Korea	7,001	5,097	161	98	1,645
Spain	10,757	5,249	2,130	990	2,388
Taiwan	3,449	1,788	262	1,399	
Thailand	8,404	6,866	227	84	1,227
Turkey	10,380	8,034	685	322	1,339
Venezuela	1,590	701	221	142	526
Yugoslavia	7,568	5,055	916	394	1,203

Taipeh. For South Korea it was assumed that there were 600,000 in the armed forces. For Thailand, the figures were adjusted on the assumption that the number of women employed in agriculture bore the same relation to male labour as in the rest of the economy. The breakdown between industries is not very reliable except between agriculture and non-agriculture.

EMPLOYMENT IN 1965

In most cases total employment and employment in agriculture for 1965 were taken from *Production Yearbook 1966*, FAO, Rome, 1967 (adjusted where necessary to conform with our population figure). In a few cases all the data were available for 1965. In countries where non-agricultural employment was not available for 1965 the breakdown was estimated from activity rates derived from census or other survey data for the nearest available year. Census and other survey data were derived from

ILO *Yearbook of Labour Statistics 1966*, Geneva, 1968, and *Labour Force Statistics 1956–1966*, OECD, Paris, 1968. Ceylon from *Economic Development 1966–68, Review and Trends*, Ministry of Planning and Foreign Affairs, Colombo, August 1967. Malaya estimates supplied by the Economic Planning Unit, Prime Minister's Department. Mexico from *La Economia Mexicana en Cifras*, Nacional Financiera, Mexico, 1966. For Thailand, it was assumed that women employed in agriculture bore the same relation to male labour as in the rest of the economy. The figures for the Philippines, Korea and Taiwan were adjusted to include the armed forces, and for Greece and Spain to include conscripts in the armed forces. Armed forces from *World-Wide Military Expenditures and Related Data*, Research Report 67–6, US Arms Control and Disarmament Agency, Washington DC, 1967 (except for Israel and Taiwan). In some cases, the data are for the labour force.

Table C–3

Employment by Sector in 1965

000's

	Total	Agri-culture	Industry	Construction transport and communi-cations	Other	Of which armed forces
Argentina	8,350	1,505	2,279	1,006	3,560	132
Brazil	25,955	12,459	4,021	2,321	7,154	200
Ceylon	3,184	1,684	322	220	958	9
Chile	2,660	691	614	287	1,068	45
Colombia	5,291	2,448	788	434	1,621	60
Egypt	8,719	4,905	919	492	2,403	180
Ghana	2,953	1,759	362	192	640	10
Greece	3,771	1,935	551	336	949	160
India	210,541	147,378	24,004	6,317	32,842	1,000
Israel	959	114	239	152	454	80
Malaya	2,599	1,310	265	139	884	29
Mexico	13,427	6,867	2,270	1,065	3,225	68
Pakistan	38,972	29,041	3,396	1,182	5,353	260
Peru	3,440	1,621	564	231	1,024	50
Philippines	10,580	6,052	1,271	666	2,592	37
South Korea	9,122	5,000	898	449	2,775	600
Spain	12,015	4,111	3,131	1,504	3,629	250
Taiwan	4,425	1,831	754	308	1,532	580
Thailand	13,223	9,720	743	336	2,424	132
Turkey	13,592	9,765	1,051	637	2,139	440
Venezuela	2,712	802	436	277	1,197	30
Yugoslavia	8,759	4,690	1,729	647	1,481	247

Appendix D

Investment and External Finance

The investment figures do not include inventories as the figures are either not available or unreliable in most cases.

INVESTMENT (Tables D–1 and D–2)

The main sources used were *National Accounts of Less Developed Countries 1950–66*, OECD Development Centre, Paris, 1968; *Yearbook of National Accounts Statistics*, 1957 and 1966 editions, UN, New York, 1958 and 1967; *National Accounts of OECD Countries, 1957–1966*, OECD, Paris; *Statistics of National Accounts 1950–1961*, OECD, Paris, 1964; *Some Factors in Economic Growth in Europe During the Fifties*, ECE, Geneva, 1964; M. Mamalakis, *Historical Statistics of Chile*, Yale Growth Centre, 1967 (mimeographed); and various official national sources. In the case of Chile and the Philippines, the figures for recent years include considerable upward revision in the estimates of capital formation, and we therefore adjusted the figures upwards for earlier years (1950–59 for Chile, 1950–61 for the Philippines) in line with the official revision for the overlap year.

The years for which data were not available for total fixed investment are shown by gaps in Table D–1. For non-residential investment there were more gaps in the information which we have filled by our own estimates. For Argentina, Brazil, Pakistan and Peru there was no information on housing investment. For Argentina and Peru we assumed that housing investment was 25 per cent of total fixed investment in all years. In Brazil we assumed a lower figure for housing, i.e. that it was 15 per cent of total fixed investment in all years (we knew that the coverage of housing construction in the Brazilian national accounts is poor and excludes most rural, and cheaper kinds of urban housing). For Pakistan, we assumed that housing investment bore the same relation to total investment as in India. For other countries except Egypt and Ghana, we had some official information on housing for most of the years. For Egypt information on some of the earlier years was taken from B. Hansen and G. A. Marzouk, *Development and Economic Policy in the UAR (Egypt)*, North-Holland, Amsterdam, 1965, p. 8.

Table D–1

Gross Fixed Investment as a Percentage of GDP at Current Market Prices 1950–67

	1950	1951	1952	1953	1954	1955	1956	1957	1958	1959	1960	1961	1962	1963	1964	1965	1966
Argentina	19·6	20·0	19·0	17·4	16·9	17·7	18·4	20·1	20·0	16·9	21·7	23·5	22·7	18·3	16·5	17·2	17·9
Brazil	13·3	16·1	15·5	13·0	16·4	14·3	13·2	13·0	13·8	16·0	16·5	17·2	16·3	16·5	14·3	10·7	12·8
Ceylon	8·7	9·3	12·0	10·1	8·7	9·7	15·1	15·3	15·9	15·6	14·7	14·3	14·6	15·2	14·4	13·1	14·1
Chile	14·5	15·4	14·9	14·7	13·0	13·4	13·3	17·2	16·7	15·4	15·4	16·9	15·4	17·1	16·6	15·9	15·6
Colombia	14·2	13·3	13·8	16·6	16·9	18·0	17·0	14·8	16·1	16·7	18·3	18·4	18·2	17·1	16·7	15·9	—
Egypt	13·7	14·0	11·8	10·3	10·5	10·5	9·3	13·8	14·4	12·5	15·5	16·6	17·8	19·7	17·8	—	—
Ghana	8·6	9·1	11·4	12·9	12·2	15·3	15·8	15·1	14·1	17·3	20·3	20·6	16·8	18·1	17·0	16·2	13·7
Greece	17·1	11·2	12·9	12·4	13·6	13·7	14·5	13·8	17·4	18·5	20·6	19·6	20·3	19·6	22·1	22·8	23·2
India	8·6	9·2	9·2	8·9	10·2	12·3	12·7	13·8	12·0	13·0	14·6	15·0	14·0	15·1	15·4	15·8	14·9
Israel	29·2	27·1	26·6	26·7	21·2	28·3	25·9	27·4	25·6	24·8	24·5	27·2	30·8	28·8	31·3	28·0	20·9
Malaya	6·2	6·6	10·3	10·0	—	9·2	11·0	12·3	11·9	10·5	12·3	14·9	17·8	17·6	17·0	—	—
Mexico	11·7	13·0	13·8	13·8	14·0	14·3	16·7	16·5	14·7	14·2	14·9	14·5	13·8	14·4	16·1	15·7	16·5
Pakistan	5·5	5·6	7·4	8·7	9·7	11·1	9·2	7·1	9·2	9·3	11·9	14·0	15·6	16·9	17·2	14·7	13·9
Peru	14·7	17·9	20·8	23·2	16·9	18·5	23·5	24·8	22·9	17·8	16·8	19·2	20·6	18·8	17·1	19·3	18·5
Philippines	10·1	9·2	8·9	9·6	9·4	9·8	11·3	12·2	11·2	11·4	13·7	17·7	17·7	18·2	20·6	20·0	19·6
South Korea	—	—	—	7·3	9·2	10·2	10·4	10·7	10·1	11·0	10·8	11·7	14·1	14·0	11·7	14·7	20·2
Spain	12·2	10·0	11·1	12·3	14·8	17·6	18·0	18·7	18·5	17·4	16·5	19·0	20·7	21·6	22·8	22·9	22·0
Taiwan	—	10·8	11·3	11·7	13·2	11·3	13·3	13·1	15·1	16·6	16·6	16·2	15·0	15·0	14·1	16·3	18·5
Thailand	—	—	12·6	14·3	14·8	13·3	13·0	14·0	13·7	14·3	15·0	15·6	18·2	21·6	21·6	21·8	22·1
Turkey	9·6	10·2	12·8	12·4	14·7	14·4	13·8	12·7	12·7	14·0	14·7	14·5	14·4	13·8	13·4	13·7	—
Venezuela	21·4	22·0	26·8	28·9	27·8	24·7	25·0	25·0	24·3	23·7	18·7	16·1	16·3	16·6	17·5	19·4	19·0
Yugoslavia	26·1	23·7	22·2	21·4	24·0	22·2	22·8	24·0	26·2	27·6	29·1	30·5	30·5	30·0	29·3	23·9	22·2

Table D–2

Gross Fixed Non-Residential Investment as a Percentage of GDP at Current Market Prices 1950–67

	1950	1951	1952	1953	1954	1955	1956	1957	1958	1959	1960	1961	1962	1963	1964	1965	1966
Argentina	14·7	15·0	14·3	13·1	12·8	13·3	13·8	15·1	15·0	12·8	16·3	17·6	17·0	13·7	12·4	12·9	13·4
Brazil	11·3	13·7	13·2	11·1	13·9	12·2	11·2	11·1	11·7	13·6	14·0	14·6	13·9	14·0	12·2	9·1	10·9
Ceylon	7·1	7·3	9·4	8·1	6·5	7·2	11·2	11·6	12·2	12·5	11·9	11·1	11·3	11·8	11·1	10·2	11·0
Chile	9·6	11·2	10·8	9·2	7·7	8·5	11·1	16·6	16·2	12·6	12·6	14·7	12·5	11·6	11·5	10·5	10·3
Colombia	11·4	10·7	11·1	13·4	13·6	14·7	13·6	11·5	12·6	12·8	14·7	14·8	14·1	12·9	12·6	12·1	—
Egypt	10·2	10·5	8·1	6·7	7·3	7·3	6·3	11·0	11·8	10·2	14·2	14·1	15·6	17·7	16·3	16·3	—
Ghana	7·4	7·8	9·2	11·6	11·0	13·7	13·8	13·2	12·3	15·1	17·7	17·9	14·7	15·8	14·9	14·1	12·0
Greece	11·7	6·5	8·1	6·9	8·2	7·7	8·6	8·8	11·4	12·9	15·0	13·9	14·1	13·2	14·9	15·2	15·6
India	7·4	8·0	8·0	7·7	8·9	10·7	11·4	12·3	10·7	11·6	13·1	13·9	13·0	14·0	14·3	14·7	13·8
Israel	15·6	14·0	16·5	17·0	13·9	17·5	17·1	17·7	17·2	16·6	17·0	18·3	19·9	19·2	21·5	18·7	14·1
Malaya	5·0	5·3	8·3	8·0	7·7	7·4	9·0	10·1	9·9	9·1	10·5	13·1	16·0	15·7	15·1	—	—
Mexico	10·8	12·2	12·7	12·6	12·9	13·3	15·3	15·1	13·5	12·8	13·4	12·4	12·4	12·9	14·4	14·1	14·8
Pakistan	4·8	4·9	6·4	7·5	8·4	9·6	8·2	6·3	8·2	8·3	10·6	13·0	14·4	15·6	15·9	13·6	12·9
Peru	11·0	13·4	15·6	17·4	12·7	13·9	17·6	18·6	17·2	13·4	12·6	14·4	15·5	14·1	12·8	14·5	13·9
Philippines	7·4	6·6	6·6	7·0	7·4	7·6	9·0	9·7	9·2	9·4	11·7	14·9	14·9	15·2	17·0	16·6	16·5
South Korea	5·7	5·7	5·7	5·7	6·7	8·4	8·6	9·2	8·8	9·3	8·7	10·0	12·4	12·6	10·1	13·0	18·1
Spain	10·3	8·4	9·7	10·7	13·1	14·6	15·1	15·4	13·2	12·1	11·9	14·6	16·4	16·8	17·7	18·9	18·6
Taiwan	9·8	9·8	10·2	10·6	11·5	9·9	11·8	11·6	13·6	14·7	14·3	14·4	13·4	12·8	12·7	14·7	16·7
Thailand	11·9	11·9	11·9	13·6	13·1	12·7	12·2	11·7	11·6	12·2	12·9	13·6	15·9	18·7	19·2	19·3	—
Turkey	6·9	7·7	9·7	9·3	10·3	10·0	9·9	9·3	9·4	10·8	11·6	11·5	11·5	11·2	10·6	10·4	—
Venezuela	20·0	19·0	23·6	24·5	24·8	21·9	21·7	22·4	20·6	21·8	16·9	14·8	14·3	14·5	14·7	15·8	15·6
Yugoslavia	22·0	21·4	19·9	18·9	20·3	19·3	19·2	19·5	20·7	22·3	22·9	23·4	22·6	22·5	24·0	19·6	18·2

We were able to examine the details of the investment estimates with national income statisticians in a few of the countries. It appeared in Brazil that the estimates probably need upward revision, most notably for construction and for agricultural investment; investment in coffee trees is not for instance included in the official figures. In Brazil the estimates are based on production and trade statistics with mark-ups for trading, warehousing, insurance and installation which seems rather low. In India, official estimates of capital formation are still very tentative. The Indian figures we have used include some items as capital goods which might well be excluded in other countries, but differences in items covered depend, of course, on the level of development of the country. In a very low income country like India some items are legitimately treated as capital goods which would not be counted as such in a developed country; 70 per cent of oil pressure lamps, 50 per cent of sewing machines, 90 per cent of radio receivers, 15 per cent of bicycles, and 50 per cent of clocks are treated as capital goods. See *National Income Statistics: Estimates of Capital Formation in India*, Central Statistical Organization, New Delhi, 1961. Argentina is a case where the estimates of capital formation are very complete in their commodity coverage, e.g. religious and funeral items are treated as capital goods, 90 per cent of cars and 28 per cent of radios and there is substantial allowance for major repairs and spare parts: 50 per cent of ship repairs, 80 per cent of locomotive repairs, and 70 per cent of mechanical repairs to automobiles are treated as capital goods. (Information supplied by CONADE, Buenos Aires.)

EXTERNAL FINANCE (Table D–3)

External finance is the amount required to meet a country's deficit in its current balance of payments, i.e. its balance on goods and services (including interest and dividends paid to foreigners). When the figures in Table D–3 are positive this means that there was a net inflow of foreign capital (or a decline in exchange reserves) and that the current balance of payments was in deficit. When the capital figure is negative this means that the current balance was in surplus and that there was an outflow of capital or an increase in exchange reserves. External finance is not the same as the 'net transfer of resources' to a country, which is the reciprocal of the balance on current account excluding payments of interest and dividends. In India in 1965 external finance equal to 1·96 per cent of GDP was required to meet the deficit on trade and services, and another 0·67 per cent of GDP to finance remittance of interest and dividends abroad. Thus India was able to use resources equal to 101·96 per cent of GDP. In the absence of external finance India would have been able to use resources equal to only 99·33 per cent of her GDP, i.e. her GNP would be 99·33 per cent of her GDP.

As far as possible the same sources were used as in Appendix B, but it was necessary to use *The Yearbook of National Accounts Statistics*, UN, New York, 1957 and 1966 editions; *International Financial Statistics*, and *Balance of Payments Yearbooks*, IMF Washington, and various national sources.

Table

External Finance as a Percentage of GDP

	1950	1951	1952	1953	1954	1955	1956	1957
Argentina	−0·93	2·45	3·06	−1·75	−0·22	1·32	1·39	2·80
Brazil	−0·75	2·84	3·75	−0·14	1·20	0·14	−0·08	1·34
Ceylon	−5·34	−3·46	7·54	2·18	−6·95	−6·80	−2·55	2·78
Chile	0·13	0·99	−0·45	0·65	0·27	−0·24	−0·09	3·04
Colombia	0·89	0·85	0·92	0·60	1·00	2·08	−0·98	−0·80
Egypt	1·27	9·96	5·02	0·84	0·67	0·54	1·59	2·91
Ghana	−9·46	−8·88	−3·49	−0·75	−13·9	−0·61	2·83	3·72
Greece	17·36	11·88	7·52	5·31	6·15	4·54	5·82	5·71
India	−0·09	1·89	0·00	0·09	0·46	0·71	3·07	3·95
Israel	25·76	18·36	24·30	22·70	19·68	22·66	24·01	19·18
Malaya	−11·80	−11·20	−7·59	−1·29	−9·72	−13·50	−7·96	−5·91
Mexico	−0·97	3·40	1·52	1·70	0·69	−0·23	1·39	3·20
Pakistan	0·56	−2·32	3·79	0·79	0·93	−0·10	2·84	2·58
Peru	−1·20	−0·15	3·48	5·00	1·47	5·70	6·35	8·35
Philippines	−0·71	1·39	1·48	1·28	1·97	3·64	1·46	4·16
South Korea	—	—	—	6·62	5·31	7·09	10·91	9·84
Spain	0·03	−0·87	1·16	1·16	0·18	1·16	1·46	1·90
Taiwan	—	4·76	5·65	5·33	8·22	3·71	7·73	5·91
Thailand	−2·85	−2·36	0·97	3·76	4·37	1·69	1·03	1·25
Turkey	0·71	1·96	3·70	2·62	2·90	2·72	1·45	0·84
Venezuela	1·86	−0·39	1·62	1·73	0·86	−0·42	2·26	6·26
Yugoslavia	2·45	3·80	3·22	5·02	2·13	2·79	1·27	4·19

D–3

at Current Market Prices 1950–67

1958	1959	1960	1961	1962	1963	1964	1965	1966
2·17	−0·14	1·70	4·12	2·15	−1·85	−0·21	−0·99	−1·23
1·37	1·84	2·40	1·30	3·08	1·32	−0·50	−1·72	0·12
2·19	3·09	3·62	1·57	2·15	2·50	2·65	−0·14	4·00
2·42	0·89	4·86	6·08	3·26	4·55	2·90	1·46	1·12
−0·28	−1·57	2·96	3·53	2·35	4·98	4·49	1·44	3·90
1·75	−0·63	0·92	5·62	6·33	7·44	4·08	5·45	3·58
−3·31	1·97	6·28	9·38	3·66	6·14	3·25	9·22	4·68
6·56	5·63	6·77	9·48	6·26	5·75	7·80	9·80	7·70
2·80	1·76	3·18	2·34	2·64	2·30	2·66	2·63	2·29
16·40	13·19	12·37	14·70	21·32	17·66	19·20	14·66	11·19
−4·04	−11·5	−9·26	−3·85	−0·97	−0·63	−0·84	−3·62	−2·87
2·57	1·38	2·50	1·69	1·06	1·33	2·28	1·79	1·56
3·50	2·60	3·72	2·44	3·91	3·81	5·83	3·88	4·37
7·71	2·50	−0·04	1·29	1·82	3·12	−0·23	3·02	1·91
1·56	0·19	2·31	2·96	7·99	0·92	3·53	1·62	−1·91
8·00	6·86	8·57	8·60	10·92	10·81	7·12	6·60	8·74
1·53	0·86	−2·86	−0·32	1·76	2·87	1·70	3·93	4·40
6·97	8·64	7·51	7·09	6·59	0·71	−0·23	3·54	0·95
3·22	2·65	1·23	−0·25	1·99	3·31	1·02	1·24	−0·38
0·87	3·03	2·77	3·03	4·03	4·45	2·00	1·09	2·99
3·68	1·20	−5·18	−5·84	−4·09	−5·09	−2·71	0·09	0·39
3·39	2·90	3·74	5·59	1·46	1·66	2·55	−0·32	−0·80

Appendix E
Foreign Trade

The figures are on a calendar year basis and show special exports f.o.b. (except for Malaya, where they include re-exports). Trade in gold and silver bullion and specie is excluded as far as possible, except for Mexico. The figures for 1880 and 1913 refer to the customs territory of the year mentioned, and from 1929 onwards to the post-war customs territory. Exceptions are India, which includes Burma to April 1937 and Pakistan through 1937. The 1929–37 figures for Israel refer to Palestine. Malaya includes Singapore to 1937. South Korea includes the whole of Korea to 1937.

1950–67: from *Yearbook of International Trade Statistics 1966*, UN, New York, 1968. 1967 from *Monthly Bulletin of Statistics*, UN, New York, March 1969.

1929–37: *Statistical Yearbook 1948*, UN, New York, pp. 326–36. This source gives figures in new dollars. 1929 and 1932 were converted to current dollars (1 new dollar equals 59·06 old cents).

1913: *Memorandum on International Trade and Balances of Payments 1913–27*, League of Nations, Geneva, p. 10.

1880: F. X. Neumann-Spallart, *Ubersichten der Weltwirthschaft, Jahrgang 1883–4*, Maier, Stuttgart, 1887; M. G. Mulhall, *The Dictionary of Statistics*, 4th edition, Routledge, London, 1899, pp. 128–55; C. Issawi, ed., *The Economic History of the Middle East 1800–1914*, Chicago, 1966, p. 373; J. C. Ingram, *Economic Change in Thailand since 1850*, Stanford, 1955; *O Brasil em Numeros*, IBGE, Rio de Janeiro, 1960 and *Annuaire Statistique du Bresil 1908–12* (for exchange rate); *Estadisticas Economicas del Porfiriato, Commercio Exterior de Mexico 1877–1911*, El Colegio de Mexico, Mexico, 1960,

Table E–1

Value of Exports f.o.b. 1880–1967

$ million at current rates of exchange

	1880	1913	1929	1932	1937	1950	1960	1965	1966	1967
Argentina	55	515	908	331	758	1,361	1,079	1,493	1,593	1,465
Brazil	101	317	461	175	350	1,347	1,269	1,596	1,741	1,654
Ceylon	20	76	139	44	124	328	385	409	357	348
Chile	74*	149	283	34	193	283	490	688	881	913
Colombia	14	33	119	64	86	396	465	539	508	510
Egypt	66	156	255	90	200	513	568	604	604	566
Ghana	1·4	26	57	23	61	192	294	291	244	278
Greece	7	23	90	33	87	90	203	328	406	495
India	327	786	1,201	402	727	1,178	1,331	1,688	1,577	1,613
Israel	—	—	9	9	32	37	211	406	477	518
Malaya	51	193	521	132	522	852	956	1,014	1,019	954
Mexico	36	150	285	97	219	521	763	1,146	1,229	1,145
Pakistan	—	—	—	—	—	489	393	528	601	601
Peru	4·5	43	134	37	92	189	431	666	763	774
Philippines	27*	48	164	95	153	331	560	794	861	812
South Korea	—	15	159	87	197	23	33	175	250	320
Spain	124	191	408	144	135	389	726	966	1,254	1,375
Taiwan	—	26	129	66	127	76	164	450	536	641
Thailand	9	43	101	46	77	304	408	622	678	685
Turkey	39	94	75	48	110	263	321	464	491	522
Venezuela	19	29	149	93	182	1,161	2,432	2,744	2,713	2,887
Yugoslavia	8*	61	139	49	144	159	566	1,092	1,220	1,252

* 1883

Index

References to tables and appendices are italicized